SOUTHERN EUROPE TRANSFORMED

SOUTHERN EUROPE TRANSFORMED

*Political and economic change
in Greece, Italy, Portugal and Spain*

Allan Williams

Harper & Row, Publishers
London

Cambridge
Hagerstown
Philadelphia
New York

San Francisco
Mexico City
Sao Paulo
Sydney

First published 1984

Harper & Row Publishers Ltd
28 Tavistock Street
London WC2E 7PN

British Library Cataloguing in Publication Data

Southern Europe transformed.
 1. Europe, Southern—History
 2. Europe—history—1945–
 I. Williams, A.M.
 910   D1051
 ISBN 0–06–318281–5

Typeset by Inforum Ltd, Portsmouth
Printed and bound by Butler & Tanner Ltd, Frome and London

The contributors

Mark Blacksell is Senior Lecturer in Geography at Exeter University.

Jorge Gaspar is Professor of Geography at the Centro de Estudos Geograficos, Lisbon University.

Salvador Giner is Head of Department and Reader in Sociology at Brunel University.

Ray Hudson is Senior Lecturer in Geography at Durham University.

P.C. Ioakimidis is currently a Special Advisor to the Ministry of Foreign Affairs, Athens.

Alun Jones is a Research Scholar in Geography at Leicester University.

Russell King is Lecturer in Geography at Leicester University.

Jim Lewis is Lecturer in Geography at Durham University.

Manuel Porto is Professor of Economics at Coimbra University and is President for the Co-ordinating Commission of the Central Region in Portugal.

Eduardo Sevilla is Professor of Rural Sociology at Cordoba University.

Martin Slater is Lecturer in Government at Essex University.

Allan Williams is Lecturer in Geography at Exeter University.

For my parents

CONTENTS

Preface

Chapter 1 **Introduction** *A.M. Williams*
1. The transformation   1
2. Historical context of development   4
3. Postwar economic development   8
4. Development and dependency   12
5. Rise and decline of dictatorial government   16
6. The postdictatorial era   21
7. Conclusion   24

PART ONE: CASE STUDIES

Chapter 2 **Greece: from military dictatorship to socialism**
P.C. Ioakimidis
1. Introduction   33
2. Historical background   34
3. Transformation of the economy   37
4. Structure of the economy   40
5. Transformation of the political system   44
6. Greece in the European Community   53
7. Conclusion   58

Chapter 3 **Italy: Surviving into the 1980s** *M. Slater*
1. Introduction   61

	2. Background	64
	3. Social transformation in the 1960s	69
	4. Developments in the 1970s and 1980s	73
	5. Conclusion: the political economy of the 1980s	80

Chapter 4 **Portugal: twenty years of change** *M. Porto*
1. Introduction | 84
2. The 1960s: European integration, emigration and colonial wars | 87
3. The Caetano Years | 94
4. The coup, April 1974 and the transition to democracy | 97
5. Post-1976, the era of parliamentary democracy | 103
6. Conclusion | 108

Chapter 5 **Spain: from corporatism to corporatism** *S. Giner and E. Sevilla*
1. Introduction | 113
2. Francoism | 115
3. The defeat of dictatorship | 120
4. The making of contemporary corporatism in Spain | 125
5. Conclusion: the rise of 'social forces' | 133
6. Appendix | 137

PART TWO: GENERAL THEMES

Chapter 6 **Population mobility: emigration, return migration and internal migration** *R. King*
1. Introduction | 145
2. Patterns of emigration | 147
3. Return migration | 157
4. Internal migration | 164
5. Conclusion: migration, the future | 173

Chapter 7 **Capital accumulation: the industrialisation of southern Europe?** *R. Hudson and J.R. Lewis*
1. Introduction | 179
2. Southern Europe in the world economy | 180

3.	International and intranational capital movements	184
4.	Forms of industrialisation	191
5.	The organisation of capital in south European industry	197
6.	Conclusion: issues for the future	202

Chapter 8   **Urbanization: growth, problems and policies**
J. Gaspar

1.	Introduction	208
2.	Postwar urbanization	211
3.	Urban social movements	214
4.	Urban policies	222
5.	Some urban issues	224
6.	Conclusions	231

Chapter 9   **Agriculture: organization, reform and the EEC**
A.R. Jones

1.	Introduction	236
2.	Agricultural populations	237
3.	Land tenure and modes of production	242
4.	Southern European agriculture and the EEC	249
5.	Conclusion: future prospects for southern European agriculture	260

Chapter 10   **The European Community and the Mediterranean region: two steps forward, one step back**   *M. Blacksell*

1.	Introduction	268
2.	Mediterranean policy within the European Community	269
3.	The second enlargement	270
4.	The overall Mediterranean approach	279
5.	European security and the Mediterranean region	284
6.	Conclusion	286

Index	289

PREFACE

The main aim of this volume is to review the economic, political, and social changes which have transformed southern Europe since the end of World War II, especially in the 1960s and 1970s. There are two major themes which run through all the contributions: the nature, extent and repercussions of economic development and the causes and implications of the demise of dictatorial government. The economic and political changes are linked and are related also to social changes associated with, for example, emigration, urbanization and secularism. In different ways the contributors have sought to disentangle these, often complex, interrelationships which lie at the heart of the southern European transformation.

In scope, the volume is limited to four countries: Greece, Italy, Portugal and Spain. It does not, therefore, seek to encapsulate the entire region and other countries bordering on the northern coast of the Mediterranean have been excluded. These four countries have been selected because, although they have distinctive features, they also share many experiences which give them an element of common identity. The dual nature of individual and common features is recognized in the structure of the book. The first part is based on case studies of individual countries while the second part investigates a number of general themes. Hopefully, this will help place each particular country in context but will also guard against over-generalization. Although the authors may have different perspectives and starting points, they have a common goal – to illuminate the profound but little-understood changes within this region.

At an early stage in preparing the volume, the West European Studies Centre at Exeter University hosted a colloquium at which preliminary versions of these papers were presented. This proved to be invaluable, informing us of the approaches being developed by our cocontributors, and helping to give shape to the final outline of the book. It was only possible to organize this meeting thanks to the generosity of the British Council, the Gulbenkian Foundation, the University of Exeter Research Fund and the Centre for West European Studies. A number of other people, whose names do not appear in this volume, also attended the seminar and their valuable contributions to our long discussions helped to clarify many ideas: these individuals were J. Beck, A. Cardoso, V. Granodos, D. Hearl, A. Glyn-Jones, S. Mennell, J. Noakes, P. Richmond and H. van der Wusten. In addition, Tom Gallagher, Ian Thompson and Stuart Woolf have also made a number of useful suggestions concerning the general outline of the volume. However, my greatest debt of gratitude is to John Naylon who has been a constant source of encouragement and has made positive suggestions at a number of stages in the preparation of the final manuscript. I am grateful to all these people but, of course, they bear no responsibility for any remaining blemishes in this volume.

CHAPTER ONE

INTRODUCTION

A.M. Williams

1. The Transformation

Before the 1950s it was appropriate to ask, 'why is southern Europe under-developed?' But this has now been supplanted by the question, 'why has southern Europe developed so rapidly?'. Baklanoff (1976) characterized the economy of the region in the 1950s: there were relatively low per-capita incomes, technological backwardness, a large proportion employed in an inefficient primary sector, a predominance of unskilled work and of small scale enterprises in manufacturing. Exports were dominated by raw materials – for example, about 70 percent in immediate postwar Greece – and imports were of high value-added manufactured goods. From the 1950s, however, there was a marked acceleration in the growth rate of the region and all the individual countries considered in this volume passed from having below to above the West European average growth rate in the next three decades (see Table 1.1). Growth does not necessarily imply a transformation and it will be argued in this and later chapters that there has been only a partial alteration of the structures of the southern European economies. Economic change has also been linked, although not by any simple causal mechanisms, with social and political change in the individual states.

The outstanding political change has been the decline or overthrow of dictatorial or military governments in all four countries; whether these were fascist regimes is considered later. These have been replaced by various types of parliamentary political systems. The change occurred first in Italy, with the military defeat of Mussolini in World War II, while in Greece there was a short military dictatorship, commencing in 1967, which ended in 1974. In

Table 1.1   **Annual average compound growth rates of real output per capita**

	1913–1950	1950–1973
Greece	0.2	6.2
Italy	0.8	4.7
Portugal	0.9	5.3
Spain	–0.3	5.2
Mean for Western Europe	1.0	4.35[1]

[1] 1950–1973 average is for both western and eastern Europe.
Source: Pollard (1981).

contrast, both Spain and Portugal had more enduring dictatorial govern-ments. In Spain, the Francoist state erected in 1939 at the close of the Civil War only formally came to an end in 1977 with the adoption of a new constitution. Portugal had the longest-standing regime, established first as a military dictatorship in 1926 and later, after 1928, reshaped as a corporate state by Salazar. This came to a sudden, though not unexpected end in 1974, after a military coup led by junior officers. Three of the countries reviewed in this book, therefore, experienced shifts from dictatorial to democratic pluralist governments within a short period in the mid-1970s. Subsequently, all have been feeling their ways, sometimes uncertainly, towards the establishment of parliamentary institutions and new political parties. Italy went through this phase two decades earlier and therefore provides a useful comparison to the other three case studies. Political change was partly caused by, as well as being a contributor to, far reaching social changes in southern Europe, associated with industrialization, emigration and urbanization.

There is, therefore, some degree of shared experience amongst all four countries examined in this book. The timing of economic development, as well as the nature of political change, provide common themes which allow the four states to be analysed together. This is the rationale for the general, thematic chapters in Part II of the volume, where the material presented reveals remarkable cross-national consistency in socio-economic trends within the region. However, there are also important differences between the four countries, for example, the significance of regionalism in Spain, the late decolonization and small size of Portugal, the belated emergence of an independent Greece (from Ottoman rule) or the early entry of Italy into the

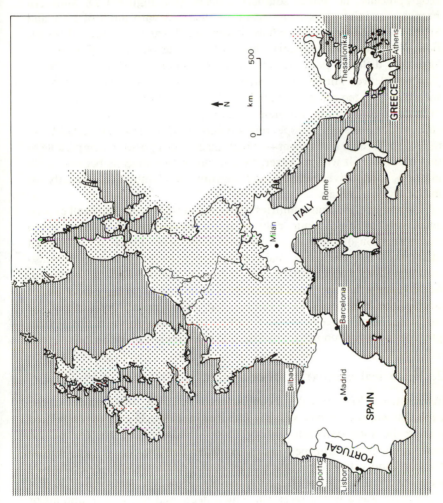

Figure 1.1 Southern Europe.

EEC. Some of these individual traits are illustrated by the detailed case studies of the four countries presented in the first part of the volume.

A case can also be established for the exclusion of other countries which, geographically, lie within southern Europe (see Figure 1.1). Southern France certainly shares many economic features with parts of Italy and Spain but, the country as a whole, is very much part of northern Europe. Both Yugoslavia and Albania, though bordering on the Mediterranean, have very different political (and, in part, economic and social) systems. This only leaves Turkey as a contender for inclusion and, as it largely lies within Asia, it too can be excluded. In the case of Turkey, however, this is not a clear-cut decision, for there are elements — such as recent large scale emigration to western Europe, relationships with NATO and the USA and the role of foreign investment — which place it in a position comparable to that of Greece. It will, however, be left out of this analysis because of its location, distinctive religion and continuing dominance (directly or indirectly) by military.

In summary, the four countries examined in this volume have all experienced substantial economic, political and social changes which amount to a transformation of their socio-economic structures. There are individual differences, not least in size and population (Table 1.2), but there are also common themes which will be explored by the contributors. It should not be surprising that there is a high degree of shared experience because, of course, these countries have similar (but not identical) positions in the world economic system. A brief outline of the evolution of this system provides a starting point for more detailed consideration of the four states.

2. Historical context of development

Wallerstein (1979) provides a concise account of the development of the capitalist world economic system. The European world economy emerged during the 'long sixteenth century' (1450–1640) and, by the end of this period, north west Europe could be considered as the core region. Within the core, individual states (such as France, Britain and the Netherlands) were involved in a struggle for supremacy. However, between 1650 and 1730 there was a world recession which decreased the global amount of surplus value available, leaving room for only one dominant state within the core: this was Britain, which ousted the Netherlands from its early dominance. After about 1760 the rate of industrialization increased dramatically in Britain and it can be argued that industrial capitalism came into

Table 1.2   **Population and area**

Country	1980 Population (millions)	Area ('000s sq km)
Greece	9.6	132
Italy	56.9	301
Portugal	9.8	92
Spain	37.4	505

Source: World Bank (1982).

existence. This provided the need to expand the capitalist system to the rest of the world, initially to provide access to materials and later to markets. Improvements in armaments and in transport technology allowed this expansion to occur and for other world systems, such as the Russian, to be subdued. During the nineteenth century the USA and Germany industrialized rapidly and challenged British supremacy within the core. Africa also became a major scene of competition between the European states and was effectively colonized in the late nineteenth century.

After this period Britain lost its dominant position in the world system, a role which was taken over eventually by the USA. The latter achieved maximum ascendancy in the two decades immediately after World War II. It assisted in the reconstruction of the devastated economies of western Europe through the programme of Marshall Aid and also considerably expanded its investment in Latin America. The USA also encouraged decolonization of Asia and Africa to weaken European capitalism overseas and to bring the ex-colonies more fully into the world system. Finally, the Bretton Woods agreement, which made the US dollar the major international reserve currency, provided an expansionary bias for the postwar world economy. Within this framework, there was remarkable recovery and expansion of the economies of western Europe, based on the 'deepening' of capital, through the adoption of new technology, and the use of cheap immigrant labour from the Mediterranean countries (Kindleberger 1967). The importance of the latter factor should not be underestimated for Bernabè (1982) estimates that immigrant labour provided approximately one-third of the growth of nonagricultural labour in the EEC. The combination of expansionary demand and lack of constraints on the supply side made for a 'virtuous circle' of growth (Paine 1982), with average annual growth rates in West Europe being in excess of 4 percent.

This remarkable expansionary phase in the world economy reached a peak in the mid-1960s. Thereafter, the hegemony of the USA was challenged by revival of the West European economies and by its consistent balance of payments deficits. In 1971 the convertibility of the dollar was suspended and the whole framework of economic growth became more hesitant. A world economy already entering recession was given a further shock by the sharp rise in oil prices in 1973–1974. The system never really recovered in the 1970s and the second 'oil crisis' in 1978–1979, following the revolution in Iran, did much to damage the prospects of growth in Western Europe (Seers 1982). Since then, there has been a major world recession in the capitalist system.

How do the countries of southern Europe fit into this schemata of world economic development? Before 'the long sixteenth century', the Italian states, Spain and Portugal had held dominant positions in the, then, essentially European economic system. They had pioneered early trade and colonization beyond Europe: the Portuguese had opened up the coastal routes around Africa to Asia, the Spanish had control of much of Latin America, and the Italian states had expanded their influence eastwards through the Mediterranean. Greece was an exception to this pattern, being incorporated into the Ottoman empire from the fifteenth to the nineteenth centuries and, consequently, having been isolated from many significant technological and social changes which occurred in western Europe (Kondonassis 1976). The country only regained independence in 1821 and its international boundaries were not really fixed until 1922. The other Mediterranean powers had, however, already outgrown their capacities to control their empires against the expansion of the northern European states. From the sixteenth century their dominant positions within Europe declined and Spain and Portugal lost control of most of their Latin American colonies in the early nineteenth century. Although Portugal and Spain retained some African territories, they were also forced to cede parts of these in the scramble to colonize that continent in the late nineteenth century (see Fage 1978).

The southern European states therefore declined into a position in the world economic system which Wallerstein (1979) terms as semiperipheral. This is a position between the periphery (characterized by low profit, low technology and low wage production) and the core (characterized by high profit, high technology and high wage production). The countries of the semiperiphery act as periphery for the core countries and as core for the peripheral countries. In the cases of Portugal and Spain, these core-periphery relationships were in some instances colonial ties. The dominant relationship, however, was the peripheral status of southern Europe in its linkages with the core of northern Europe. Typically, the south provided the north with raw materials (such as fruit and vegetables) in return for manufactured goods. This pattern is not, however, quite as simple as has been portrayed. Some regions within southern Europe industrialized at a relatively early stage and there were important textile industries in both Catalonia and Lombardy-Piedmont in the late eighteenth century. More geographically widespread and diversified industrialization did not, however, occur until the late nineteenth century when in Spain, for example, there was the growth of metallurgical industries in the Basque region to set alongside the Catalan textile and food processing sectors (Wright 1977). During the first half of the twentieth century the process of industrialization received set-backs in all the countries of southern Europe. Apart from the general effects of the interwar recession, the Civil Wars in Spain (1936–9) and Greece (1945–8) and the Second World War in Italy severely disrupted production in these countries. Portugal was least affected, isolated to some extent by the autarkic policies of the Salazar regime and actually benefiting from new export opportunities during the 1939–1945 war (Baklanoff 1978).

After World War II all four countries experienced rapid rates of development. In part this was due to their linkages with the core economies, which expanded rapidly during this period, but it was also partly the result of state economic policies. The actual process of development is considered in more detail in the following section; here, it is sufficient to note that it led to a shift in status from semipheriphery towards core status. There were differences between the four countries and the process was more complete in Italy and Spain which now, arguably, can be considered as parts of the core. In contrast, the process is less complete in Greece and Portugal. However, despite these differences between the four states, there are sufficient similarities in their experiences to mark them as a distinctive group of semi-peripheral economies, differentiated in important respects from other semiperipheral economies such as Taiwan or Brazil. This distinctiveness – which is, however, qualified by their overall role within the world capitalist system – stems from their geographical location which influences the nature of their relationship with the northern European core. In particular, they have distinctive patterns of emigration (more likely to be short term), and tourism (extensive and generating relatively low expenditure per capita), have the potential for becoming components of specifically European investment strategies by multinational corporations (for example, as in the car and chemical industries), are and could become members of the EEC, and have special geopolitical importance as the southern perimeter of NATO.

3. Postwar economic development

All the countries of southern Europe have recorded very high growth rates in the postwar period (Table 1.3) with average annual growth in GNP per capita being between 4 and 6 percent in all but Italy. Only Japan, amongst OECD members, has recorded higher growth rates during the same period. There have been even higher rates of growth over shorter time spans, for example, over 7 percent per annum in Spain between 1960 and 1973. Aggregate economic changes have been accompanied by substantial sectoral shifts in the distribution of the labour force (Table 1.4). There has been a decline in the relative importance of agriculture and a massive shift of employment to industry and services. The extent of these shifts varies amongst the four countries but they have probably been greatest in Spain and least in Greece and Portugal. Italy experienced this transformation earlier but, even so, has seen a sizeable reduction in the relative importance of agriculture. Although there is something of a dichotomy between, on the one hand, Italy and Spain and, on the other hand, Greece and Portugal, the overall trends have been similar.

It has been argued that it is the shift from relatively low-productivity agriculture to relatively high-productivity urban–industrial activities which accounts for the growth of these economies. In the case of service employment this is controversial, for many such jobs – say, in bars or cafes – can have low productivity, while others are 'created' by the state as part of clientelistic networks (see the chapters on Greece and Italy). However, the role of service employment as a generator of growth should not be underestimated. Tourism, in particular, has made an important contribution to national economic growth as well as to the transformation of some regional economies – notably the zones bordering the Mediterranean. Elsewhere, the expansion of public sector employment and office jobs has contributed to economic growth. Less controversy surrounds the role of industrialization, usually considered to be the major source of growth, and drawing labour from agriculture to work in more efficient, higher value added manufacturing activities. However, the shift from agriculture to industry is not always straightforward; on the one hand, industrial pollution can lower the capacity of agriculture, especially where there is diffuse industrialization as in northern Portugal or central Italy, while, on the other hand,

Table 1.3 Gross National Product Per Capita

	1980 (dollars)	Average annual growth 1960–80 (percentage)
Greece	4380	5.8
Italy	6480	3.6
Portugal	2370	5.0
Spain	5400	4.5

Source: World Bank (1982).

Table 1.4 Sectoral distribution of the labour force in 1960 and 1980

	Agriculture		Industry		Services	
	1960	1980	1960	1980	1960	1980
Greece	56	37	20	28	24	35
Italy	31	11	40	45	29	44
Portugal	44	24	29	36	27	40
Spain	42	15	31	40	27	45

Sources: World Bank (1982).
OECD Economic Surveys for Greece, Italy, Portugal and Spain.

industrial wages can be a source of investment in agriculture, especially in cases of part-time farming. Nevertheless, expansion of the manufacturing sector has been an outstanding feature of southern European development which needs to be examined in some detail.

The low cost of labour was an important precondition for rapid industrialization. In Spain, Greece and Portugal low wages were 'guaranteed' by the dictatorial regimes which neutralized the trade unions: for example, Spain had its Basic Labour Law of 1939 effectively making trade unions illegal (Mérigo 1982), while in Portugal the constitution of the *Estado Novo* set up *grémios*, state controlled syndicates, in place of trade unions (Baklanoff 1978). In combination with the surplus of labour available in the economy (in the agricultural sector), these conditions kept wages at low levels until at least the final years of the Francoist and Salazarist regimes (Tsoukalis 1981). In Italy the reserve of labour in the South, which could be drawn to work in northern industries, helped to maintain wages at relatively low levels (Wade 1979).

In addition, there was a shift from autarkic to internationalist economic policies. Whilst extreme autarky was forced on Spain between 1946 and 1950, through its isolation by the United Nations (although Franco may have chosen a similar strategy anyway), Portugal and Greece 'opted' for this mode of development. All three countries isolated their economies, to some extent, through protective tariffs and quotas, and encouraged import-substitution. There was also a high level of state control; for example, in both Spain and Portugal there were strict systems of industrial licencing and price controls. The periods of autarky were important because they provided opportunities for general recovery and the establishment of important new industries, after periods of disruption during civil wars (in Spain and Greece), and during the Great Depression (in Portugal). However, autarkic policies eventually proved to be restrictive to growth, as the economies expanded and became more complex. International agencies such as the IMF and the OECD also pressed for the 'opening' of these economies as means of ameliorating their mounting balance of payments deficits (Tsoukalis 1981). The timing of these reorientations varied but was more or less complete in all cases. Greek policy changes stemmed from 1953 when there was a 100 percent devaluation of the drachma and foreign investment was encouraged. Spain joined the World Bank and the IMF in 1958, adopted a Stabilization Programme in 1959 (to reduce budget deficits) and devalued the grossly overvalued peseta in the same year. Portugal, partly as a consequence of the demands of the colonial wars on its exchequer (which reduced the capacity for domestic investment), entered EFTA in 1959 and in 1965 liberalized foreign investment controls. An important symbol of this changing economic orientation can be seen in relationships with the EEC. Each country sought and eventually obtained special trading relationships: Greece in 1962, Spain in 1970 and Portugal in 1972. The experience of Italy, of course, is rather different, having had an open economy since the end of World War II and having been a founder member of the EEC. However, even in Italy there was a change of emphasis in the economy over time and Rey (1982) considers that it was the growing importance of exports over internal demand which was the critical factor in the 'economic miracle' of 1958–1963.

Internationalization involved three main elements: foreign investment and technological transfer, emigration and tourism. Foreign investment located in the region both to utilize low cost labour and to gain access to national markets. In addition, third parties, such as North American corporations, were able to improve access to EEC or EFTA markets through locating in southern Europe, since this lay within their tariff boundaries.

The nature of this capital flow is discussed more fully in Chapter 7; here it is sufficient to note that the transfer of technology was sometimes more important than the simple input of investment funds (for example, see Rolo 1977; Nikolinakos 1982). Emigration was not a new phenomenon in southern Europe but it changed in nature during the 1950s and 1960s (see Chapter 6) when expansion of the West European economies provided demand for labour from southern Europe. This led to shorter-distance, shorter-duration emigration, replacing traditional long-haul emigration to the Americas. Improvements in transport technology also led to intra-continental travel becoming markedly cheaper so that there was '. . . a moving geographical frontier within which host country employers could draw on reserve labour supplies' (Paine 1982, p212). By the early 1970s, emigrant remittances had reached very substantial levels and in Portugal and Greece were equivalent to more than half the value of merchandise exports (World Bank 1981b). This made an important contribution to the balance of payments of these countries but there was a tendency for remittances to be directed to consumption rather than production (see Chapters 6 and 7). The third major 'international' element was the growth of tourism which grew at rates in excess of 13 percent per annum in the 1960s (Boissevain 1979). Tourism was based on the climatic and environmental attractions of the Mediterranean coast, on reduced costs of international travel, and on increased real incomes and leisure time in northern Europe (Pearce 1981). As with emigrant remittances, receipts from tourism made an important contribution to balance of payments accounts, being equivalent to over 30 percent of merchandise exports in the mid 1960s. However, tourism also brought cultural conflicts, environmental pollution, low-wage and seasonal employment, so its real benefit to these countries is contentious (de Kadt 1979).

Growth in southern Europe was already slowing down by the early 1970s in response to the reduced growth of the world economy. This was evident, especially in a reduction of tourist receipts and in the demand for emigrant labour. The oil crisis, and resultant sharp rise in energy costs in 1973–1974 (and later in 1979) only served to accentuate this trend. The same was true of the economic consequences of the demise of dictatorial government in Greece and Portugal in 1974 and in Spain in 1975. Political uncertainty in Spain and Portugal certainly discouraged foreign investment, while a series of strikes to try to improve living standards, disrupted production and pushed up labour costs and prices in all three countries. As a result, there was a 'vicious circle': investment fell, inflation rose and unemployment increased. These events, however, only reinforced existing tendencies within the region, as is evident, for example, in comparing Spain and Italy: the growth of GDP in the former fell from 6.1 to 2.8 percent between 1953–1973 and 1973–1979 and in Italy there was a remarkably similar decline, from 5.3 to 2.6 percent (Boltho 1982).

Developments in the Italian economy were not dissimilar to those observed elsewhere in southern Europe. The years 1963–69 had been a period of stable economic growth with modest wage increases. However, there was growing frustration amongst the working class stemming from worsening conditions of work and of housing (Marcelloni 1979). These tensions erupted in the 'hot autumn' of 1969 (the political implications of which are discussed in Chapter 3). The economic outcome of a series of strikes was higher wages, the 1979 Workers Statute (limiting the right of employers to declare redundancies) and improved working conditions. As a result, there was a sharp rise in real wages as well as declining productivity. Investment fell, inflation rose, the balance of payments deficit worsened, and the lira was devalued against the dollar by 15 percent in 1973. This pattern was repeated in the experiences of the other southern European states, two or three years later. Some of the more recent features of all four economies are summarized in Table 1.5.

4. Development and dependency

Southern Europe has been classified as semiperiphery and its relationship with the core, particularly northern Europe, is one of dependency. Selwyn has stressed that what he calls the periphery of Europe (but we have termed the semiperiphery of the world economic system) has a number of distinctive characteristics. The central feature is '. . . the lack of effective local control over the use of resources. The major economic decisions – what to produce, where and how to produce it, the origin of inputs, the marketing of outputs, what to consume, what to invest, where to invest it – all these will either be entirely taken in the core or will be profoundly influenced by decisions in the core. This, indeed, is what we mean by dependence' (Selwyn 1979, p37). There is a lack of local innovation and reliance on imported ideas and technology, poor linkages within the periphery (note the weak trade between Greece and Italy or between Spain and Portugal), poor information flows within the periphery in comparison to core-periphery flows, migrant flows from periphery to core and reverse flows of tourists. King (1982) has argued that all these characteristics are present in

Table 1.5 Recent economic indicators

Country	Growth of GDP 1975–80 (percentage)	Average Rate of Inflation 1970–1980 (percentage)	International Balance of Payments 1981 ($ millions)
Greece	4.4	14.4	–2,216[2]
Italy	3.8	15.3	–8,117
Portugal	5.2[1]	16.6	–1,048[2]
Spain	2.2	15.9	–5,095[2]

Source: OECD Economic Surveys for Greece, Italy, Portugal and Spain.
Notes: [1] Influenced by the sharp fall in production in 1975.
[2] Data for 1980.

the relationship between northern and southern Europe. Multinational companies with headquarters located in the core region are important in all these economies, although it should be noted that Italy and, to a lesser extent, Spain and Greece have their own multinationals. The multinationals of the core region can occupy a key role in the development of the southern European economies, which are also heavily reliant on tourist receipts and emigrant remittances from the core. These linkages are, however, sensitive channels whereby fluctuations in the core economies are transmitted to southern Europe.

The constraints that dependency imposes on national development strategies are most clearly illustrated in the case of Portugal where, following the coup of 1974, there was an attempt to delink from the world economy and establish a more autonomous socialist economy. Economic and political changes disrupted production and caused great uncertainty which contributed to a disastrous rate of economic growth; tourism and emigrant remittances fell precipitately, foreign banks insisted on prompt payment of obligations, there was an outflow of capital and, eventually, balance of payments and foreign exchange crises (see Chapter 4). The IMF was approached for assistance and it granted Portugal a loan, only on condition that earlier egalitarian trends (in agriculture and industry) were reversed and that a package of austerity measures were adopted. It is no doubt true that smaller economies, such as Portugal and Greece, are potentially in positions of greater dependency because limited internal markets and, perhaps, lack of natural resources, limit their scope for alternative strategies (Seers 1981). However, the example cited does illustrate some aspects of the dependency relationships in all the southern European countries.

In addition to these general features of dependency, there are also a number of other common characteristics of the southern European economies. Despite a decline in agricultural employment, the four countries still have substantial farming sectors. There is a tendency for these to be polarized between *minifundia* and *latifundia* (see Chapter 9) and to have low productivity. Only Italy has experienced any effective land reform and this, arguably, was initiated for political rather than for economic reasons (Allum 1981). The backwardness of agriculture has, traditionally, constrained development because of the reduced potential market for industrial goods, while more expensive food has increased the cost of labour reproduction. The most acute case is Portugal which, in recent years, has had to import more than half its food requirements. However, there have been changes, notably in moves to commercialize and modernize agriculture in both Spain and Italy.

Another major feature of these economies is the dualistic nature of industry, polarized between large numbers of relatively small and internationally uncompetitive enterprises and a few large enterprises; the latter may be owned by national private capital, state capital (note the IRI holdings in Italy and INI holdings in Spain), or foreign capital. Direct state involvement has been least in Greece and Portugal but this has changed, to some extent, in recent years. In Greece the state, through acquisition of the Commercial Bank (to add to its control of the National Bank) exercises a dominant influence on the availability of investment while, in Portugal, banks and many large manufacturing companies were nationalized in 1974 and 1975. The dominance of small companies can indicate a relatively inefficient and undercapitalized sector and certainly the difficulties experienced by Greece since accession to the EEC confirm this. However, segmentation of the economy, diffuse industrialization and expansion of the informal sector, can be logical responses to problems of capital accumulation. For example; there has been growth of the informal sector in Italy in response to a rise in wage levels after the 'hot autumn'. Firms in this sector mainly employ young women and older men on piecework, and operate outside the framework of labour legislation relating to wages and job security (Bernabè 1982). Therefore, care must be taken in making inferences about the nature of small firms in such economies. Another characteristic is the existence of relatively large service sectors. Certainly, in both Greece and Italy, these include large numbers of 'artificial jobs', created as part of clientelistic networks and contributing little to value added (see Chapters 2 and 3).

There are also very high levels of regional disparities in the southern European economies: for example, in the mid-1970s, it has been estimated that the four countries under review all featured amongst the six European states with the highest levels of regional variation in GDP (Nicol and Yuill 1982). The processes of uneven regional development in these countries are linked to their dependency status, for tourist and emigrant flows, foreign investment and information flows are all spatially selective. Growth tends to be concentrated in a few core regions, leaving large, relatively poor agricultural regions. The former often suffer from housing shortages and a number of other symptoms of rapid urbanization (see Chapter 8), while the latter have high ratios of noneconomically active populations and little productive investment (see Chapter 9). Both the national and international context are important for understanding changes in these regions. As King (in Chapter 6) reminds us, migration from the south of Italy works at two levels: there is internal migration to the north and international emigration, but the consequences for the areas of origin are similar.

Finally, before ending this brief review of economic development, the recent debate about 'the new international division of labour' can be noted. Fröbel et al (1980) have argued that in the 1970s there was a pronounced shift of investment from the core region to the newly industrialized countries (NICs), including much of southern Europe. There were three preconditions for this shift: the availability of a nearly inexhaustible supply of cheap and flexible labour, the subdivision of the production process so that there are many fragmented operations which require minimal levels of skill and are locationally flexible, and the development of improved transport techniques to allow international decentralization of production. In Europe, the increasing social costs of employing emigrants in the core region has also encouraged the relocation of employment in the south. This hypothesis has been criticized by, amongst others, Paine (1979, 1982) who considers it to be over simplistic. International relocation is not necessarily the only response which can be made to changes in the conditions of production, and the aims of supplying growing demands in national markets or establishing platforms for export to North Africa or the Middle East have also been important (see Chapter 7). On one point, however, both sets of protagonists are agreed: the emergence of the new international division of labour does not imply any lessening of dependency, for many important features, such as control of technology and the location of management and research remain unaltered.

5. Rise and decline of dictatorial government

The economic transformation of southern Europe in the postwar period was preceded by or accompanied by radical political changes as dictatorial governments were established and then dismantled. There is considerable variety in the political experiences of the individual countries, as there was also in their economic development but, again, there is a substantial element of shared experience. Giner (1982), a useful starting point for analysis of these political developments, considers that the southern European countries have all passed through four major phases: oligarchic rule and extreme popular exclusion, bourgeois consolidation and continued popular exclusion, fascist or fascistisant dictatorships and political pluralism within advanced capitalist corporatism.

The initial phase of oligarchic rule was probably over by the mid-nineteenth century in southern Europe, excepting Greece, where *tzakia* (control by the nobility) lasted until the late 1860s (Mouzelis 1978). This was a phase when the still relatively small and weak bourgeoisie group were excluded from political power by the elites of the *ancien régime*. However, the growth of trade and industry and of towns, saw an expansion of the bourgeoisie during the nineteenth century and they dominated most governments until the early twentieth century. There was usually a split between what loosely were termed the liberal and conservative wings of the bourgeoisie political movements: examples are the Venizelists and non-Venizelists in Greece (Mouzelis 1978) or the Progressives and Regenerators in Portugal (Gallagher 1983). However, despite differences of opinions on some issues – such as the role of the monarchy or the church – these groups shared a number of common goals. They sought to encourage industrial expansion and diversification, which usually involved protectionist economic measures as, for example, in Italy in the 1880s and in Spain in the 1890s. They also sought to 'modernize' the state but, on the one hand, they compromised with the upper classes (particularly in failing to implement agrarian reforms) and, on the other hand, they allowed only limited expansion of the franchise so that the working classes and even parts of the lower middle class were still excluded from power. The failure to reconcile these conflicting interests led to the growth of extraparliamentary opposition both in the trade unions and amongst openly revolutionary groups. Eventually, economic and political contradictions made the continuation of these regimes in their present forms impossible and all passed, however briefly, through periods of dictatorial rule in the early and mid-twentieth century.

A number of factors contributed to the rise of dictatorial government. First, as late industrializing nations, these economies had dependency relationships with the economic cores, with high levels of foreign capital penetration in their national markets, transport networks and even their manufacturing sectors. The weak state apparatus of bourgeois government was not in a position to control these intrusions, which meant that strong dictatorial governments could be advocated by some groups as a means of national advance. The southern European states also found themselves manipulated mercilessly by the core powers in the colonial sphere. The establishment of new colonies or the development of existing ones became an increasingly important means of economic expansion but this, of course, conflicted with the requirements of the USA, Britain, France and Germany. Therefore, Spain found itself denuded of its remaining important colonies in Latin America after 1898, Portugal was forced to cede claims on territories in Southern Africa to Britain and Italy launched an abortive military excursion to colonize Abyssinia. The experience of Greece was rather different, for its attention was focussed on a struggle with Turkey in order to achieve national unification (see Chapter 2). However, the Asia Minor 'disaster' of 1922 meant that Greece also experienced a major military defeat. The significance of these defeats lies in the way that they reinforced awareness of dependency while also redirecting political attention from external to internal affairs.

It can also be argued that dictatorial government became a requisite for guaranteeing capital accumulation, in the face of growing pressure from labour on surplus value. In all four cases, growth of trade union activity, disruption of production and high wage settlements can be observed. There was, therefore, a common interest amongst many elements of the middle and upper classes in a political restructuring which would allow for change in the conditions of production. Dictatorial government also seemed to offer a more stable economic future for white-collar and lower middle class groups who were amongst the worst affected victims of inflation. Finally, periods of political instability – with large scale public meetings, some forms of civil strife and a succession of weak and ineffective governments – usually preceded the rise of dictatorial government. Such conditions existed in Italy and Portugal in the 1920s, in Spain in the 1930s and in Greece before the Metaxas coup. Given this conjuncture of circumstances, dictatorial forces were able to forge alliances with the church, with bourgeois groups apprehensive of bolshevism or the consequences of instability, and with upper class groups (such as the monarchy or landowners) who wished to seek a destruction of left-wing forces.

The actual mode whereby dictatorial regimes were established varied considerably and only the briefest details can be presented here (see Delzell 1970). In Italy, Mussolini formed his first parliamentary government in 1922 after the 'March on Rome' by the blackshirts had pressurized the King into appointing him Prime Minister; this was followed in 1925 by a coup which made parliament subject to direct control by Mussolini. In Portugal, there was a military coup in 1926 and, after two years of direct military rule, the armed forces delegated government to the civilians. Salazar became Minister of Finance in 1928 and took over as Prime Minister in 1932. In Spain, the establishment of Franco's dictatorial government in 1939 was preceded by three long years of bitter civil war, during which the coalition of right-wing forces overthrew the democratically elected Republican government. The pattern in Greece was different: there was the brief Metaxas dictatorship, 1936–1940, and then, in the face of attempts to modernize the state, there was a reactionary military dictatorship, 1967–1974. A fuller discussion of some of these events can be found in Part I of this volume.

Thus far the term dictatorial rather than fascist has been used for these regimes. The 'pure' concept of fascism implies a political culture centred on a chief figure, class domination linked to single party control, extreme nationalism, systematic removal of all opposition, autarkic economic policies, a myth of cultural superiority and extreme anticommunism. None of the four southern European cases matches these criteria completely and Cassells (1975) argues that there were two distinctive branches of fascism: one, radical and totalitarian (epitomized by Nazi Germany) and the other, prevalent in southern Europe, which was really under the control of conservative interests. Italy was probably the closest to a pure fascist model because there was strongly personalized rule. However, Mussolini actually kept the Fascist Party in abeyance and did little to challenge the power of church, army, aristocracy, industrial capitalists or southern landed interests (Smith 1982). In Spain, the government represented reactionary ruling class interests but fascists were 'domesticated' and eventually distanced from power. In Portugal, the constitution of the New State established full-scale corporatism in principle and there were attempts to set up a nationalist youth movement but, essentially, Salazar's regime was conservative and backward-looking rather than fascist (Lucena 1976; Wiarda 1973). Greece under the Colonels bore less resemblance to a fascist state than the other countries.

Nevertheless, some fascist elements can be observed in all these cases

(Giner 1982). There was class domination, for although the state claimed to serve all interests, it was actually controlled by coalitions of right-wing groups whilst working class organizations were neutralized. The latter action was an important precondition for rapid postwar industrialization. Permissible ideologies were severely restricted and political pluralism was limited to the ruling classes. Anticommunism was a common theme but, otherwise, the precise ideology of the ruling class changed over time. A good illustration of this is the way Spain redefined its position vis-à-vis western Europe in light of the defeat of the axis powers in World War II (Carr and Fusi 1979). Another common feature of these countries is that the state exercised control through a service class. 'Loyal' members of all classes could be used to fill intermediate positions of authority and their recruitment was facilitated because the state was the only major source of relatively secure and well-paid jobs. This, of course, contributed to 'over-expansion' of the service sector in these economies, although the experience of Greece before the Colonels and of Italy after Mussolini suggests that the role of a service class is not exclusive to dictatorial regimes. Finally, these states relied on political cooption rather than mass political mobilization (as in 'pure' fascism) for their support; only Mussolini's Italy appeared at all 'fascist' in this respect. Therefore, the southern European countries did have some fascist features, especially in the early years, but they are probably better characterized as dictatorial regimes. On the other hand, they were not totalitarian states for their ability to reshape social structure was limited and they did not employ total surveillance and repression methods. This was one reason which contributed to the relative lack of obstacles during the later transition to political pluralism (see Chapter 5).

The dictatorial regimes of southern Europe had varying durations: the rule of Metaxas (1936–1940) and of the Colonels (1967–1974) in Greece was shortest, then came Francoism in Spain (1939–1975) and Mussolini in Italy (1922/1925–1943) but, by far the longest-surviving, was Salazar in Portugal (1926/1928–1974). Why did these dictatorial regimes eventually come to an end? In Italy the answer is largely tied up with military defeat in World War II, although pressure against the regime had emerged earlier (Di Palma 1982). In the other cases, three considerations seem to have been important: social change and economic requirements, the lack of a social base for the regime, and the continuity of conservative forces in the postdictatorial era.

In a way it can be argued that the dictatorial regimes contributed to their own downfalls, especially in Spain and Portugal. Economic policies set out initially to establish a stable context for private capital accumulation with state support in the forms of protectionism, infrastructural provision and direct investment in industry. The resultant economic growth was however constrained by the limitations of autarkic policies and there was pressure from sections of the bourgeoisie for 'opening' the economies. Eventually, there was a shift to internationalization which provided the stimulus for more rapid growth. However, this had important repercussions for the regimes: emigration and tourism brought about awareness of conditions in other countries and contributed to modernization of attitudes and demands for greater democracy. There was an expansion of the middle classes, who saw that their interests could be better served in a pluralistic political system; while, for industrialists, the logical extension of opening the economy was eventual accession to the EEC, which would only be feasible after establishment of more democratic rule. Finally, the very expansion of these economies meant that they became too complex to be administered within existing political frameworks. Together, these contradictions within the regimes created enormous pressure for change and in their final years there was already a relaxation of dictatorial rule. There were, for example, important strikes and political demonstrations in both Spain and Portugal in the early 1970s.

The dictatorial regimes were unable to resist these pressures for change because they lacked broad social bases. Therefore, at the time of crisis, the ruling elites were isolated and unable to defend their positions. By this stage the ideological legitimization of the regimes had also been exhausted and in both Spain and Portugal in the early 1970s there were confused switches in state policies – for example, in the attempts by Caetano to 'liberalize' Portugal (see Chapter 4). In addition, the armed forces were unable to resist the move to parliamentary democracy because they were socially hetero-geneous and unable to act in a unified manner (Harries-Jenkins 1978). This was notably the case in Greece where the military faction led by Brigadier Ioannides overthrew Colonel Papadopoulos when he attempted to liberalize the regime (see Chapter 2).

Finally, in many cases the ruling classes of the dictatorial regimes did not 'fade away' with the restoration of parliamentary rule. Instead they became reorganized as 'respectable' conservative parties, operating within new political institutions. After all, Francoist politicians actually prepared the new constitution for Spain and dominated the first post-Franco parlia-mentary government, while influential members of the New Democracy party in Greece were survivors from the pre-Colonels era, and many of the leaders of the Aliança Democratica in Portugal had been 'liberal' members of the Assembly under Caetano. There was, therefore, a substantial element of continuity in personnel between the two political eras and, indeed, it is argued in Chapter 5 that corporatism still survives in post-Franco Spain. Elsewhere, it has also been argued that corporatism survives in the Portuguese state (Wiarda 1979), that there is '. . . considerable institutional continuity between fascism and the Republic. . . .' in Italy (Donolo 1980) and that the military handed over power to Karamanlis in Greece precisely in order to retain their dominant position (Mouzelis 1980).

The precise conditions under which dictatorial government came to an end were as varied as they had been during their initiation. Military defeat and the death of Mussolini paved the way for the imposition of parliamentary democracy in Italy after World War II; the debacle of a military disaster in Cyprus led to the Colonels handing over power to the civilians in Greece; and the death of Franco in 1975 saw a peaceful transfer of power in Spain. Events in Portugal were more remarkable: a group of junior military officers carried out a coup in April 1974 and there was then an attempt to create a left-wing revolution but, by 1976, power had been institutionalized in a pluralist framework.

6. The postdictatorial era

Comments on the postdictatorial era will be kept relatively brief because this is the period on which Part I of the volume is focussed. Again there are common themes and individual features to be noted in the experiences of southern Europe. Almost 10 years have passed in Greece, Portugal and Spain since the end of dictatorial rule and, as yet, it is still difficult to generalize about their experiences. In contrast, over 40 years have passed since the death of Mussolini and there is a wealth of commentary on Italian politics.

The outstanding feature of the Italian experience has been the resilience of the Christian Democrats who have formed a seemingly permanent coalition of parties, creating an 'imperfect one-party system' (Allum 1981). Christian Democrat support has two main bases: first, their ideological position, reinforced by the Church's anticommunism and, secondly, their use of the State. The power of the State was used initially to repress working class organizations, such as trade unions, and to fragment the basis of working class politics. The Christian Democrats have also 'occupied the State' (Donolo 1980) and are able to manipulate patronage. This has been especially important in the South where, immediately after the war, the DC had a very poor electoral base. Patronage however has been openly exploited (42 percent of public expenditure is on 'social security') to build up a clientelistic network which usually delivers over 40 percent of the vote in the country. The first major challenge to the ruling coalition came in the Hot Autumn of 1969 which contributed to a growth of working class activity as, for example, in urban protests (Marcelloni 1979). In the 1979 municipal elections the DC lost control of many areas, even in the South, but by 1980 seemed to have recovered its position.

The experiences of the other southern European countries have been rather different. First, there has been a concern in all three countries to return the armed forces to the barracks and to exclude them from political institutions. In Greece this was probably the major achievement of the ND governments, although it was managed only by highlighting external conflicts and increasing the resources devoted to the military (see Chapter 2). In Portugal the coup by the Armed Forces Movement brought about the downfall of the dictatorial regime and played a dominant role in the transition to parliamentary democracy. They were given a permanent role in the new constitution in 1976 (dominating the Council of the Revolution which was the ultimate arbiter in constitutional matters) but were finally 'depoliticized' when the Constitution was amended in 1982. The exclusion of the military has been most painful in Spain and it has proved extremely difficult to shift some of their entrenched interests. Matters came to a head in the attempted coup led by Tejero in 1981. This led the government to modify many of its modernizing and democratizing policies – for example, with respect to regionalism and family law – but there are still fears of a future coup (see Chapter 5). For a fuller review of the legacies of dictatorial government, see Di Palma (1982), Malefakis (1982), Maxwell (1982) and Psomiades (1982).

Another common theme has been the attempt to establish new political parties in the political vacuum created by the demise of the dictatorships. Usually, elements of the liberal wings of the previous governments have combined with conservative democrats to form right-wing parties (such as the ND in Greece, the PSD and CDS in Portugal and the Popular Alliance Party and Centre Party in Spain), the Communist Party has emerged from clandestine roles to form small, but important groups on the left and 'new' Socialist Parties have hurriedly been created to contest elections. The actual pattern of electoral results has varied but has usually involved right-wing governments assuming power initially and being replaced by Socialist governments in the 1980s. Both Greece and Spain fit this model, but the position in Portugal is more complex because of the nature of the coup of 1974 and of the electoral coalitions which have been formed. Portugal (fifteen governments in nine years) is similar to Italy (44 governments in 37 years) in having a remarkably rapid turnover of governments if not in real shifts in the disposition of power.

One remarkable feature is that, in 1983, as the balance of power seems to be swinging rightwards in northern Europe, all four southern European states simultaneously have Socialist governments for the first time. Papandreou in Greece, Craxi in Italy, Soares in Portugal, and González in Spain all head socialist governments (although within coalitions in Italy and Portugal) at the time of writing. The conjuncture of social, political and economic events which have brought this about still needs to be analysed, although the papers in this volume give some clues as to its nature. Certainly there are elements of reaction to the failure of right-wing parties to 'solve' mounting economic and social problems and rejection of traditional modes of clientelism in all four cases.

Equally remarkable has been the near total eclipse of the Communist Party in southern Europe, especially in those countries recently emerged from dictatorial regimes. In recent elections the Communist parties in Spain and Greece have each only received about 10 percent of the total vote, while the Portuguese Communist Party has obtained some 17 percent. The Italian party has, of course, been more successful, receiving between about 25 and 34 percent of the votes cast. This eclipse is notable because the Communist parties usually formed the focus for clandestine opposition to the dictatorial regimes and sometimes, as in Civil Wars in Spain and Greece, assumed heroic resistance roles. Their different fortunes are not simply to be explained in terms of whether they are Eurocommunist or Stalinist in outlook: the Italian and Spanish parties are renowned for their Eurocommunist standpoints but obtained, respectively, the largest and smallest shares of popular support of all four southern European case studies. Instead their electoral disappointments stem from the restricted regional and sectoral bases of their support and the peculiarities of each party's position within its own national political context (Gallagher 1979; Kohler 1982; Prevost 1981). An interesting question concerning the shifts from dictatorial to democratic, and Conservative to Socialist governments is whether there have been changes in the political elites and in patronage/clientelism in these countries. Some of the arguments advanced in this book suggest that the rise of PASOK in Greece has brought a change in the system of political recruitment, while in Spain many positions of authority have remained in possession of Francoist appointees. In Portugal, there was a more dramatic change of personnel following the events of 1974.

There are also some similarities with respect to the policy issues which have preoccupied governments in the region. Foreign affairs have been prominent, especially in Greece which has been concerned to reduce its political dependency on the USA and strengthen its negotiating position vis-à-vis Turkey (see Chapter 2). However, the dominant foreign policy issue in Greece, Portugal and Spain has been accession to the EEC (see Chapters 2, 9 and 10). At present, Greece is involved in renegotiating its terms of accession while detailed negotiation of the membership of the Iberian countries seems deadlocked, largely because of the opposition of France and, to a lesser extent, Italy. Domestic policy issues are more varied, with regionalism being prominent in Spain, land reform and opening of the banking system being important in Portugal, and further changes in clientelistic networks and authoritarian practices being controversial in Greece. However, all four countries have had the common experience of trying to implement economic policies (to reduce unemployment and increase growth) and social policies (to extend the welfare state and change family law and women's rights) at a time when there are considerable short-run constraints on their economies (discussed earlier, see Table 1.5).

7. Conclusion

Finally, turning from the present to the future, it is interesting to contemplate some of the problems that are likely to preoccupy governments, whether right-wing or socialist, in southern Europe during the remainder of the 1980s. With no pretence of being comprehensive, five issues are highlighted here which are likely to be contentious:

1. Future trends in the world economy are extremely difficult to predict but there seems to be no immediate prospect of easing the short-term problems of the southern European economies or, in the cases of Greece and Portugal, of changing their positions of dependency. There may be greater pressures for protectionism, especially for sensitive industrial products, but the most likely boost for these economies will come from either renewed emigration flows (perhaps to new destinations or even within the semiperiphery) or a sharp increase in foreign investment as part of further shifts in the international division of labour. As ever, the semiperiphery has to identify an appropriate production niche between

the newly industrialized countries of the Third World and the core economies. Overall, it is feasible to foresee a widening rift between Italy and Spain on the one hand, becoming more firmly established as part of the core, and Greece and Portugal, still struggling to complete this economic transformation.

2. To some extent, prospects for the southern European economies are dependent on the outcome of negotiations within the EEC and between it and the Iberian applicants. As this point is covered fully in Chapters 9 and 10, here it is sufficient to stress that key issues are the status of Mediterranean agriculture (the level of support for Mediterranean producers as opposed to the terms granted both to nonmember Mediterranean countries and, internally, for temperate products), and the level of net transfers to be effected through the regional, social and other 'quota' funds. In view of the initially not entirely favourable Greek experience of EEC membership, the Iberian applicants (as well as the Community) are likely to proceed very cautiously with negotiations. Of course, it can be argued that the Iberian countries (as was earlier the case with Greece) are effectively already economically integrated with the EEC, and that membership is essential to give them a voice in policy making in Brussels. In view of attempts by some EEC countries to block out emigrant labour and some of the more sensitive industrial exports, membership may in fact be of considerable economic significance.

3. The political implications of membership may turn out to be more important than the economic ones. Certainly arguments were initially advanced to suggest that Community membership was an essential means of guaranteeing fledgling democracies. With time, and the growing stability of the new democratic regimes, these arguments have less appeal. Instead, the significance of membership is that it will bring a clear and enlarged international role for the applicants. Greece has certainly found this to be an advantage, although it has sometimes chosen to differ with overall Community attitudes. In Portugal, there are still some who see a special role for the country, using links with the ex-colonies, to be an intermediary between western Europe and the Third World. However, few (to the right of the Communist Party) challenge the view that Portugal's future lies in Europe. Spain's case is similar to Portugal's, with traditional links with Latin America offering an important complementary rather than alternative role.

4. Although the transition to parliamentary democracy seems relatively secure, there is still considerable progress to be made in democratizing

subnational level institutions. Italy has started to grasp the problems of regional government but the detachment of the DC party from the local state, especially in the South, seems a near-insurmountable task. Moderation of the role of patronage in local government is also an issue in Greece, while Portugal, which had virtually no effective local government in 1974, has only taken some of the initial steps necessary for establishing democratic local and regional government. The problems are likely to be greatest in Spain because, although the Constitution allows for a remarkable level of regional autonomy, there is no evidence that this will be sufficient to appease the more radical Basque separatist groups and yet, at the same time, devolution remains a sensitive issue for some military factions.

5. An issue which is likely to become more important in future is environmentalism. To some extent rapid growth rates in industry have been achieved at the cost of permitting severe pollution. The effects that Mediterranean countries' petrochemical industries have on their surrounding regions is well documented and need little elaboration. It is not simply the quality of the landscape which is being affected: In Tarragona the oil and petrochemical industries have greatly reduced the potential of the surrounding agricultural regions (Garcia 1982) and there are estimates that the net value added of paper pulp mills in Portugal is negative (because of their pollution of agricultural water supplies). Opposition to further large scale complexes of potential pollutant industries has grown in recent years, as Hadjimichalis and Varou-Hadjimichalis (1980) report in their study of the proposed development of Pylos.

The contradiction for the state is that antipollution measures may deter foreign investors who will locate instead in other Mediterranean countries. Environmental problems are not restricted to industry— tourism brings its own forms of pollution and, as is argued in Chapter 8, environmental issues have been the focus for the organization of many urban political movements (for example; see Ceccarelli 1982).

References

Allum, P. (1981) Thirty years of Southern policy in Italy, *The Political Quarterly*, Vol. 52, pp314–323.
Baklanoff, E.N. (1976) Mediterranean Europe: Perspective on a developing region,

in E.N. Baklanoff (ed) *Mediterranean Europe and the Common Market*, Alabama, University of Alabama Press.

Baklanoff, E.N. (1978) *The Economic Transformation of Spain and Portugal*, New York, Praeger.

Bernabè, F. (1982) The labour market and unemployment, in A. Boltho (ed) *The European Economy: Growth and Crisis*, Oxford, Oxford University Press.

Boissevain, J. (1979) Tourism and the European periphery: the Mediterranean case, in D. Seers, B. Schaffer and M.L. Kiljunen (eds) *Underdeveloped Europe*, Sussex, Harvester Press.

Boltho, A. (1982) Growth, in A. Boltho (ed) *The European Economy: Growth and Crisis*, Oxford, Oxford University Press.

Carr, R. and Fusi, J.P. (1979) *Spain: Dictatorship to Democracy*, London, Allen and Unwin.

Cassells, A. (1975) *Fascism*, Arlington Heights, A.H.M. Publishing Corporation.

Ceccarelli, C. (1982) Politics, parties and urban movements: Western Europe, *Urban Affairs Annual Reviews*, Vol. 22, pp261–276.

Delzell, C.F. (1970) *Mediterranean Fascism 1919–1945*, New York, Macmillan.

Di Palma, G. (1982) Italy: Is there a legacy and is it fascist? in J.H. Herz (ed) *From Dictatorship to Democracy: Coping with the Legacies of Authoritarianism and Totalitarianism*, Westport, Greenwood Press.

Donolo, C. (1980) Social change and transformation of the State in Italy, in R. Scase (ed) *The State in Western Europe*, London, Croom Helm.

Fage, J.D. (1978) *An Atlas of African History*, London, Edward Arnold.

Fröbel, F., Heinrichs J. and Kreye, O. (1980) *The New International Division of Labour*, Cambridge, Cambridge University Press.

Gallagher, T. (1979) The Portuguese Communist Party and Eurocommunism. *Political Quarterly*, Vol. 50, pp205–218.

Gallagher, T. (1983) *Portugal: A Twentieth-Century Interpretation*, Manchester, Manchester University Press.

Garcia, D. (1982) Agricultural change in an industrializing area, Tarragona, Unpublished paper presented to the National and Regional Development in the Mediterranean Basin Conference, Durham.

Giner, S. (1982) Political economy, legitimation and the State in Southern Europe, *The British Journal of Sociology*, Vol. 33, pp172–199.

Hadjimichalis, C. and Varou-Hadjimichalis, D. (1980) Penetration of multi-national capital into backward regions: a policy analysis in Greece, *Antipode*, Vol. 12, pp17–24.

Harries-Jenkins, G. (1978) Armed Forces and European society, in S. Giner and M.S. Archer (eds) *Contemporary Europe: Social Structure and Cultural Patterns*, London, Routledge and Kegan Paul.

Kadt, E. de (1979) *Tourism: Passport to Development?*, Oxford, Oxford University Press.

Kindleberger, C.P. (1967) *Europe's Postwar Growth*, Cambridge, Mass, MIT Press.

King, R.L. (1982) Southern Europe: Dependency or development?, *Geography*, Vol. 67, pp221–234.

Kohler, B. (1982) *Political Forces in Spain, Greece and Portugal*, London, Butterworth.

Kondonassis, A.J. (1976) Greece in E.N. Baklanoff (ed) *Mediterranean Europe and the Common Market: Studies of Economic Growth and Integration*, Alabama, University of Alabama Press.

Lucena, M. (1976) *A Evolução do Sistema Corporativo Português*, Lisbon, Perspectivas e Realidades.

Malefakis, E. (1982) Spain and its Francoist heritage, in J.H. Herz (ed) *From Dictatorship to Democracy: Coping with the Legacies of Authoritarianism and Totalitarianism*, Westport, Greenwood Press.

Marcelloni, M. (1979) Urban movements and political struggles in Italy, *International Journal of Urban and Regional Research*, Vol. 3, pp251–268.

Maxwell, K. (1982) The emergence of Portuguese democracy, in J.H. Herz (ed) *From Dictatorship to Democracy: Coping with the Legacies of Authoritarianism and Totalitarianism*, Westport, Greenwood Press.

Mérigo, E. (1982) Spain, in A. Boltho (ed) *The European Economy: Growth and Crisis*, Oxford, Oxford University Press.

Mouzelis, N.P. (1978) *Modern Greece: Facets of Underdevelopment*, London, Macmillan.

Mouzelis, N. (1980) Capitalism and development of the Greek State, in R. Scase (ed) *The State in Western Europe*, London, Croom Helm.

Nicol, W. and Yuill, D. (1982) Regional problems and policy, in A. Boltho (ed) *The European Economy: Growth and Crisis*, Oxford, Oxford University Press.

Nikolinakos, M. (1982) Internationalization of Production, Location of Industry and the Deformation of Regional Development in Peripheral Countries: the Case of Greece, unpublished paper presented to the National and Regional Development in the Mediterranean Basin Conference, Durham.

Paine, S. (1979) Replacement of the West European migrant labour system by host foreign investment in the European periphery, in D. Seers, B. Schaffer and M.L. Kiljunen (eds) *Underdeveloped Europe*, Sussex, Harvester Press.

Paine, S. (1982) International investment, migration and finance: Issues and policies, in J.A. Girão (ed) *Southern Europe and the Enlargement of the EEC*, Lisbon, Economia.

Pearce, D. (1981) *Tourist Development*, London, Longman.

Pollard, S. (1981) *Peaceful Conquest: The Industrialization of Europe 1766–1970*, Oxford, Oxford University Press.

Prevost, G. (1981) Eurocommunism and the Spanish Communists, *West European Politics*, Vol. 4, pp69–84.

Psomiades, H.J. (1982) Greece: from the Colonel's rule to democracy, in J.H. Herz (ed) *From Dictatorship to Democracy: Coping with the Legacies of Authoritarianism and Totalitarianism*, Westport, Greenwood Press.

Rey, G.M. (1982) Italy, in A. Boltho (ed) *The European Economy: Growth and Crisis*, Oxford, Oxford University Press.

Rolo, J.M. (1977) *Capitalismo, tecnologia e dependência em Portugal*, Oporto, Editorial Presença.

Seers, D. (1981) Development options: the strengths and weaknesses of dependency theories in explaining a government's room to manoeuvre, in D. Seers (ed) *Dependency Theory: A Critical Reassessment*, London, Frances Pinter.

Seers, D. (1982) The second enlargement in historical perspective, in D. Seers and

C. Vaitsos (eds) *The Second Enlargement of the EEC: The Integration of Unequal Partners*, London, Macmillan.

Selwyn, P. (1979) Some thoughts on cores and peripheries, in D. Seers, B. Schaffer and M.L. Kiljunen (eds) *Underdeveloped Europe*, Sussex, Harvester Press.

Smith, D.M. (1982) *Mussolini*, London, Weidenfeld.

Tsoukalis, L. (1981) *The European Community and its Mediterranean Enlargement*, London, Allen and Unwin.

Wade, R. (1979) Fast growth and slow development in South Italy, in D. Seers, B. Schaffer and M.L. Kiljunen (eds) *Underdeveloped Europe*, Sussex, Harvester Press.

Wallerstein, I. (1979) *The Capitalist World Economy*, Cambridge, Cambridge University Press and Editions de la Maison des Sciences de l'Homme.

Wiarda, H. (1973) The Portuguese corporative system: basic structures and current functions, *Iberian Studies*, Vol. 2, pp73–80.

Wiarda, H. (1979) The corporatist tradition and the corporative system in Portugal: structured, evolving, transcended, persistent, in L. Graham and H. Makler (eds) *Contemporary Portugal: The Revolution and its Antecedents*, Austin, Texas University Press.

World Bank (1981a) *World Development Report 1981*, Washington, Oxford University Press on behalf of the World Bank.

World Bank (1981b) *International Migrant Workers' Remittances: Issues and Prospects*, Washington, World Bank.

World Bank (1982) *World Development Report 1982*, Washington, Oxford University Press on behalf of the World Bank.

Wright, A. (1977) *The Spanish Economy 1959–76*, London, Macmillan.

PART ONE

CASE STUDIES

CHAPTER TWO

GREECE: FROM MILITARY DICTATORSHIP TO SOCIALISM

P.C. Ioakimidis

1. Introduction

There is no doubt that the 1970s and early 1980s can be characterized by years of radical change in Greek politics and society. Greece entered the 1970s under an oppressive military dictatorship led by Colonel George Papadopoulos; by the early 1980s, however, it has acquired what appears to be a stable, workable democratic system and, for the first time in Greek political history, a radical socialist government.

Underlying these developments were profound changes in the Greek economy and society. In economic terms, Greece ceased being a backward, closed economy dominated by agriculture, for the rate of capitalist development was quite spectacular until the late seventies. Gross National Product (GNP) per capita rose from 632 US dollars in 1962 to 4380 in 1980, and the share of the industrial sector in Gross Domestic Product (GDP) rose from 25.9 percent in 1962 to 32.0 percent in 1979 while that of agriculture dropped from 22.7 percent to 18.0 percent. Also important were the changes which affected social institutions and values: the family, the church, male–female roles, patron–client relations, the mass media and such pervasive psychological traits as mistrust, insecurity and individualism underwent a transformation during the past fifteen years (Campbell and Sherrard 1968; Legg 1969). In addition Greece joined the European Economic Community in 1981 as its tenth member, an event symbolizing the far-reaching changes which occurred in the politico-economic system during the 1970s.

Of course while the changes which took place in the political sphere in the

1970s represent a clear departure from the past, developments in the economy during the same period involved the acceleration of trends and processes which had begun to be manifested in the 1960s. An exception to this is of course the accession of Greece to the European Community, an event, though, with wider implications – social, political and cultural – than merely economic ones. In a rather schematic way, one could argue that in the 1970s Greece advanced its political development in the form of democratizing its political system whereas in the 1950s and 1960s it was primarily preoccupied with economic growth.

Nevertheless, important as the above-mentioned changes are, they have not made Greece a 'modern' state in the West European sense of the term. As is demonstrated in the following pages, Greece, like other Mediterranean countries, exhibits a dualist socio-political formation with modern structures and institutions coexisting with traditional elements (or what pass for traditional elements).

2. Historical background

Modernization and national unification have been two of the fundamental goals which have preoccupied the modern Greek state ever since its inception as an independent unit, in 1829. Nevertheless, neither of these two goals has been entirely fulfilled even today. Modernization in the form of westernization – that is, organizing political life and institutions along western lines – became the cherished policy of intellectuals and Greeks of the *diaspora* who assumed power as soon as the Greek independent state was born: '. . . despite the weak capitalist development and the nonexistence of a strong western-type autochthonous bourgeoisie' (Mouzelis 1978a).

Because of the nonexistence of capitalist conditions, and the resistance presented by the 'traditionalists' who argued in favour of developing indigenous institutions inherited from the Byzantine tradition, the westernization policy could not be successfully carried out. To a considerable degree, the subsequent evolution of Greek political history has been shaped by this conflict between the 'westernizers' and the 'traditionalists' (Mouzelis 1978a). It must be noted, however, that the categories 'westernizers' and 'traditionalists' do not correspond fully to the conventional dichotomy between left and right.

Simultaneously with the persuance of a modernization policy, the Greek state had to strive for the accomplishment of a further fundamental goal, national unification. Indeed national unification became the first policy priority and, under the slogan *Megali Idea* (Great Idea), the basic ideological orientation of the nascent state (Dakin 1972). This policy had of course been dictated by the fact that the Greek state, established in 1829, incorporated only a tiny part of the territories considered historically, nationally and culturally as belonging to Greece.

For almost a century (1821–1922) considerable economic and political resources were devoted to advancing national unification (Dakin 1972). This prolonged process of unification not only prevented the political elites from channelling sufficient economic resources to the modernization policy but also prevented the building of strong and legitimate central political institutions; as any new territorial addition to the Greek state tended to disrupt existing political processes and balance (Legg 1969). Moreover, the exigencies of the unification policy (that is, to expand and secure the frontiers of the new state) forced Greece to rely heavily on the support of the major powers of the day, and this left a pervasive legacy of dependency (Tsoukalas 1969).

The unification policy, as conceived in the nineteenth century, came to an end in 1922 with the military defeat of Greek forces in Turkey in the Asia Minor disaster, and the subsequent deportation of 1.5 million Greeks from Asia Minor to the Greek mainland. By that time, however, Greece had achieved a considerable degree of unification by acquiring the Ionian Islands, Thessaly, Crete, Macedonia, Epirus, the Aegean Islands and western Thrace. Even so, the perennial problem of establishing undisputed frontiers was not irrevocably resolved, as is demonstrated by the present conflict between Greece and Turkey over the Aegean and Cyprus.

Military defeat, and the influx of 1.5 million destitute Greeks, ushered in a period of sharpened social conflicts, political instability, military intervention in politics and authoritarian government (Metaxas's regime 1936), with minimal attention being paid to the problems of economic and political modernization (Dafnis 1955; Veremis 1974). Internal conflicts and external political factors led the country into a fully-fledged civil war in the late 1940s and, in this, the left-wing and radical forces, which had constituted the major resistance force against the German occupation, were annihilated. The victorious right-wing forces, assisted by the USA, imposed a semi-parliamentary system in which the monarchy and the military were invested with decisive political authority (Campbell and Sherrard 1968; Tsoukalas 1969). At the same time, a set of rules known as *parasyntagma* (parallel constitution), greatly restricted the activities of the left, while anticommunism became an official ideology of the ruling political groups. The

Communist Party was outlawed and was forced to operate outside Greece, although its popular support declined steeply anyway in the aftermath of the civil war.

This political system lasted virtually unchanged until the early 1960s. By that time, however, a new middle class had emerged as a result of the processes of economic development, urbanization and the expansion of education services. This new middle class began to press for political participation, institutional changes in the balance of power and a wider share in the fruits of economic growth. In 1963 this class, in alliance with disgruntled sections of the peasantry, brought to power the Centre Union Party, led by George Papandreou, which began to apply a cautious policy of liberalization. However, no matter how cautious and moderate the approach, this policy soon brought the Centre Union Party into open conflict with the monarchy and the army, whose power was threatened (Tsoukalas 1969, Clogg 1979). In July 1965 the King, in violation of the constitution, dismissed the Centre Union from power and installed a puppet government, thus throwing the country into a political crisis which lasted nearly two years.

Early in 1967 it appeared, however, that the crisis was about to be resolved by means of holding general elections (scheduled for May) as the Centre Union demanded. By that time, however, the Centre Union Party had been transformed into a more radical political force under the influence of Andreas Papandreou. The party advocated, among other things, the subjugation of the military to civilian rule and a drastic reduction in military expenditure (Papandreou 1966). Given the prospect of the Centre Union coming to power, the military, led by Colonel G. Papadopoulos, stepped in and imposed a dictatorial regime. In other words, military intervention constituted a reaction to the modernization process. Its main aim was to prevent the transformation of society and the political system from a semiparliamentarian, praetorian state into a genuine participatory democratic system, in which the electorate would hold ultimate political power. It was, as Huntington (1968) would have called it, a 'guardian-type' military intervention led by traditionalist-minded officers who aimed to frustrate the modernization process.

The military regime was not supported by any distinctive social class, the exceptions being the tiny, though economically powerful, group of shipowners and internationally-oriented financiers, as well as some highly conservative sections among the peasants. The rest of the population at first showed apathy which was transformed gradually into passive opposition, while intellectuals and students emerged as the most effective resistance to the regime.

The dictatorship collapsed in July 1974 for three main reasons: a) the failure to rally to its support any sizeable social group upon which it could rely for legitimizing its rule; b) the inability to deal effectively with any of the social and economic problems which faced the country; and c) the lack of internal unity among the ruling junta with respect to the policies to be pursued or the type of political system to be established on a permanent basis. Indeed, internal disunity was so pervasive that when Papadopoulos attempted to liberalize the mode of dictatorial rule in 1973, he was promptly overthrown by other officers led by Brigadier Ioannidis. The military was finally forced to return power to civilian politicians in July 1974, when it became clear that it was utterly unable to handle the crisis with Turkey which had been provoked by an attempt to overthrow President Makarios of Cyprus. With the collapse of the dictatorship, a government of national unity led by former Prime Minister Karamanlis was formed.

3. Transformation of the economy

Greece has witnessed rapid rates of growth during the postwar years, yet this growth has not altered fundamentally either the peripheral character of the Greek economy or the peculiar nature of Greek capitalism. The latter still exhibits built-in structural weaknesses which can not be overcome merely by good management policies (Delivanis-Negreponti 1979).

Rather schematically, the year 1953 can be taken as the turning-point in the postwar development of the Greek economy. In that year, the conservative government, led by Alexander Papagos, introduced the first set of policy measures which seriously aimed to promote economic growth and, more specifically, to advance industrialization of the Greek economy. Among these measures were: a devaluation of the Greek drachma by 50 percent and the introduction of special legislation (law 2687) for attracting foreign capital. In terms of economic philosophy, the government professed strong attachment to the principles of liberal economy, free enterprise and a free market economy, a philosophy consistent with its anticommunist political ideology and the prevalence of American influences. This policy orientation and philosophy was, by and large, adhered to by all subsequent governments until the rise to power of the first socialist party, PASOK, in 1981.

In practice, however, policy and philosophy were not always in accord; for in spite of the ideological emphasis on the free economy, the state came to play a crucial role in the process of economic development in the postwar years. The pervasive involvement of the state in the economy took the following forms: a) direct investment in infrastructure; b) special incentives and aids to private industry; c) control of finance to the private sector through the banking system; and d) direct participation in the economy by means of setting up public enterprises and utilities (Tsoukalis 1981). Even when the state could not play a direct economic role, it exercised an indirect influence through the banking system. The latter, virtually under the control of the state, channelled funds to projects not on the basis of vigorous economic criteria, but, more often than not, on the basis of political expediency. Consequently, political clientelism played a major role in the formulation of economic policy decisions (Kolmer 1981).

In pure economic terms, the strategy pursued by all governments until 1981 was geared to promoting 'outward-looking industrialization'. This strategy actually resulted in increasing the dependency of the economy on imported capital and technology and in the establishment of import-substitution industries. Eventually this strategy gave rise to serious balance of payments problems which the economic policy-makers tried to solve by promoting tourism and encouraging emigration (Giannitsis 1979). During the period of the military dictatorship (1967–1974), there was some shift of emphasis in economic policy to developing the sectors of construction, tourism, commercial activities and services in general, in an attempt to produce more rapid rates of growth (Karagiorgas 1978).

With regard to the sources of growth, investment rates were quite high for the period 1966–1977. Investment, which represented 15.5 percent of gross expenditure in 1956, rose to an average of 22.3 percent for the period 1964–1973 and 18.9 percent for the period 1974–1977 (Giannitsis 1979). However, the allocation of investment among the various economic sectors failed to solve the fundamental problems of the Greek economy, or to create the base for sustained and balanced growth. More specifically, in the period 1951–1975, 30.6 percent of total investment (or 43.3 percent of private investment) was absorbed by the housing sector and only 14.1 percent by the manufacturing sector and 11.3 percent by agriculture (the remainder being in infrastructure, energy and transport). In overall terms, investment in manufacturing as a percentage of GDP was the lowest among all OECD countries during the period 1960–1976.

Not surprisingly, the bulk of the foreign capital inflow to Greece – which for the period 1953–1979, is estimated at 1403.3 million dollars as registered under law 2687 (Papandreou 1981) – was invested in the industrial sector (68.9 percent for this period). Within manufacturing, foreign capital was concentrated at first in some of the strategic advanced technology sectors such as chemicals, plastics, petroleum products and base metals. Accordingly, during the 1960s multinational firms were the main exporters of nontraditional products. However, in the period 1971–1979 the share of foreign capital invested in the above-mentioned sectors dropped to 50.9 percent. Yet, at the same time, foreign capital began to penetrate successfully the traditional sectors of the Greek economy, such as textiles, food, beverages and clothing (Giannitsis 1980). Consequently, as Giannitsis (1979) argues, industrial growth was based not on the rational utilization of the productive factor which the country possessed in abundance, namely labour, but on capital which had to be imported. Indeed, labour leaving agriculture was encouraged to seek employment in western Europe, principally West Germany, and between 1961 and 1971 the net number of migrants was 543,000. Besides economic considerations, this policy also served political goals in that it contributed to diffusing social and political tensions.

Indigenous capital was directed to traditional areas of production involving low or intermediate technology (foodstuffs, textiles, etc.) while foreign capital was mainly concentrated in sectors of more advanced technology. Even the state, despite its widespread involvement in the economy, systematically neglected to promote investment in the manufacturing sector. In the period 1964–1975 state investment in that sector represented only 1.4 percent of total investment of fixed capital (Giannitsis 1979).

Despite these reservations, in pure quantitative terms, the rates of growth in the 1960s and early 1970s were spectacular. To begin with, between 1962 and 1977 the average annual rate of increase in GNP was 6.6 percent, as compared with 3.8 percent for the EEC. During the same period industrial production increased by an average annual rate of 9.0 percent (4.1 percent for the EEC) (Zolotas 1978). The rate of increase of total exports was also impressive, being 9.7 percent per annum between 1971 and 1977, at constant prices. Exports of manufactured products increased even faster, with the result that the share of manufactured goods in total exports increased from 11 percent in 1961 to over 53 percent in 1978. The composition of GDP also changed, and the share of agriculture fell from 22.7 percent in 1962 to 14.3 percent in 1979, while the share of secondary production rose from 25.9 percent in 1962 to 33.0 percent in 1979. As a result of these developments, GNP per capita which in 1962 stood at only 632 US dollars (at constant 1970 prices and exchange rates), representing 34.6 percent of the EEC average, had reached 4380 dollars or 46 percent of the Community average in 1980. This clearly suggests that, although narrowed, the income gap between Greece and the Community remains wide.

4. Structure of the economy

Despite the spectacular rates of growth in recent decades, the economy in the early 1980s is in serious structural crisis. The crisis manifests itself in persistently high rates of inflation, a widening deficit in the balance of payments, rising unemployment and stagnation in productive investment. Although the international economic crisis has adversely affected the performance of the Greek economy, the present economic predicament is primarily due to structural weaknesses. This is evident, because when the international economic environment began to improve at the end of 1982, the Greek economy continued its downward path: GDP stagnated (falling by 0.2 percent in 1981 and rising by a meagre 0.2 percent in 1982), inflation continued to run at around 20 percent and unemployment rose to 8 percent.

The structural weaknesses and problems confronting the Greek economy today are the direct result of the economic strategy which the country has followed since the early 1950s. As already stated, this strategy aimed at industrialization based on imported capital and technology, and, while the state played a paramount role in the economy, it failed either to channel investment to the manufacturing sector or to produce a coherent policy for the balanced development of the economy. These failures become even more apparent in the postjunta period (1974–1981). The economic policy of that period was based on a '. . . traditional mixture of fiscal expansion and over-accommodating monetary policies', with overexpansion of the housing sector (Kolmer 1981). In the years 1976 to 1979, while manufacture absorbed around 17 percent of total investment, the housing sector absorbed 44 percent. As a result, the role of the housing sector has grown so important that it is exceedingly difficult for any government to pursue an industrial policy independent of the housing sector.

Overexpansion of the housing sector has been accompanied by parallel expansion of the services sector. Although the phenomenon has deep historical roots (Mouzelis 1978a), the expansion of services in the postwar period has been the product of the economic policy of developing tourism and, to a lesser extent, shipping. The phenomenon assumed a dramatic dimension in the postjunta period. According to the OECD (1982), there has been a significant shift in the pattern of growth after 1975 in that the services sector came to contribute up to three-quarters of the increase in GDP as compared with only one half before 1975. The Minister of National economy, Arsenis (1982), stressed recently that if this trend persists, and the structure of the services sector does not change, then the whole process of development could come to a halt.

As noted, overexpansion of the services sector is related to the rapid growth of tourism and, to a lesser extent, shipping and the flow of funds from Greek emigrants abroad. The invisibles accruing from these sectors contributed significantly to alleviating the balance of payments problems, but they also produced a number of distorting phenomena in the socio-economic system. To begin with, by fostering overexpansion of the services sector, invisibles have contributed to leading Greece into a peculiar phase of deindustrialization before even reaching the stage of industrial maturity. Furthermore, a services sector fed by invisibles constitutes a precarious and weak foundation for the economy. This became abundantly clear recently when, as a result of politico-economic factors, the flow of invisibles declined considerably (see also Chapter 7).

Secondly, receipts from tourism, shipping and emigration, generated consumption patterns not commensurate with domestic productive capacities, with the consequent effect of increasing imports. In an indirect way, therefore, invisibles contributed to accentuating the balance of payments problems. Thirdly, from a social and political point of view, invisibles imbued some social groups with rising expectations as regards their levels of consumption, thereby increasing the pressures and demands on the social and political system. Some of the difficulties which the PASOK government is now facing, in introducing a policy of economic reform, are related to the resistance of these groups. Fourthly, a considerable amount of invisibles and especially emigrants' remittances were used for purchases of houses, largely in the area of Athens (see Chapter 6). This has contributed to the expansion of housing and population, with the undesirable effects (pollution, traffic congestion etc.) which have turned Athens into an 'uninhabitable city'.

As regards the industrial and agricultural sectors, these clearly illustrate the structural weaknesses of the economy and the failures of economic strategy. In the first place, industry contributes only 32 percent of GDP. Agriculture contributes 16 percent and employs 37 percent of the labour force while the corresponding figures for the European Community as a whole are 4 percent and 8 percent respectively (Eurostat 1981). Productivity both in the agricultural and industrial sectors is substantially lower than in the EEC as a whole. This is precisely due to a failure to channel sufficient resources into these sectors.

Greek industrial structure is characterized by fragmentation, with small and medium-sized, family-owed units being dominant except in the tobacco and chemicals sectors. It is estimated that 99 percent of all firms employ less than 50 persons and 93.5 percent less than 10. However, while small and medium firms provide 63 percent of all industrial jobs, their share of industrial net value added amounted only to around 40 percent in 1974, and they produced almost entirely for the domestic market. In contrast, almost 60 percent of total exports in 1974 came from the 100 largest firms (German Development Institute 1978). Alongside this fragmented traditional industrial sector there exists a technologically advanced sector based on, or controlled by, foreign capital. In this respect capitalist development in Greece exhibits traits similar to those encountered in certain Latin American countries whose economic structure is characterized by a dualist pattern of development (Mouzelis 1978a).

As regards agriculture, farm holdings are very small, almost three quarters of holdings being between 1–5 ha. and 93 percent being less than 10 ha. Even in terms of agricultural land in use, 43 percent is on holdings of 1–5 ha. Agricultural productivity, as measured by value added per employed person, is also low, being 10 percent lower than that of Italian agriculture and 30 percent below that of Ireland (Pepelasis 1978).

The prevalence of small, family-owned units, in both industry and agriculture tends to increase the level of self-employment in the economy. Thus, while in the OECD as a whole in the mid-1970s the self-employed and unpaid family workers accounted for 10 to 20 percent of total employment, in Greece they represented approximately 60 percent. In part this is due to the large weight of agricultural employment. Nevertheless, when this is excluded the situation becomes even more striking. The proportion of self-employed in the rest of the economy is close to 35 percent, which is not only considerably above that of OECD countries at similar levels of development, but also above that of many developing countries (Delivanis-Negreponti 1979). Self-employment is not in itself a problem, especially in a period of rising unemployment, but it is related to the so-called informal economy. In Greece it is estimated that the informal economy generates a total income equal to 25 percent of the GDP at factor cost (Delivanis-

Negreponti 1981), and that this escapes full taxation.

One of the most serious effects of the economic strategy pursued over the past 30 years is that it has led to a very unbalanced pattern of development (see Chapter 8). As the OECD (1981) observed, '. . . over the past three decades practically the whole growth of the Greek economy took place in the two urban areas of Athens and Thessaloniki, and the greater part in the Athens area'. Demographic changes highlight the gravity of the problem caused by this pattern of development. The population of Greater Athens increased from 1.85 million in 1961 to 3.02 million in 1981. That is to say; the population of Athens increased by 63.4 percent while the population of the whole of Greece increased by only 16.1 percent! Similar demographic developments were observed in the area of Thessaloniki, where population increased from 544 400 in 1961 to 871 600 in 1981, an increase of 60.1 percent. As a result of these developments, Athens now comprises 31.1 percent of the total population, while Athens and Thessaloniki together comprise 38.3 percent of the total population or 66 percent of the population living in urban areas, '. . . a degree of concentration not paralleled in any other OECD country' (OECD 1981).

Inevitably the overconcentration of population in Athens and Thessaloniki was paralleled by the depopulation of most of the other regions of the country. In the period 1961–1981 the population of the Peloponnese fell by 7.7 percent, the Ionian Islands by 14.1 percent, Epirus by 8.0 percent, Thessaly by 4.4 percent, Thrace by 7.6 percent, Aegean Islands by 12.5 percent and Crete by 5.5 percent. The region of Macedonia as a whole shows misleadingly an increase of 11.9 percent in its population thanks to the dramatic rise in the area of Thessaloniki. Other areas of Macedonia suffered the worst declines, for example, Drama 21.7 percent, Florina 22.3 percent and Kilkis 20.6 percent.

Apart from demographic data, other indicators highlight the problem of unbalanced development. Thus, 47.3 percent of all private investment, 73 percent of industrial units and 49 percent of industrial labour are concentrated in the area of Athens (OECD 1981). Social indicators also show the gravity of the situation; for example, while there is one doctor for every 215 persons in Athens, this declines to one for 14 000 in the rest of Greece (excluding Thessaloniki). The distribution of income is also uneven: whereas in the Greater Athens and Thessaloniki areas output per head is estimated to be equivalent to 124 percent and 108 percent of the national average, in the seven regions not containing major cities, the level ranges between 56 percent and 85 percent of the national average (OECD 1981).

The role of the state in the process of economic development was referred to earlier, but the expansion of its economic functions especially after 1974 has been so dramatic that it has become a structural problem for the economy. Mouzelis (1978a) speaks of 'tight state control over the whole social formation' while Papandreou, the socialist Prime Minister, considers that 'the part of the economy controlled by the state is so great that it has no parallel in any other European country'. The practice of *rousfeti* or patron–client relationships has been a major contributing factor to widening the economic functions of the state: many politicians used to exchange safe appointments in the public sector for votes, which led to dramatic over-staffing of state institutions. Thus the number of public servants increased from 65 000 in 1956 to 175 000 in 1980 (Kolmer 1981). Overstaffing was accompanied by a dramatic increase in public expenditure, for example, from 110 billion drachmas in 1974 to 731 billion in 1982. If the expenditures of social security institutions and local government and the interest on the national debt are added, then the total expenditure of the public sector amounts to 42 percent of the GNP. Some commentators, however, argue that the public sector as a whole controls around 60 percent of the GNP.

High public expenditure obviously does not necessarily imply the existence of an advanced welfare system. On the contrary, Greece still devotes a relatively low share of expenditure to social welfare. In the mid-1970s, Greece spent a lower share of its GDP on social welfare than any other OECD country (OECD 1982). In part this is because, confronted with acute external problems, Greece devotes an extremely high proportion of its GNP to military expenditure which, at around 7 percent, is the highest of all NATO countries. In addition, rising public expenditure means increasing deficits in the general budget which, together with the rising deficits of the public enterprises and utilities, fuel inflationary pressures and absorb capital resources which could otherwise have been used for productive investment.

5. Transformation of the political system

The restoration of democracy

The seven-year military dictatorship and the problems it created for Greece internally and externally served at least one beneficial purpose: it persuaded the bougeoisie that the political system had to be freed from the authoritarian elements, institutions and processes inherited from the period of civil war. In other words, the experience of the dictatorship made it clear that political modernization was a political necessity and also the only way to accommodate social and economic pressures.

The New Democracy (ND) Party which was formed by Karamanlis and other conservative politicians, adopted this modernizing ideological posture, termed 'radical liberalism', thus making an important break with the ideological theses of the past. At the same time, there was a realization that Greece needed changes in the parochial structure of its socio-economic system. PASOK, the Panhellenic Socialist Movement, the Party established by Andreas Papandreou and other radical figures in September 1974, came to advocate precisely this.

The contribution of Karamanlis and the ND party, which remained in power from November 1974 to October 1981 (winning the 1974 and 1977 elections), can be said to be the demilitarization and democratization of the political system. The first reforms of Karamanlis's administration were the legalization of the Communist Party (KKE) and the abolition of the so-called *parasyntagma*, the 'extraordinary legislation' allowing widespread discrimination against left-wing forces. Moreover, a referendum confirmed (by 69.2 percent) the abolition of the monarchy, and a new constitution making Greece a presidential parliamentary democracy was drawn up by parliament. In a sense these reforms, along with the relaxation of Greece's links with NATO and the United States, marked the end of an era in Greek politics which started with the outbreak of the civil war in 1944.

One fundamental precondition for the democratization of the political system was the drawing of firm boundaries between civilian and military institutions, restricting the role of the latter to securing the defence of the Greek territory. The experience of military rule, which ended with the debacle in Cyprus, had taught the bourgeoisie that involvement of the military in the political process, however limited, is liable to culminate in its direct assumption of power. Consequently, a broad consensus emerged on the need for keeping the military completely outside the political arena, an entirely novel attitude in modern Greek politics.

Nevertheless, the transition from a system of fully-fledged military dictatorship to one of democratic civilian government might not have been so swiftly or smoothly achieved if the danger of an immediate war with Turkey had not loomed so large in the political background. One consequence of this was that all the major political forces agreed on the need for devoting more resources to the modernization and expansion of military institutions. Ironically enough, the return of the civilian political elite to power, far from resulting in a restriction of the military's corporate strength, heralded a drastic rise in the proportion of public funds going to the military. In 1975, for instance, defence expenditure rose by 46.5 percent over 1974 levels and has continued to rise ever since. These increases were voted almost unanimously in parliament, the only exception being the Communist Party. At the same time, by evoking the urgent need for reinforcing the defence of the Greek borders, the government succeeded in physically removing from Athens all the army forces, including the elite units used for political control during military rule. With the military's corporate interest and image largely protected and its power and attention concentrated on the Greek borders, the civilian government was able to take some vital steps in the democratization process, such as organizing elections in November 1974 – the first in a decade. This is perhaps the first time in modern world history that a military dictatorship was succeeded by a completely demilitarized civilian system.

The New Democracy remained in office for six years until October 1981. In May 1980, however, Karamanlis left party politics to be elected by parliament as President of the Republic for a five-year term. The liberal George Rallis succeeded him as leader of the Party and Prime Minister. After the initial measures for restoring democracy, it can be argued that the ND failed to proceed either in the direction of further democratizing the political system, or in the direction of introducing social and economic reforms. Indeed, over time, the Party became more conservative in outlook, abandoning its liberal ideological postures in favour of more paternalistic and authoritarian policies (though Rallis personally was committed to liberal policies). For instance, the Party stopped short of freeing radio and television from tight state control or of opening these to free political discussion. It also failed to modernize the archaic structure of the Greek bureaucracy or to abolish the patron–client system.

However, the ND governments under Karamanlis and, to a lesser extent, under Rallis had to devote considerable energy and resources to foreign policy issues. Apart from joining the European Economic Community, which Karamanlis set as his first foreign policy goal (see below), he had also to deal with Greece's relations with Turkey, both within NATO as well as over the Cyprus question. Relations with Turkey had reached crisis point as a result of the invasion of Cyprus in July 1974, its claims over the continental shelf of the Aegean and over airspace. Within NATO and the USA the situation became very strained because the Greek public blamed both for the establishment of the military dictatorship and the Turkish invasion of Cyprus. Indeed, to placate public feeling, the government withdrew

Greece from the military wing of NATO in August 1974 and later initiated negotiations for revising the status of American military bases in Greece. Grece rejoined the military wing of NATO in 1980 but at the time of writing the status of the bases had not yet been decided.

The rise of PASOK to power

The election of October 1981 proved a catalyst in Greek politics. In that election the Socialist Party, PASOK, founded only seven years earlier and advocating radical *allaghi* (change) in Greece's socio-economic structure as well as in its external relations, captured an absolute parliamentary majority to form the first socialist government in Greek history. PASOK received 48.07 percent of the votes and 172 seats (out of a total of 300) in parliament, while the ND was relegated to second place with 35.88 percent of the votes and 115 seats. The only other party which gained representation in parliament was the Communist Party (KKE) with 10.94 percent of the votes and 13 members. The centre parties (EDIK and KODISO) as well as the Eurocommunist (KKE Interior) Party were virtually annihilated, electorally (see Table 2.1).

As Tsoukalas (1982) points out, the results of the 1981 election reflect important changes concerning the 'typology' and the structure of political forces in Greece. For the first time in Greek political history, it appears that there is a party system made up of three parties corresponding to three distinct ideological and political positions and that the 'structural absence' of socialist and social-democratic parties from the political arena is at an end.

PASOK drew its support from the main urban areas (Athens, Thessaloniki) as well as from rural areas and less developed regions such as Macedonia and Epirus. In fact Dretakis (1982) observed that the rate of increase of PASOK's electoral strength between 1974 and 1981 was most impressive in traditionally conservative (rural) areas. Thus, PASOK increased its strength ninefold in Zakinthos and Kastoria, sevenfold in Rodopi and Florina, and sixfold in Fthiotida and Fokida. The fact that PASOK, a radical socialist party, managed to establish an electoral base in such 'backward' and politically conservative rural areas as the southern Peloponnese, Epirus and Thrace is indicative of the far-reaching changes which have affected the socio-political structure of the Greek countryside, as well as the general desire for change in Greek politics.

Some commentators have branded PASOK as a party of 'rural protest'

Table 2.1 Results of the 1974, 1977 and 1981 elections in Greece

Parties	1974 Election		1977 Election		1981 Election	
	% of votes	Seats Parliament	% of votes	Seats Parliament	% of votes	Seats Parliament
New Democracy	54.37	220	41.84	171	35.88	115
PASOK	13.58	12	25.34	93	48.07	172
KKE			9.36	11	10.94	13
KKE es (CP Interior)					1.35	
EDIK.			11.95	16	1.69	
EK (Centre Union)	20.42	60				
KODISO.			10.61	9	0.71	
Others	11.67	8			1.36	

precisely because of its widespread support among the rural population. But, in view of the increase in PASOK's electoral strength throughout the country, it is clear that this is inaccurate. Empirical research shows that in the 1981 election PASOK managed to appeal practically to all socio-economic groups both in the urban centres and in the countryside (Loulis 1981b) though PASOK's urban vote came predominantly from the lesser bourgeoisie (small shopkeepers, artisan and white collar workers). In the rural areas PASOK captured votes from EDIK (Centre Party) as well as from the ND.

It has been argued that PASOK is an entirely new political formation, substantially different from any other party in Greek political history in terms of its programmatic principles, ideological pronouncements and organizational structures (Elefantis 1981). Although, for some, PASOK can be said to be effectively synonymous with its charismatic leader Andreas Papandreou (Mouzelis 1978b, Elefantis 1981), the party has by now developed an organizational structure and ideological position quite independent of the personality of its leader. Apart from the Communists, no other party in modern Greek history has managed so decisively to break out of the clientelistic pattern or to build such an organizational base.

The Party claims to represent the nonprivileged strata which comprise practically the whole Greek population save the economic oligarchy. It is indicative that PASOK does not call itself a party but a 'movement' based on Marxist methodology and theory, whilst resolutely rejecting 'the bureaucratic state socialism of the Eastern block'. Seen from this basic ideological posture, PASOK seems more to resemble the Populist movements of the Third World than the socialist or social-democratic parties of Europe (Mouzelis 1978b).

PASOK sees itself as the agent of historically demanded change and of the socialist transformation of Greek society. Its ideological creed rests on three fundamental principles: national independence, popular sovereignty and social liberation. Greece is viewed as a country belonging to the capitalist periphery and this has stunted its capacity for self-sustained growth and fostered exploitation, its capital and technology being controlled by the economic core (North America, specifically the United States, and Western Europe). The resulting social structure requires a small oligarchic elite, both socially and politically, which acts as an agent for foreign interests. Such dependency is obviously antithetical to the end of self-sustained growth (Papandreou 1978). Socialization of some sectors of the economy while still supporting private initiative in other sectors 'with special emphasis on small and medium sized business concerns' and the creation of 'agricultural industrial cooperatives of a new kind', are fundamental principles of PASOK's economic policy.

In the realm of foreign policy, the declared ideological goals were: a) complete withdrawal of Greece from NATO; b) the removal of American bases from Greek soil; c) withdrawal from the EEC following a referendum; and d) strengthening Greece's relations with the Balkan, Arab and Mediterranean countries.

Changes in the political elite

One of the most far-reaching developments in Greek politics after the downfall of the military dictatorship relates to the renewal and modernization of the Greek political elite in terms of its composition and ideological identity and to the transformation of the traditional patterns of political recruitment. Seen against the background of predictatorial Greek politics, this is an extremely important change. Writing in the 1960s, Legg (1969) pointed out that '. . . the opportunity for real political power in Greece is slight. There have always been few elective offices. Except in 1910 there has always been a small turnover in higher positions; and within the top leadership group most offices have been consistently held by a few durable figures'.

Generally, it was very difficult for an 'outsider' to penetrate the political elite or to reach elective or bureaucratic offices. With marginal exceptions, only persons born into traditional political families could aspire to political careers. Whenever there was a change in the composition of the political elite, it was the direct or indirect result of violent action (for example, the military intervention in politics in 1909) rather than the result of the 'ordinary' political process.

The profound changes that have affected the composition of the political elite in the 1970s are reflected first and foremost in the transformation of the membership of the parliament, for which there is reliable statistical data (although it seems clear that what happened in this group applies, by and large, to other political groups). To begin with, as Table 2.2 shows, in the parliamentary election of 1964, 161 members out of 300 (53.66 percent) were elected for a fourth time to parliament whilst 41 were elected for a third time; this means that 202 members (67.32 percent) already had long careers in politics. Only 37 members (13.33 percent of the total) were elected for the first time. By contrast, in the election of 1974 – the first election after the collapse of the military dictatorship – 184 members (61.33 percent) were

Southern Europe Transformed – Tables (2)

Table 2.2 The age structure of the Greek parliament

	1964		1974		1977	
	No.	%	No.	%	No.	%
CATEGORY 'A'						
Elected for first time	37	13.33	184	61.33	115	38.33
Elected for second time	61	20.33	16	5.33	106	35.33
Total	98	33.66	200	66.66	221	73.66
CATEGORY 'B'						
Elected for third time	41	13.66	25	8.33	13	4.33
Elected for fourth time	161	53.66	75	25.00	66	22.00
Total	202	67.32	100	33.33	79	26.33

Source: Metaxas (1981).

elected for the first time, while 16 members (5.33 percent) were elected for a second time; that is, two-thirds of the members of parliament were new-comers to politics. This modernizing trend continued in the election of 1977; 221 out of 300 members (73.66 percent) were elected either for a first or a second time, while only 79 members (26.33 percent) were elected for a third or fourth time. The same trend seems to have persisted in the 1981 election when the Party captured its majority. The overwhelming majority this has yet been conducted.

Both the major parties, PASOK and the ND, acted as agents for the renewal of the political elite. In 1974 67.9 percent of ND's representatives were elected for a first or for a second time and this percentage remained stable in the 1977 election. The fact that this occurred with the New Democracy, a party of conservative ideology and structure, is remarkable (Metaxas 1981), although a number of their key individuals had been in parliament since the end of the civil war. As regards PASOK, it is appro-priate to examine the profile of its parliamentary members after the 1981 election when the Party captured its majority. The overwhelming majority of the members – that is 150 out of 170 – had entered parliament after the collapse of the military dictatorship.

The emergence of a new, younger political elite is also reflected in the age of the deputies (MPs) elected after the collapse of the military regime. In 1964 only 30.33 percent of the deputies were under 50 years of age, while 69.66 percent were aged 50 or over. In 1974 the percentage of those under 50 rose to 43.33 percent while those in the second category dropped to 56.32 percent. Although the tendency towards the emergence of a young genera-tion of parliamentarians is quite clear, the majority of the deputies were still in the 50-plus age-group. This relationship was however overturned after the 1977 election, when 51.66 percent of the deputies were under 50 years of age (Metaxas 1981, Perdikaris 1981). This trend persisted in the 1981 election, after which 59 percent of parliamentarians were aged under 50. PASOK is currently the party whose members in parliament have the lowest average age, 48 in 1981 compared to 51 for the ND and 59 for the KKE.

All these changes indicate the relative decline of traditional patterns of political recruitment and, more specifically, the decline of the political family as an institution of political recruitment. As already noted, a rela-tively limited number of traditional political families used to provide the members of the political elite in the broader sense of the term (parliamen-tarians, top administators, diplomats etc.). More often than not, an elected politician was succeeded in his constituency by his son or nephew or another close relative, thereby ensuring the continuity of the family in political life. This phenomenon was primarily due to the structure of the Greek social and political system and more specifically, to the pattern of clientelistic politics. It was quite common for a retiring politician to leave the clientelistic network which had sustained him in parliament as an inheritance to a relative who could then get elected quite easily to parliament, irrespective of competence or ideological suitability. This does not necessarily mean that all channels to political careers were blocked for young aspirants of humble origin. In fact, two of the most influential political leaders of the postwar era, Karamanlis and Papandreou, originated not in established, political families but in poor agricultural families.

However, in general terms, the role of the political family in providing the top political leadership remained paramount in the political system which was in operation before 1967. One study has demonstrated that 40 percent of the members of parliament elected in 1964 originated in established political families. However, this percentage dropped to 26.6 percent in the parliament which was elected in 1974 and to 19.6 percent in 1977 (Perdikaris 1981). The downward trend seems to have persisted in the election of October 1981.

Although these radical changes have not been accompanied by changes of the same magnitude in the social and professional origins of the political elite, the latter trends are also positive. Lawyers of the upper middle class still dominate the elective political elite, but other professional groups more closely associated with the economic development of the country have made their way into parliament. Economists, technicians, civil engineers and planners are among those who entered parliament after 1974. The rise of these groups to political prominence is also reflected in the composition of the PASOK government which is overwhelmingly made up of people with technocratic backgrounds. The recent revision of electoral law (abolition of cross preferences, etc.) will probably contribute to eroding further the traditional pattern of political relations and to changing even more deeply the social profile of the political elite.

6. Greece in the European Community

Having joined the EEC as its first associate member in 1961, for both economic and political reasons (Yannopoulos 1975), Greece opted in 1975 for full membership of the European Community. By that time, the

Table 2.3 Greek trade with the EEC

Year	Imports		Exports	
	Million $	% of total	Million $	% of total
1961	272.4	38.1	68.4	30.7
1967	526.8	44.4	200.4	40.4
1973[1]	1,739.0	50.1	799.0	55.0

[1] With the enlarged Community.
Source: Bank of Greece.

economy's dependency on the EEC market had grown considerably, mainly as a result of the tariff liberalization arrangements laid down in the association agreement. As Table 2.3 shows, while in 1961 only 38.1 percent of total exports went to the EEC, by 1973 this figure had risen to 50.1 percent. Similarly, imports from the EEC countries, which in 1961 represented 30.7 percent of total Greek imports, rose in 1973 to 55.0 percent. Economic reasons, and, above all, political considerations, prompted Karamanlis to seek full membership of the EEC in June 1975. The negotiations, which began a year later, resulted in the signing of the Act of Accession in 1979 which enabled Greece to become a full member of the Community on January 1, 1981.

For its accession to the EEC, Greece accepted the so-called *acquis communautaire*, that is, the whole body of policies and regulations which the Community had produced up to January 1, 1981. Greece appeared so anxious to join the Community that it did not raise some questions which might have delayed the negotiations. The main aim of long and painful negotiations was not the modification of the *acquis communautaire* but the formulation of transitional arrangements to allow Greece to adjust smoothly to Community conditions and to enable the Community to absorb the effects of the entry of a new member. In the previous enlargement (with the UK, Denmark and Ireland) the transitional arrangements acted exclusively for the benefit of the newcomers, as compensation for their acceptance without any modification of Community policies. However, in the Greek case a number of the arrangements aimed to protect the Community from the impact of the admission of a new and relatively underdeveloped country (see also Chapter 10). As a general rule, the transitional arrangements for the complete application of Community policies to Greece are of a five-year duration. They commenced on January 1, 1981 and will end on December 31, 1985 with two notable exceptions: a seven-year transitional period is provided for the incorporation of peaches and tomatoes into the Common Agricultural Policy (CAP), as well as for the free movement of labour between Greece and the EEC. In a number of cases, the transitional period is limited to two or three years or there is no transitional period at all as, for example, with the right of establishment and free provision of services.

Greece has been a member of the Community for only two years which is rather a limited period for any meaningful assessment of the impact of Community membership on the Greek economy and political structure. Nonetheless, some trends which have already become apparent afford a basis for discussion. Accession to the European Community was seen by the New Democracy and by Karamanlis himself as a decisive step towards strengthening Greece's external position, consolidating democratic institutions and modernizing the socio-economic system. In other words, the paramount reasons which prompted Karamanlis to seek Community membership were political (Karamanlis 1979). He hoped that, by joining the EEC, Greece would be able to relax its dependency on NATO and the United States (which, from the mid-1940s, had served as a 'protector power') and develop a more influential role in European affairs. With hindsight, it seems that Karamanlis attached far greater political significance to the Community that the Community itself felt it possessed. The emphasis on the political necessity for joining the EEC relegated economic considerations to a secondary place. The economic implications of accession were never considered seriously and this partly explains why Greece pushed so hard to join the EEC.

At the same time PASOK, the main opposition party (from 1977), had projected such passionate ideological opposition to the Community itself and to Greece's entry that it hardly afforded any basis for rational discussion of the likely economic and political implications. Total opposition to Greece's entry was also expressed by the Communist Party (KKE). Only smaller parties such as the Eurocommunists and the social-democratic KODISO tried to rationalize the discussion on the EEC, although to no avail. In contrast, accession to the EEC and 'Europeanization' of the socio-economic system appeared to serve as an alternative political ideology for conservative political forces, following the bankruptcy of the anti-communist pseudoideology which had been their exclusive political credo since the end of the civil war. It is possible to suggest, that the 'ideology of accession' and accompanying overtones concerning the role of Greece in

Europe were clumsy responses to filling the ideological vacuum which emerged after the collapse of the *Megali Idea* (Theodoropoulos 1979).

In retrospect it is clear that the significance attached to Greece's accession to the Community was grossly exaggerated and certainly was not borne out by events. Of course, participation in the Community has had a certain modernizing influence on administration and a positive socializing impact on the behaviour of Greek civil servants. It is also true that Greece, especially under the PASOK government, has made its voice heard within the mechanisms of European Political Cooperation (EPC) over a number of important international issues. This seems to have influenced positively the 'psychological identity' of the country. The decisions by Greece not to support the dispatch of European forces to Sinai in October 1981 and not to endorse commercial sanctions against Poland after the declaration of martial law – issues discussed in the framework of EPC – complicated the shaping of common community positions. However, for Greece these were acts of great political significance in that they demonstrated the ability of the country to play a distinctive role in international affairs. Nevertheless, the expectation that, as a result of Community membership, Greece would be able to lessen its dependency on NATO and the USA did not materialize. The PASOK government is now trying to develop a new, more symmetrical, relationship with the USA and NATO, but this owes more to the party's policy than to Community membership.

The economic implications of Community membership have become more apparent during the past two years. One should of course distinguish between the so-called budgetary implications and the wider economic implications. The budgetary implications refer merely to the position of a member state in the financial system of the Community (whether it is a net beneficiary), whereas in order to assess the overall position, it is imperative to take into account the trade flows which result from the customs union and a number of other less quantitative factors.

Greece has made substantial gains out of the Community's budget during the first two years after accession. In 1981 it received 170 million ECUs in 'net receipts' while in 1982 this figure jumped to 630 million and is estimated to reach 700 million in 1983. The bulk of this money came from the Agricultural Fund (FEOGA), a smaller part from the Regional Fund and only a tiny part from the Social Fund (Ioakimidis 1983). More importantly, this budgetary gain is almost completely offset by the adverse impact of trade liberalization on the balance of payments. While Greek exports to the EEC fell in 1981 by 2.2 percent, imports from EEC countries increased by a staggering 37.5 percent. As a consequence, the overall trade deficit with the Community countries doubled in 1981 to 2.5 billion dollars and in the first 10 months of 1982 it reached 4.9 billion dollars. As The Economist (January 15, 1983) stated, '. . . far from boosting Greek industry and exports, membership of the EEC since January 1981 has opened the floodgates to imports of European manufactures and food'.

Most pervasive has been the impact of Community membership on the agricultural balance of payments. In 1981, for the first time, Greece's agricultural balance of payments with the EEC showed a substantial deficit. While in 1981 Greece had a surplus of 6.8 m. drachmas in the agricultural balance of payments with the Community, this was turned into a deficit of 10.9 m. drachmas in 1981, the first year of accession. Agricultural imports from EEC countries, which in 1980 were 9.5 percent of total imports, reached 16.6 percent in 1981. This dramatic deterioration in the Greek agricultural balance of payments is directly related to the operation of Community rules, which forced Greece to divert imports of agricultural products from low cost, third countries to high cost, Community countries. At the same time, opening of the Greek market enabled the more efficient Community farmers to push exports of a number of items, including meat and dairy products (see Chapter 9).

The opening of the national market has been extremely painful for Greek manufacturers. A number of manufacturing sectors have shown that they were not at all prepared to face the competition of the most efficient Community manufacturers or to adjust smoothly to Community rules. Greek industry is not uncompetitive because of accession to the EEC but Community membership has accentuated existing problems to such an extent that an increasing number of manufacturing establishments have already collapsed. The worst affected enterprises are in the traditional labour-intensive sectors, such as shoes, clothes, furniture, textiles and spirits. Imports of these products from Community countries (mainly Italy) increased by as much as 200 percent in some cases, while exports either fell or stagnated. Confronted with this deteriorating situation, Greece took drastic measures in January 1983:

1. It devalued the drachma by 15.5 percent to improve the competitiveness of exports.
2. It obtained permission from the Commission to impose, for one year, import restrictions on a number of products.

At the same time, the government has entered into a dialogue with the Commission for a more thorough restructuring of Greece's relations with the Community.

7. Conclusion

Greece is currently in a transitional stage of economic and political development which makes it exceedingly difficult to assess the prospects even for the immediate future. Nevertheless some concluding remarks are possible and some trends can be outlined.

No doubt the peaceful change of government with the rise to power of PASOK is an important event not least because it demonstrates the capacity of newly-founded political institutions to absorb political change. PASOK has already introduced a number of serious institutional reforms in the social and political system, including abolition of antidemocratic legislation inherited from the period of the civil war, official recognition of the wartime resistance, lowering the voting age to 18, abolition of cross-preference voting, partial reform of the civil service, radical review of the education system especially at university level, and reform of family law, recognizing both equality of the sexes and civil marriage. However, the promised electoral reform (simple PR) and the lifting of state control over the trade unions and radio and television have not yet been implemented.

In foreign policy, however, PASOK has been forced by harsh realities to moderate or even abandon some of the radical theses it advocated while in opposition. It seems that PASOK has relinquished its pledge to organize a referendum on whether Greece should remain in or leave the EEC; instead, it is trying to obtain better terms for the protection of the Greek economy within the Community. Similarly, there is an attempt not so much to break as to restructure Greece's relations with the USA and NATO. To this end, negotiations have been reopened for revising the status of the American bases in Greece though, at least ideologically, the government remains committed to their eventual removal. Relations with Turkey remain deadlocked, owing mainly to the refusal to Turkey to drop its claims over the Aegean. PASOK has also made attempts – some quite successful – to develop Greece's relations with the Balkan and the Arab states as well as with the developing countries. Therefore, in general terms it seems that Greece's international position and orientation will not change radically in the immediate future, though it will pursue a more open and multi-dimensional foreign policy. In other words, Greece will remain in western institutions, including the EEC and NATO, although its attention will continue to be directed towards its eastern neighbour, Turkey.

With respect to the economy, it is clear that there is an urgent need for structural reforms: development of some industrial sectors, promotion of regional development so as to arrest overconcentration of economic activities around Athens, curbing bureaucratic state intervention in the economy and reducing the dependency of the economy on imported capital and technology. PASOK, committed to the socialist transformation of the economy, has presented a draft five-year plan which provides for such reforms as well as for the socialization (involving worker participation) of key sectors of the economy. Nevertheless implementation of such a plan appears to be fraught with difficulties in the face of continuing economic stagnation and the resistance of well-entrenched interests. Therefore, economic and social policies are bound to be a central issue in future political debate.

References

Arsenis, G. (1982) *Summary of the Statement at the Annual Shareholders Meeting*, Athens, Bank of Greece.

Campbell, J. and Sherrard P.H. (1968) *Modern Greece*, London, Ernest Benn.

Clogg, R. (1979) *A Short History of Modern Greece*, London, Cambridge University Press.

Couloumbis, T.A. (1980) Greek American relations in transition, *Hellenic Review of International Affairs*, Vol. I, p7–24.

Dafnis, G. (1955) *I Hellas Metaxi ton Dio Polemon 1923–1940*, Athens, Ikaros.

Dakin, D. (1972) *The Unification of Greece 1770–1923*, London, Benn.

Delivanis-Negreponti, M. (1979) *Analysi tis Hellinikis Oikonomias*, Athens, Papazisis.

Delivanis-Negreponti, M. (1981) *I Helliniki Oikonomia*, Thessaloniki, Paratiritis.

Dretakis, M.G. (1982) *Parliamentary Elections 1974, 1977, 1981*, Athens.

Elefantis, A. (1981) PASOK and the elections of 1977: The rise of the populist movement, in H.R. Penniman *Greece at the Polls; The National Elections of 1974 and 1977*, Washington, American Enterprise Institute for Public Policy.

German Development Institute – GDI – (1978) *European Community and Acceding Countries of Southern Europe*, Berlin GDI.

Giannitsis, T. (1979) Provlimata anaptixis tis hellinikis oikonomias, *Oikonomia kai Koinonia*, Vol. 1, pp26–45.

Giannitsis, T. (1980) Polyethnikes epicheiriseis kai exagogikes sheseis tis helladas, *Oikonomia kai Koinonia*, Vol. 2, pp21–30.

Huntington, P.S. (1968) *Political Order in Changing Societies*, London, Yale University Press.

Ioakimidis, P.C. (1983) Dio chronia entaxeos stin EOK, *Oikonomikos Tachydromos*, Vol. 13, pp47–53.

Karagiorgas, D. (1978) Oi Oikonomikes Synepeies tis Stratiotikis Dictatorias in Sp Papaspiliopoulos (ed) *Meletes Pano stin Sychroni Helliniki Oikonomia*, Athens, Papazisis.

Karamanlis, C. (1979) *The Ideal of a United Europe in Greece and the EEC: Political, Economic and Cultural Aspects*, Athens, Epopteia.

Karras, H. (1981) 1964–1981: Continuity and change, *Anti*, Vol. 193, pp11–15.

Kohler, B. (1982) *Political Forces in Spain, Greece, Portugal*, London, Butterworth.

Kolmer, K. (1981) *The Greek Economy at a Crucial Turning Point: Political Reality versus Social Aspirations in The New Liberalism: The Future of Non-Collectivist Institutions in Europe and the U.S.*, Athens, Centre for Political Research and Information.

Legg, K.R. (1969) *Politics in Modern Greece*, Stanford, Stanford University Press.

Loulis, J.C. (1981a) *The Greek Conservative Movement in Transition: From Paternalism to Neo-Liberalism, in The New Liberalism. The Future of Non-Collectivist Institutions in Europe and the U.S.* Athens, Centre for Political Research and Information.

Loulis, J.C. (1981b) Pos kai yiati oi hellines psifisan to 1981, *Epikentra* Vol. 22, pp4–29.

Metaxas, A.I.D. (1981) Biokoinoniki kai politismiki chartografia tis voulis, *Epitheorisi Politikis Epistimis*, Vol. I, p11–56.

Mouzelis, P.N. (1978a) *Modern Greece: Facets of Underdevelopment*, London, Macmillan.

Mouzelis, P.N. (1978b) The Greek Elections, *New Left Review*, Vol. 108, pp59–74.

OECD (1981) *Regional Problems and Policies in Greece*, Paris, OECD.

OECD (1982) *Economic Surveys*, Greece, Paris, OECD.

Papandreou, A. (1966) *Democratia kai Ethniki Anagennisis*, Athens, Fexis.

Papandreou, A. (1978) *PASOK Positions*, Athens, PASOK.

Papandreou, B. (1981) *Polyethnikes Epicheiriseis*, Athens, Gutenberg.

PASOK (nd) *Diakyrixi Kyvernitikis Politikis*, Athens, PASOK.

Pepelasis, A. (1978) The structure of Greek agriculture and the expected impact upon entering the community, *La Grèce et la Communauté*, Edition de l'Université de Bruxelles.

Perdikaris, E. (1981) O rolos tou koinonikou metachimatismou stin exelixi tis koinoniologikis synthesis tis voulis. *Epitheorisi Politikis Epistemis*, Vol. I, pp57–79.

Theodoropoulos, B. (1979) *Aspects of Accession in Greece and the EEC: Political, Economic and Cultural Aspects*, Athens, Epopteia.

Triantis, S.G. (1965) *Common Market and Economic Development*, Athens, Centre of Planning and Economic Research.

Tsoukalas, C. (1969) *The Greek Tragedy*, London, Penguin.

Tsoukalas, C. (1982) To genikotero noima ton eklogon kai oi prooptikes tous, *Epitheorisi Politikis Epistimis*, Vol. 2, pp135–153.

Tsoukalis, L. (1981) *The European Community and its Mediterranean Enlargement*, London, Allen and Unwin.

Veremis, Th. (1974) *O Rolos tou Stratou stin Politiki*, Athens, Exantas.

Yannopoulos, G.N. (1975) Greece and the European Economic Communities: The First Decade of a Troubled Association, London, *Sage Research Papers*.

Zolotas, X. (1976) *Greece in the European Community*, Athens, Bank of Greece.

Zolotas, X. (1978) *The Positive Contribution of Greece to the European Community*, Athens, Bank of Greece.

CHAPTER THREE

ITALY: SURVIVING INTO THE 1980s

M. Slater

1. Introduction

At first glance, it may seem inappropriate to place Italy in the same socio-economic and political category as other countries of southern Europe. Unlike the others, Italy has experienced continuous democratic rule since the end of World War II. She also plays an important international role. During the 1950s, the country was one of the six founder members of the European Community and today, her government regularly attends the summit meetings of the seven major western industrial nations. Rapid economic growth in the late 1950s and 1960s turned Italy into one of the world's leading industrial powers with multi-national corporations such as Fiat, Pirelli, and Olivetti competing successfully in world markets. In addition, smaller industrial concerns producing consumer durables experienced remarkable growth. The northern industrial triangle, defined by the cities of Genoa, Milan, and Turin, has become one of Western Europe's richest regions, comparable to any in France, Germany, or the Benelux countries. In recent years, economic growth has spread to other regions in north-eastern and central Italy. With industrialization has come the growth of the working-class and the development of a powerful workers' movement. The industrial militancy of the late 1960s and early 1970s in Italy paralleled similar developments in northern Europe. In many other respects, Italy shares the same social, economic, and political experiences as any other urbanized, industrialized society in Western Europe.

Despite the similarities with northern Europe, many aspects of Italian politics and society remain typical of southern Europe. The Mezzogiorno, in particular, conforms to the stereotype of a traditional Mediterranean society, since, in terms of economic development, it has languished behind other regions. In the rural areas, an agricultural population, now depleted by successive emigrations, continues to eke out an existence on mountainous and often unproductive land. Like other parts of Italy, the South is a traditionally urbanized society. But, unlike the northern cities, those in the South have not experienced high levels of industrialization, and the urban working class makes up only a small proportion of the total population. Instead, the service sector is over-inflated, corresponding to the model of Third World cities. Much of the service sector consists of public administration workers, dependent for their livelihood on state funding. The importance of the public sector, especially in the South, has encouraged the development of clientelistic patterns of political participation. Until the 1950s, patronage was exercised by wealthy local notables but since then, political parties have increasingly exercised patronage through the expansion of state spending (Allum 1981). The Christian Democrats, as the dominant party of government throughout the postwar era, have used their control of state resources to consolidate their position in the South, as well as in some other regions.

The manifestations of a Mediterranean 'culture' are not confined to southern Italy for clientelistic patterns also exist in the North. Furthermore, Italian democracy as a whole seems to be little more stable than in other countries of southern Europe. Italians still appear to be distrustful of politicians and the governmental process. Corruption in high places is a recurring theme of the past 35 years. Unlike the countries of northern Europe, the working class has not been fully integrated into the governmental process. Although the Socialist Party joined the governing coalition in 1963, the Communist Party, representing the majority of the working class, remained excluded. It still remains excluded today, despite attempts to accommodate it during the 1970s. The sharp political divisions reflect the deep social and economic divisions that characterize Italy. Rapid industrialization, migration, and urbanization have created a series of intractable problems in both urban and rural areas that today test to the limit the capacities of the political system.

The contrasts visible in Italian society make it both typical and atypical of southern Europe. Italy remains in many respects a traditional Mediterranean society, yet it is also firmly part of the modern industrialized world. It is, in fact, a country of both continuity and change. These contrasts have not made the task of government easy, and help explain the high level of cabinet instability during the postwar era. Since the late 1960s, Italy has, in a very real sense, become even less governable than it was in the past. The social and economic systems displayed new forms of instability which threatened the political system. For the past ten years, the state has teetered on the brink of collapse. Yet miraculously it survives. The situation might best be described as one of permanent instability.

What are the changes which have made Italy so much less governable in the 1970s than in the past? Certainly, the crisis of governability has not been limited to politics. Economic problems of inflation and unemployment have aggravated the political crisis. Inflation has remained in double figures since the oil price increases of the early 1970s and today it stands at about 13 percent. Unemployment is at 9 percent (or 11 percent allowing for short time working) while Italian industry, having to rely on the import of most of its raw materials, has been vulnerable to the vagaries of the international economy. The relatively labour-intensive nature of Italian industry, compared to northern European competitors, proved disadvantageous following the great increase in union militancy from the late 1960s onwards. During the 1970s, the union movement developed new forms of participation, and now plays a central role in economic policy-making. Pressure for change has not come from the unions alone; the growth of terrorism, of both left and right, has threatened to undermine civil society. Far more demands have been made upon the political system than was previously the case, and by groups that have become far more powerful.

The political crisis has been marked by the steadily loosening grip of the Christian Democrats on the reins of political power. The Christian Democrats remain the largest party but in 1981 for the first time, a non–Christian Democrat, Giovanni Spadolini, leader of the Republican Party, led the Italian government. Following the June 1983 elections, in which the Christian Democrats lost votes to moderate parties of the centre, Bettino Craxi has become Italy's first Socialist Prime Minister. The past 10 years of crisis have also been marked by the growth of protest politics. This involved:

1. The electoral rise of the right in 1972.
2. The rise of the left, notably the Communists, in the mid-1970s.
3. The rise of the Radicals in 1979.
4. In the 1980s, it is the turn of the smaller parties of the centre, presenting themselves as the main alternative to Catholicism and Communism.

One of the results of this development is the breakdown of accommodation between political parties. During the 1950s and 1960s there were
numerous coalition crises but, they were all resolved without resource to
new elections by accommodation among the parties. Since 1968, however,
no parliament has run its full course. The last four elections, in 1972, 1976,
1979, and 1983, have all been premature. Though the parties of the centre
and centre-left continue to govern Italy, their hold on government has
become increasingly unstable.

To some extent, it might be said that the crisis of government has also
been affected by the vast increase in mechanisms of political participation
during the 1970s. In the 1960s, legislative and municipal elections were the
major forms of citizen participation. In the 1970s, we have seen:

1. The spontaneous development of new channels of participation such
   as workers' councils and neighbourhood councils.
2. The implementation by the government of democratic reforms such
   as regional government and schools' councils.
3. The further development of existing mechanisms of participation that
   had fallen into disuse. Thus, the referendum was revived in 1974 as an
   important device in the policy-making process. In the past ten years, it
   has been used to great effect by issue-orientated interest groups, and
   also by the Radical Party.
4. There have also been new forms of participation through the development of direct action, in the form of mass demonstrations, strikes, and
   terrorism.

The political and civil crises of the 1970s and 1980s have their roots in the
social and economic transformation that took place during the 1960s. The
'Hot Autumn' of 1969 was the major catalyst of change. In the following
sections, I will look first at the background to the transformation of the
1960s, moving on to explain how the socio-economic changes of that period
relate to later political changes. In dealing with changes in the 1970s, I will
focus, in particular, on unions, the party system, and new forms of participation.

2. Background

There are several strands of Italy's ongoing crisis of governability. Certain
economic and political aspects can be traced back to the early postwar

period and beyond. At the political level, the fundamental problem in Italy is the lack of accommodation between the two major political subcultures, Catholicism and Socialism (Barnes 1977). As a result, the working class has been imperfectly integrated into the political system.

The dominance of Socialism and Catholicism in the postwar era has been one of the legacies of fascism. The advent of a fascist dictatorship discredited the traditional political elites. Though they survived the fascist period in the guise of the present day Liberal and Republican Parties, they never again enjoyed widespread political support. The implications were important, for it meant there was no possibility for a party of the bourgeoisie to dominate postwar politics.

Instead, the Christian Democrats, building a bridgehead to state power through the Church, emerged as the dominant political force, aggregating the interests of the bourgeoisie and other social groups. The signing of the Lateran Pacts in 1929 had ended the 60-year isolation of the Church from political life. It also gave the Church a privileged position in the cultural life of the nation, establishing Catholicism as the state religion. Far from compromising Catholicism with fascism, the Lateran Pacts consolidated Catholic strength. Thus, Catholics emerged from fascism with a solid organizational base from which they could develop their own political party, the Christian Democratic Party.

The fascist experience also had a major impact on the left in Italy. The Socialists had entered the fascist period as a divided movement. In 1921, the party had split with the formation of the Communist Party. After 1920, in fact, the Socialist Party had shown little appetite for revolutionary action, though this was not always apparent from the rhetoric of party leaders. The division of the socialist movement was important in so far as it paved the way for the eventual integration of the Socialist Party into the postwar political system. By the 1960s, the Communist Party stood alone as the major antisystem party on the left. Both the Communists and the Socialists emerged from fascism with considerable credit because of their opposition to the dictatorship. The Communists, in particular, gained support from their role in the Resistance Movement, and the martyrdom and intellectual contribution of Gramsci. The experience of fascism also fostered, within the Italian socialist movement, a strong commitment to political liberties. Certainly, in the north and central regions, the Communists and Socialists emerged from the war as a major, and sometimes the dominant, political force. It was in these regions that they had led the Resistance movements. The South, in contrast, had had no internal resistance movement, and was liberated by external forces. There, the local notables remained in control, and there was little penetration by the mass parties.

The final legacy of the fascist era was the continued existence in Italy of the nondemocratic right. Drawing its support from the lower ranks of the civil service, parts of the South, and more recently, discontented youth, the extreme right remains an isolated group in Italian politics, despite attempts in the 1980s to define itself as the 'new right'.

By the end of World War II, patterns of political loyalties had been firmly established and the dominance of the Christian Democrats was soon apparent. The Truman doctrine and the advent of the Cold War resulted in the exclusion from the government of the Communist Party in 1947. This exclusion provoked a further split in the ranks of the Socialist Party. In 1948, a majority of Socialists joined ranks with the Communists in opposition to the Christian Democratic government. A smaller group broke away, forming the Social Democratic Party. The choice for the Socialists was whether to be prosystem or antisystem and the majority chose to be antisystem.

Throughout the entire postwar era, Christian Democrats have dominated the political system. The Christian Democratic Party is much broader than the old Popular Party, which it effectively replaced. It unified the traditions of both liberal and social catholicism. It is representative of all social classes, being both a bourgeois and a working-class party. Though a religious party, it is rather more than that. The decline of the traditional bourgeois parties meant that the Christian Democrats were seen as the main rallying point for the bourgeoisie. Its anticommunist stand has ensured the continuing support of the middle class. This anticommunism was already apparent in the 1948 elections in which the Christian Democrats won an absolute majority of votes. It also reemerged as a potent force in the mid-1970s. Historically, the main regional base of Christian Democratic support was in the 'white' zones of the north-east. Through their control of the state apparatus, however, the Christian Democrats have built up their levels of support in southern Italy. Southern notables wielding political power have either disappeared or been integrated into the Christian Democratic Party.

From 1948 to 1963, the Christian Democrats governed in coalition with parties of the political centre. They remained the dominant partner in coalitions which were formed with the Liberals, Republicans, and Social Democrats. In a sense, this period saw the first rapprochement between Catholicism and socialism in so far as the Social Democrats were now integrated into the governing majority.

It could not be claimed that this period was one of governmental stability in Italy. Changes in government were almost as frequent as in the French Fourth Republic. But, there was no threat to the authority of the state. The Communists, and to a lesser extent the Socialists, constituted a potentially powerful opposition. Indeed, in some regions, mainly in central Italy, the Communists were the largest party. However, they remained politically isolated, and were excluded from the governmental process.

International developments explained much of the Communists' and Socialists' isolation. During the years of the Cold War, the Christian Democrats, and their allies, brought Italy firmly into the Western fold. The first step was NATO membership, with the establishment of important NATO bases on Italian territory whilst the second step was membership of the European Communities. In 1952, under the leadership of de Gasperi, the Italian government joined the Coal and Steel Community, and in 1958, Italy became a member of the EEC and Euratom. The economic arguments in favour of joining these communities were hardly compelling. Certainly the ECSC gave Italy access to raw materials, while both it and the EEC provided export markets. At the time that membership was mooted, however, there was genuine concern that Italy's nascent industries would suffer from Community competition. Therefore the fact that Italian industry gained significantly from the expansion of aggregate demand that came with Community membership was viewed as a bonus (Graziani 1972). The fundamental motive for joining the Communities was political (compare this to the Greek experience – see Chapter 2). It gave Italy a greater voice in world affairs, and integrated the country firmly into the West European political system. The existence of a large pro-Soviet Communist Party gave these political arguments special force.

In economic terms, Italy had emerged from World War II with a largely rural economy. Like other countries, the war had had a disruptive effect on industry. The main structural feature of the economy was the divide or duality between North and South, and between the modern and traditional sectors. The underdevelopment of the South had its origins, at least in part, in the pattern of Italian Unification. Unification in 1861 had been achieved by the Piedmontese elite. The result of this northern hegemony was a disproportionately heavy tax burden for the South, and premature exposure to the more efficient economy of the North. Since these disadvantages were combined with a latifundia land tenure system that defied reform, it is no surprise that the South failed to fulfill its promise of development (see Mountjoy 1973; Eckaus 1961).

The fascist experience did little to change the major economic divide between North and South. The antiurbanization laws proclaimed by the Fascists had only a marginal impact. More important was the state of the international economy during the 1930s which hindered industrial growth and cut off the outlets of emigration, particularly from the South. The economic collapse of the 1930s did, however, produce an important side-effect which was to have political and economic consequences in the post-war era. In 1936, the collapse of Italian industry closely followed by the collapse of their major creditors, the banks, forced the state to take direct control over large parts of the manufacturing and banking industries. The long-term result was to place great powers of patronage in the hands of those who controlled the central state apparatus. Over the past thirty years, the Christian Democrats, as the dominant governing party, have used this resource to their advantage. They have expanded the state sector still further, leading to the growth of large numbers of parastatal organizations, such as the *Cassa per il Mezzogiorno* (the major state funding agency for southern development). This vast patronage network has been particularly important in consolidating Christian Democratic power in the South (Caciagli and Belloni 1981; Chubb 1981; Littlewood 1981). There, the state sector is of disproportionate importance compared to the more industrialized northern regions.

During the early postwar years, economic growth proceeded at a moderately rapid rate. Between 1953–1957, GNP increased at an annual rate of 5.5 percent (Postan 1969), but, from 1952–1958 employment grew by only 8 percent (Lutz 1962). Even in major industrial cities such as Milan and Turin, the actively employed population increased only slowly. Unlike the nations of northern Europe, Italy did not reach full employment until the early 1960s. During the 1950s, levels of unemployment remained high, while under-employment and hidden unemployment were serious problems, especially in the South which, in fact, was a vast reservoir of labour (Graziani 1978). Millions emigrated from rural poverty, but few went to Italy's own industrial regions (King 1976). Instead, they went to the Americas, Australia, and northern Europe (see Chapter 6).

The pattern of economic growth during the 1950s provided the conditions for social and political stability. Emigration also provided a useful safety valve for the political system. In the industrial regions, the isolation of the political representatives of the working class was matched by the weakness, ideological divisions, and political dependence of the trade-union movement. The 1944 Pact of Rome had seen the unification of the

Italian trade-union movement into the CGIL (*Confederazione Generale Italiana del Lavoro*). As a result of the Cold War, the movement split three ways. The CGIL remained as the union of Communists and left-wing Socialists. The CISL (*Confederazione Italiana dei Sindacati dei Lavoratori*) was formed in 1948 as a Catholic workers' union with close links to the Christian Democratic Party. Finally, the UIL (*Unione Italiana del Lavoro*) brought together Socialists, Social Democrats, and Republicans. Closely tied to the political parties, the unions had little scope for independent action. In many large factories, such as Fiat, union members, especially those belonging to the CGIL, were actively discriminated against. Unions had virtually no contractual power in the work-place. Indeed, wage contracts were always negotiated at the confederal level, since union representatives in the work-place were not recognized by employers.

The lack of working class power during the 1950s was understandable in view of the Cold War, the various ideological divisions, and most of all, the state of the labour market. Not till the 1960s did the balance of power within the political system begin to change.

3. Social transformation in the 1960s

Against the background of relative stability during the 1950s, social and political change came with economic expansion. Membership of the European Community in 1958 had opened up new markets for Italian industry and the following years were a period of international integration (Rey 1982). In addition, as Kindleberger notes, Italy's labour reserves were an important factor contributing to economic growth. Between 1958–1962, the annual rate of economic growth touched 8 percent. This was the period that became known as the years of the 'economic miracle' (Kindleberger 1965) (see also Chapter 1).

Economic growth brought about a profound socio-economic transformation in Italy and it dramatically changed the occupational structure. In 1950, 40.8 percent of the Italian work-force was employed in agriculture, 31.8 percent in industry and 27.4 percent in other activities, mainly services. By 1964, the proportion employed in agriculture had declined to only 25.4 percent; that in industry had increased to 40.8 percent and that in other activities, to 33.8 percent (D'Antonio 1973). During the 1960s and 1970s, the proportion employed in agriculture has continued to decline: by 1980 agriculture, industry and services accounted respectively for 11, 45 and 44 percent of the labour force. Within the industrial sector, the fastest expanding industries were the more technologically advanced ones; auto-mobiles, petrochemicals, and metallurgy. The more traditional sectors experienced a relative decline (D'Antonio 1973).

The locus of growth was the northern industrial triangle. Despite the efforts of the *Cassa per il Mezzogiorno*, the South remained relatively underdeveloped. From its foundation in 1950 till 1957, the *Cassa* prin-cipally funded agricultural projects, such as the land reform programme (King 1973), which was seen as a prerequisite for southern industrialization (see Chapter 9). Later, it funded the provision of industrial infrastructure, and also offered a series of financial incentives for industrial investment. The programmes have continued in one form or another into the 1980s (Ronzani 1980). The lack of success of the *Cassa*'s programmes is evidenced by the continuing gap in living standards between the North and the South. It is also evidenced by the massive rates of emigration from the South. Far from stemming the emigration tide, the development programmes of the late 1950s and 1960s coincided with the increase in migratory flows away from the southern regions (King 1981).

Migration in the South has created two kinds of problems. First, it has led to rural depopulation, particularly in the more inaccessible mountainous regions. Agricultural land is often under-utilized in these regions. Second, it has led to an over-expansion of many southern cities, which have played host to large numbers of rural migrants. The lack of industrial job oppor-tunities in these cities has meant that the new migrants have swelled the ranks of an unproductive service sector. Government policy has been directed towards the stimulation of economic growth in a number of southern cities, designated as poles of development. The main policy instrument has been compulsory investment by state-owned industries. However, many of the projects, such as the steel works at Taranto and the oil-based industries at Siracusa, have been poorly integrated into the local economies; they are capital intensive and have not had the hoped-for multiplier effects, either on local firms or their hinterlands.

The process of economic development profoundly transformed social and economic life in southern Italy although it is possible to agree with Wade (1979) that there has been 'fast growth but slow development'. As a result, the traditional gap between produced and disposable income remains (Fano and Sardoni 1979), and it is bridged by state transfer payments (Wade 1979). In 1980, the South with 35.6 percent of the Italian population produced 23.9 percent of GNP but had 27.9 percent of dispos-able income. Consumption levels have also been maintained by emigrants remittances. In gross terms, the mean per capita income of the South, expressed as a percentage of that of the North, increased from 41 to 59 percent between 1951 and 1971 (King 1981). However, as Schneider, Schneider and Hansen (1972) have argued, this represents 'modernization without development'. Many social groups are marginalized from production, depending instead on the distribution of patronage.

In contrast, economic development has led to radicalization of the northern working class. Several factors contributed to this radicalization. The first was the tightening of the labour market. By 1963, following the years of the 'economic miracle', unemployment stood at a record low of 2.6 percent. For the first time unions began to exert serious contractual power in the work-place. The 1963 wages' contracts resulted in major pay increases for many categories of workers (Weitz 1975; Giugni 1971).

Accompanying this tightening of the labour market was mass immigration to the industrial regions, urbanization, and industrialization. With regard to immigration, the industrial regions of the north-west had depended initially on local migration from the surrounding agricultural regions. Later, northern industries, in their labour-recruitment drives, switched first to the north-eastern regions of the country, and by the late 1950s to the South. It is estimated that over 5 million southerners migrated to the industrial regions around Milan and Turin over the 25 year period from 1955–1980. The cultural divide between North and South in Italy and the scale of internal migration meant that a major change took place in the social and ethnic composition of the northern Italian working class. Further, the very process of migration led directly to the breaking down of traditional family and community ties. A process of secularization was underway, reinforced by other aspects of economic growth.

The speed of the urbanization which accompanied this process gave rise to serious social problems. Migrants settled in poor housing in the peripheral areas of the major industrial cities and social infrastructure was grossly inadequate. Bianchi argues that the poor integration of migrants into the urban environment of Turin was to contribute to their later militancy in 1969 (Bianchi et al 1970; Della Setta 1978).

The nature of industrialization was also an important contributory factor to the radicalization of the working class. The late 1950s and early 1960s saw a major reorganization of the work processes in northern Italian factories. Increasing mechanization and division of labour led to the employment of large numbers of low and semiskilled workers. A process of proletarianization was taking place. During the 1960s, then, there grew up in northern

Italy a new class of low-skilled southern migrants, alienated both from the industrial environment and from the urban environment. Furthermore, they were in many senses, removed from traditional cultural ties influencing their behaviour. It is not too dramatic to say that a powderkeg was being created (Bianchi et al 1970).

The changing social environment in Italy had an impact on politics by the early 1960s. New demands for housing, schools, and other social infrastructure needed to be met (see Chapter 8). Under the leadership of Moro, the Christian Democrats moved towards an accommodation with the Socialist Party. The Socialists, under Nenni's leadership, had moved reluctantly towards sharing government with the Christian Democrats and the parties of the centre. It was preferable to remaining in isolation with the Communists. In 1963 the Socialists entered a centre-left coalition led by the Christian Democrats. This period also saw a rapprochement between Socialists and Social Democrats; the two parties merged in 1965.

The experience of government was not entirely happy for the Socialists. On the positive side, they were able to gain access to large areas of public patronage. A Socialist, Mancini, became minister of public works, the classic ministry for the dispensation of patronage. On the negative side, the Socialists became tarred with the brush of corruption and immobilism. As junior coalition partners, the reforms they were able to achieve were very limited and, meanwhile, the Communists became the main voice of opposition on the left.

The ineffectiveness of the Socialists was immediately apparent from the new government's response to the union victories of 1963. Responding to a downturn in the international economy, a series of deflationary measures were put into effect. Over the next few years unemployment increased and by the time of the 1966 wages' round, union strength had been considerably diminished. Only modest wage increases were awarded. Thus the centre-left coalition continued to be based on the policy of exclusion of the working class.

After 1966, the economy improved to the extent that by 1968/69, full employment was reached once again. This time the impetus for change could not be halted. Matters came to a head in the 'hot autumn' of 1969. The importance of the 'hot autumn' was that it served as a catalyst for political and social change in Italy. After this, a government policy based on the exclusion of the working class was no longer possible.

There had already been a taste of the 'hot autumn' in 1968. In that year, a radical students movement had developed in Italian universities. Far more important, towards the end of the year, a series of wildcat strikes had broken out amongst low-skilled migrant workers in some of the large Milanese and Torinese factories. What seemed particularly radical about the conflict was:

1. The existence of councils expressing workers' demands directly on the shopfloor.
2. The egalitarian nature of many of the grievances.

The new mood of radicalism was even more apparent the following year. In 1969, the metal workers' contract came up for renewal and over 4 million workers came out on strike. The same forms of organization developed as in 1968. New radical demands were made, bringing into question not just salaries, but the whole organization of work, investment programmes, and skill systems within the work-place (Pizzorno et al 1976).

The importance of the movement lay mostly in the fact that it constituted a grass-roots protest against the prevailing system of industrial relations in Italy. It also by-passed the traditional union structure, whose ideological divisions seemed so irrelevant to the problems of workers in the factory. Whether one was a Communist, Socialist, or Catholic made little difference to the basic problems one faced as a worker on the shop-floor, or as a migrant facing problems of housing, transport, or ethnic discrimination within the urban environment. Government and employers effectively ceded to workers' demands which, it was estimated, added 28 percent to the costs of Italian industry over the next three years (Giugni 1971).

4. Developments in the 1970s and 1980s

The early 1970s were marked by the economic effects of the 'hot autumn'; industrial wages rose by almost 20 percent in 1970 alone and the number of hours worked fell by about 12 percent by 1974. Consumer prices rose quickly as labour productivity declined. In addition, as the lira continued to be overvalued, exports became less competitive and the growth of GDP slowed down considerably. As the country is heavily dependent on imported oil (equivalent to approximately 70 percent of energy needs) the oil crisis had a severe impact on the economy. However, devaluation of the lira allowed exports to remain buoyant and this sustained growth in the face of weak domestic demand (Rey 1982).

The political changes brought about by the 'hot autumn' can be distinguished in terms of the way the protest movements were mediated by:

1. The trade union movement, and its effect on the industrial and political system and their impact on political life in the 1970s.
2. The party system.
3. The mechanisms of participation which developed directly and indirectly from the 'hot autumn'.

Unions, economics and politics

It is important not to lose sight of the fact that the 'hot autumn' was a protest movement not just against the government, but the entire political and industrial establishment. The latter included the trade unions as much as it included industrialists. In factories such as Fiat in Turin, about 90 percent of the delegates elected to the new factory councils claimed no political or union affiliation.

The most important development was that trade unions managed to regain control of the protest movement at an early stage. This resulted in the consolidation of trade union strength, and also changed the nature of the union movement. During the 'hot autumn' and in 1970, the old structures of union representation had existed alongside the grass-roots workers' councils. Either because of the extreme weakness of the union movement, or alternatively, through the foresight of trade-union leaders, the unions abandoned their traditional organization and integrated the new structures into the union movement. In mediating the protest movement, the trade-union movement developed a programme of social reforms, on issues such as housing, education, health and transport. Though ultimately this reform movement met with fairly limited success, it was nonetheless important in that it made the unions major protagonists in the political arena. In pursuing this course of action, the unions effectively by-passed the major political parties, denying their legitimacy as representatives of working class interests, although, by the mid-1970s, the political parties had regained an initiative of their own.

The option of deflationary policies has no longer been realistic as a means of bringing wage increases under control. In a sense, inflationary wage increases were institutionalized in 1975, when unions negotiated an index-linked pay agreement with employers. This provided for automatic pay increases in line with rises in the cost of living as measured by an agreed 'basket of goods'. There is no doubt that other factors have contributed to the high levels of inflation in Italy, notably the oil price increase of 1973 and the level of aggregate demand. However, the high cost of labour, together with the increasing difficulties associated with laying-off labour, has been an important element in the inflationary spiral. This process has led to a loss of competitivity in Italian industry, particularly in the large scale public and semipublic enterprises. A partial response to this crisis has been the growth of diffuse industrialization (Arcangeli et al).

The changing balance of power within the productive system has contributed to the growth of corporatism in Italy. Unions are now a central part of economic, and indeed social, policy-making (Regini 1979; Salvati and Brosio 1979). Over the past few years, no prospective Premier called upon to form an administration, has thought it wise to ignore the unions' viewpoint. Consultations have taken place before an administration was formed.

In 1978, the famous 'svolta sindacale' occurred in which union leaders expressed their willingness to negotiate with government and employers. This has culminated in the 1983 agreement to limit the full impact of index-linked pay increases, by increasing pay at 15 percent less than the rate of inflation. The Craxi government is currently committed to seeking further reductions. Four factors were important in explaining this change in union strategy:

1. There is no doubt that unions did now see inflation and the economic crisis as a problem for the working class. The concessions they made were from a position of strength, and in return for a central role in economic policy-making.
2. The high cost of labour had led directly to the segmentation of the labour market. The most dynamic sector of the Italian economy during the 1970s has been the small firm, often linked to big capital through subcontracting (see Chapter 7). Unlike large firms, small firms have been able to employ a largely nonunionized workforce. The very strength of this sector has threatened to compromise the claim of the unions to represent the productive element of society, the working class.
3. The collaboration of the Communist Party (PCI) in the government majority in 1978 may also have influenced the decision of union leaders to pursue a policy of cooperation.
4. Strikes led by autonomist unions in some sectors of industry and public enterprise threatened the hegemony of the trade union movement.

Changes in the party system

The immediate effects of the 'hot autumn' on the party system were to place the centre-left coalition in crisis. The Socialists felt seriously compromised by their participation in government and though they did not withdraw from the government coalition immediately, the party underwent a leftward shift. However, by 1974, aware of the growing strength of the Communist party, and angry that the DC had sided with the neofascists on the divorce issue, it was no longer prepared to participate in a centre-left coalition.

The Christian Democrats, for their part, also experienced a leftward shift within the Party in the early 1970s. The results of the 1972 elections were not disappointing to the Christian Democrats but they revealed that there was a considerable right-wing backlash against the increasing power of the trade-union movement and of the working class in general. Parties that had stood on a right-wing platform had been successful at the election and, for example, the neofascists (MSI-DN) who had recently joined forces with the Monarchists became the fourth largest party in Italy with 8.9 percent of the vote.

The reaction of the Christian Democrats to the 1972 elections was to shift markedly to the right and this was given impetus in 1973 by the election of Fanfani as general secretary of the Party. Under his stewardship, the DC in the 1976 elections pursued a strongly anticommunist line. Despite the leftist gains, the Christian Democrat vote remained stable, while the extreme right lost support. Quite clearly, the Christian Democrats were selling themselves as a rallying point for right-wing forces. This development was important for it was further evidence of the breakdown of traditional political culture in Italy. The Christian Democrats, with the growing trend towards secularization, could rely less and less on the vote of regular churchgoers. It was having to depend on its attraction as a right-wing conservative party.

On the left of the political spectrum, the immediate aftermath of the 'hot autumn' had been disarray. As previously mentioned, the Socialists had been compromised by their role in government. The Communists, on the other hand, had played no role in leading the conflicts, which had been grass-roots movements. By the 1972 elections, they had still not formulated a coherent strategy for integrating the protest movement. Thus the elections did not result in any gains for the left since the protest movement was not being mediated through the parliamentary system.

The PCI had long realized the importance of a strategy of alliances with other social and economic groups in order to broaden its appeal. The results of the 1972 elections revealed the need for the party to pursue such a strategy with greater force. In 1973, Berlinguer announced the PCI's strategy of 'historic compromise'. The compromise was to be an alliance between the Communists and all the other democratic parties in Italy. Such an alliance, argued the Communists, was the best way to tackle Italy's pressing social and economic problems.

There were several reasons why the Communists saw the 'historic compromise' as their best strategy. First, the experience of the Marxist Allende government in Chile had shown the difficulties faced by a democratically elected left-wing regime in holding on to power against right-wing forces. Second, the increase in terrorism combined with the success of neofascist parties in the 1972 elections pointed towards a need for solidarity among democratic parties, that is, the lessons of the interwar years had been well learned. Third, social conflicts in the late 1960s had shown the irrelevance of ideological divisions to the basic problems of low pay, poor housing and lack of schools which working people had to face. Finally, the 'historic compromise' was an admission that Catholicism *did* exist in Italy. If the Communist party wished to solve the problems of working people, it had to admit that many members of the working class were Catholic and supported the Christian Democratic Party.

The 'historic compromise' strategy was spectacularly successful and it put both the Socialists and the Christian Democrats on the defensive. The former were no longer prepared to participate in government without the participation of the Communists whilst the latter could not form a government without the Socialists. The Communists presented themselves to the electorate as the Party whose participation was vital for the resolution of Italy's social, economic, and civil crises. As a Party that had not participated in central government, it also stood as a Party of efficient, incorruptible administrators. The first sign of the success of the Communist strategy came in the 1975 regional elections and this new trend was continued in the general election of 1976, the Communists obtaining a greatly increased share of the vote, 34.4 percent, while the DC held steady at 38.7 percent.

Following the 1976 elections, it soon became apparent that no government was possible without Communist collaboration. The Socialists, having made no gains in the election, were less willing than ever to participate in government without the Communists. A centre coalition on the other hand, could not provide sufficient parliamentary support. The problem for the Christian Democrats was that they had fought the election on an anticommunist ticket. They could hardly turn around and invite the Communists into government. Eventually, under the leadership of Andreotti, a Christian Democratic government was formed which relied on the external support of the Republican, Liberal, and Social Democratic Parties, and the abstention of the Socialists and Communists. In return, the Communists were consulted on the programme proposed by the government to deal with the economic and civil crisis. Andreotti also discussed his economic plans with the trade-union leadership.

The Communists now became victims of their own success. Denied full participation in government, they were, because of their 'historic compromise' strategy, obliged to accept accommodation with the Christian Democrats even at a fairly minimal level. With the government pursuing an austerity plan, they now faced the prospect of losing popularity among their traditional supporters within the working class. They also became identified with the political establishment.

Poor results in the May 1978 municipal and provincial elections showed the risks inherent in the Communists' strategy, for they were no longer seen as an important source of change within the political system. In 1979, the Communists withdrew from supporting the government; they demanded full participation in the cabinet. With the Christian Democrats unwilling to make this concession, early elections took place. The result was the decline of the Communists' vote to 30.4 percent. The main gains were made by left-wing parties, pursuing a more antiestablishment line than the Communists; thus the Radical Party tripled its vote to 3.4 percent.

Following the 1979 election, the Communists continued to call for a 'historic compromise'. However, the relative weakness of the PCI now opened up possibilities for the Socialists to take over the political initiative lost by the Communists. Under the dynamic right-wing leadership of Craxi, the Socialists have managed to present themselves as an alternative to the doctrinaire socialism of the Communists and to the inefficiency and corruption of the Christian Democrats. The Socialists are thus attempting to take up the mantle of change within the Italian political system. They are no longer prepared always to play the role of junior coalition partners and since the late 1970s Craxi has had ambitions of holding the premiership. Following the 1983 elections, Craxi's ambitions have finally be realized, albeit within a centre-left coaltion.

New forms of participation in politics

The final effect of the 'hot autumn' which we have identified is the movement towards new forms of political participation in the state. These are of several types:

1. Those that grew spontaneously and directly from the workers' conflicts in the late 1960s. These included the workers' councils, providing the work-force with democratic structures of participation within the workplace and the neighbourhood councils which acted as pressure groups for social change within the urban environment.
2. The regional councils which came into being during the 1970s. Regional government had been provided for in the 1948 constitution but it had not been implemented. It had been opposed by the Christian Democrats as it was seen as giving a new power base to opposition parties. For the same reason, the Communists argued strongly in favour of regional reform. The reform law was finally passed in 1972 largely in response to the demand for greater openness within the system. The regions have indeed provided important power bases for the Communists and also the Socialists, notably after the 1975 elections. However, the reality of regional government has not proved as advantageous as the opposition believed. First, the regions still have fairly limited powers as a result of the non-implementation of regional government statutes by the central government. Secondly, access to political power and patronage has also involved Communists in taking on the responsibility for failures in social policy.
3. The referendum that was brought in during the 1970s. Not used since 1946, it was resurrected in the early 1970s by the Movement for Life which tried unsuccessfully to abrogate the 1970 abortion laws. Since then, it has been used particularly by the Radical Party on mainly civil libertarian issues.

Outside these more formal mechanisms of participation, the social transformation of the 1960s and the 'hot autumn' led to the development of more informal and extraparliamentary forms of participation. Since the 1960s, there has been a significant increase in the level of strike activity in Italy. Strikes are used not just to achieve contractual gains in the workplace, but also as a means of achieving certain social and economic objectives in the world of politics. Finally, the events of the late 1960s have produced a form of extralegal participation that has been welcomed by few Italians — terrorism. The worst excesses of terrorism occurred significantly during the period 1976–1980 when the major parties within the political system could all be regarded as members of a political establishment. Thus Moro, one of the main proponents of closer links between the Christian Democrats and the Communists was murdered in 1978, and the Bologna station bombing, in which 84 people died, took place in 1980.

5. Conclusion: the political economy of the 1980s

The new Italian government, like its predecessors and other western governments, is faced with major problem of creating the conditions for sustained economic recovery. A major failing of previous governments, and particularly of the recent Spadolini government, has been their inability to control inflation and unemployment (compare this to the Portuguese experience — see Chapter 4). Under the subsequent Christian Democratic government, led by Fanfani, some progress was made in limiting wage increases through the reform of the wage indexation agreement. No-one doubts, however, that any new government will soon come under intense pressure on the wages' front.

The growth of international trade during the past 20 years, helped by international trading agreements such as GATT and the creation of supra-national trading organizations, such as the European Economic Community, has made it increasingly difficult for governments to formulate a national economic strategy. Italy is particularly vulnerable to changes in the international economy. She is a signatory of GATT and, of course, a member of the EEC. She imports most of her raw materials, paying for them through the export of finished manufacturing goods. Having little control over raw material costs, the Italian government can aim for little more than helping to improve the export performance of Italian industry. It can best achieve this goal by making industry more efficient, thus reducing labour costs.

In seeking to achieve its goal of increasing productivity, and hence Italy's competitive position vis-à-vis third countries, there are two ideal strategies:

1. *The laissez-faire model* of reducing the role of government, controlling spending to reduce inflation, but at the same time creating higher unemployment. This strategy will increase labour productivity, but will involve some social costs.
2. *The corporatist model*, seeking broad consensus between government, business, and unions over wages and prices with the objective of

increasing productivity whilst minimizing the social costs (compare this to the Spanish experience – see Chapter 5). In the case of Italy, the pursuit of either strategy is limited by the political developments of the past few years.

The first solution is risky, given the strength of the trade-union movement, the development of more popular and radical forms of political participation, and the strength and nature of the political opposition on the left. The Communist Party provides a credible alternative government given its level of popular support. In the event of an Italian government pursuing a hard-line antiunion strategy, the Communists might well be capable of forming a government with dissenting coalition partners. It would not, however, be a government that would be acceptable to bourgeois interests, nor to Italy's allies.

The second solution is the one that most closely corresponds to that of recent Italian governments. Regular consultations over economic policy now take place between government, business, and the trade-union movement. However, this consultation has been forced on the Italian government as a result of the increasing union strength of the 1970s. The consultation process, though, is still imperfect, since the political representatives of a major section of the working class, the Communist Party, remains excluded from the governmental process. This exclusion means that there is no solid basis for corporatism within the Italian political system. Indeed, the kinds of concessions currently required of the working population in terms of lower pay increases and public expenditure cuts (to control the public deficit) are such as to place severe strain on the social and political system. Under these circumstances, alternative means of popular participation seem likely to flourish.

Among other complications it is clear that the recent and proposed enlargement of the EEC will pose one of the greatest challenges for the future. Initially, Greek accession has benefited agricultural and industrial exports from Italy, but the membership of Spain will pose rather different problems. Spain will offer competition in agricutural products, including most fruit and vegetables but especially wine, olive oil and citrus. Italy's well-publicized problems in exporting its surpluses of wine to France, for example, can only be exacerbated by this. As accession of the three other southern European states will surely also weaken Italy's share of the regional and social funds, further enlargement must be viewed with great reservations.

The general international context also causes concern for the prospects of industrial expansion. Italian growth has been based on successful adaptation of production to the requirements of international markets. The 'hot autumn' initially destroyed the flexibility of the labour market in responding to these, and eventually encouraged diffuse industrialization. Whether further adjustments can be made in the 1980s, given changes in the international economic system (see Chapter 7) remains to be seen. Perhaps the largest question mark of all hangs over the heavy industrial complexes established in the South. Such projects have relatively short production cycles and it will require an enormous political commitment by the State to renew them within the region at the end of the century. At the moment this political commitment clearly does not exist, as evidenced by the policy pronouncement of the head of the IRI, Romano Prodi.

This brings us to a final point, the inevitability or otherwise of the persistence of North–South disparities. Certainly the employment structure of the latter has changed but King (1981) still estimates that southern unemployment levels are about 50 percent above those of the North. Matters will not be assisted by the slow down in emigration which, traditionally, accounted for up to half the income of villages in some remoter areas. Instead, it is likely that the South will increasingly become a welfare region, dependent on State transfers. It is in times of crisis that the State is least able to maintain these and when, consequently the associated system of political patronage comes under most strain.

References

Allum, P. (1981) Thirty years of southern policy in Italy, *The Political Quarterly*, Vol. 52, pp314–323.

Arcangeli, F., Borzaga, C. and Goglio, S. (1980) Patterns of peripheral development in Italian regions 1964–1977. *Papers of the Regional Science Association*, Vol. 44, pp19–34.

Barnes, S.H. (1977) *Representation in Italy*, Chicago, University of Chicago Press.

Bianchi, G., Aglieta, R., Merli-Brandini, P. (1970) *Delegati Operai: Ricerca su Nuove Forme di Rappresentanze Operaie*, Rome, Quaderni ISRIL.

Caciagli, M. and Belloni, F.P. (1981) The new clientelism in Southern Italy: the Christian Democratic Party in Catania, in S.N. Eisenstadt and R. Lemarchand (eds) *Political Clientelism, Patronage and Development*, London, Sage.

Chubb, J. (1981) The social bases of an urban political machine: the Christian Democratic Party in Palermo, in S.N. Eisenstadt and R. Lemarchand (eds) *Political Clientelism, Patronage and Development*, London, Sage.

D'Antonio, M. (1973) *Sviluppo e Crisi del Capitalismo Italiano 1951–1972*, Bari, De Donato.

Della Setta, P. (1978) Notes on urban struggles in Italy, *International Journal of Urban and Regional Research*, Vol. 2, pp303–329.

Eckaus, R.S. (1961) The North–South differential in Italian economic development, *Journal of Economic History*, Vol. 20, pp285–317.

Fano, D. and Sardoni, C. (1979) The fiscal crisis of the State: notes on the Italian case, *Capital and Class*, Vol. 8, pp46–57.

Giugni, G. (1971) Recent trends in collective bargaining in Italy, *International Labour Review*, Vol. 104, pp307–350.

Graziani, A. (1972) *L'Economia Italiana 1945–1970*, Bologna, Il Mulino.

Graziani, A. (1978) The Mezzogiorno in the Italian economy, *Cambridge Journal of Economics*, Vol. 2, pp355–372.

Kindleberger, C. (1965) *Europe's Post War Growth*, Cambridge, Mass., MIT Press.

King, R. (1973) *Land Reform: the Italian Experience*, London, Butterworth.

King. R. (1976) Long range migration patterns in the EEC: an Italian case study, in R. Lee and P.E. Ogden (eds) *Economy and Society in the EEC*, Farnborough, Saxon House.

King, R. (1981) Italy, in H.D. Clout (ed) *Regional Development in Western Europe*, Chichester, Wiley.

Littlewood, P. (1981) Patrons or bigshots? Paternalism patronage and clientelist welfare in Southern Italy, *Sociologia Ruralis*, Vol. XXI, pp1–18.

Lutz, V. (1962) *A Study in Economic Development*, London, Oxford University Press.

Mountjoy, A.B. (1973) *The Mezzogiorno*, Oxford, Oxford University Press.

Pizzorno, A. (1976) *Lotte Operaie e Sindicator in Italia (1968–1972)*, Vols I–VI, Bologna, Il Mulino.

Postan, M.M. (1969) *An Economic History of Western Europe 1945–1964*, London, Methuen.

Regini, M. (1979) Labour unions, industrial action and politics, *West European Politics*, Vol. 2, No. 3, pp44–61.

Rey, G.M. (1982) Italy, in A. Boltho (ed) *The European Economy: Growth and Change*, Oxford, Oxford University Press.

Ronzani, S. (1980) Regional incentives in Italy, in D. Yuill, K. Allen and C. Hull (eds) *Regional Policy in the European Community*, London, Croom Helm.

Salvati, M. and Brosio, G. (1979) The development of market politics: industrial relations in the seventies, *Daedalus*, pp43–71.

Schneider, P., Schneider, J., Hansen, E. (1972) Modernization and development: the role of regional elites and non-corporate groups in the European Mediterranean. *Comparative Studies in Society and History*, Vol. 14, pp328–350.

Wade, R. (1979) Fast growth and slow development in Southern Italy, in D. Seers, B. Schaffer and M.L. Kiljunen (eds) *Underdeveloped Europe*, Sussex, Harvester Press.

Weitz, P.R. (1975) Labour and politics in a divided movement: the Italian Case, *Industrial and Labour Relations Review*, Vol. 28, pp226–242.

CHAPTER 4

PORTUGAL: TWENTY YEARS OF CHANGE

M. Porto

1. Introduction

The beginning of the 1960s was a turning point for Portugal. Events during this period formed the basis for important developments that led to clear changes in Portuguese political and economic life in the mid-1970s. Therefore, the whole of these two decades can be considered a period of change, perhaps among the most interesting in the history of Portugal. But, of course, it is also important to take into account developments in earlier periods, especially the first three decades of the Salazar regime. Only in this way can we fully understand the dramatic changes that have occurred in this small State located on Europe's western periphery.

Both the creation of the Republic in 1910, and the emergence of the Salazar dictatorship after 1926, were mainly political transformations. However, the main bases of social and economic support for the new leaderships were different in both instances: in the first, an urban bourgeoisie influenced by international developments and, in the second, more conservative groups with landed interests. According to Saraiva (1974, p57), '. . . the Republic had been the victory of the city over the land – Salazar is going to create the revival of an agrarian and provincial order. The Republic had been the victory of an urban petty-bourgeoisie in ascendancy – Salazar is going to base power on the large land-owner aristocracy. The Republic had represented, "openness to Europe" – Salazar is going to enforce a nationalism content with itself'. Despite these differences, in neither case was the social and economic structure of the country changed by political reorganization.

It seems clear that, at least during the early decades, Salazar wanted to preserve Portugal, as far as possible, as a rural society. Greater industrial and financial opportunities were progressively created but were only available to a small number of entrepreneurs, who were able to develop large-scale industrial projects. This also reinforced the role of the private commercial banks, sometimes owned by the same groups. All industrial investments were conditioned by the 'control of industry acts' (leis 1956 from 1937, and 2052 from 1952) which, in fact, acted as a powerful brake on new initiatives. In many cases potential investors from outside the large groups could not obtain the financial assistance required to launch new enterprises. As Gallagher stresses (1983, p138), '. . . industrial growth was opposed where it might jeopardise the traditionalist goals of the State. Such economic retardation was a conscious goal, in order to hold back trade unionism, secularism, mass politics, urbanisation, consumerism and other modernising trends. Salazar was not only antiliberal but also anticapitalist in several key respects'.

Although economic opportunities were restricted, important efforts were made to change infrastructural conditions. There were significant public investments in roads and viaducts, ports, dams, power production and public buildings in a policy of fomento (development) in which Duarte Pacheco, Minister of Public Works from 1932 to 1934 and from 1936 to 1943, had a pioneering role. Attempts by some Ministers of the Economy, such as Daniel Barbosa (1947–1949) and Ferreira Dias (1958–1962), to promote industrial and agricultural modernization also had a positive influence (see Marques 1980).

As a result both of State policies and favourable world economic conditions, the Portuguese economy grew rapidly in the last decade of this period (1951–1960), when the annual compound rate of increase in Gross Domestic Product (GDP) was 4.4 percent – with an increase of 6.2 percent in industrial production and 5.3 percent in the services sector, but only 1.1 percent in agricultural production. This was an important precursor for the following decade, together forming 20 years when '. . . the Portuguese economy underwent the most far-reaching and rapid change of its history' (ILO 1979, p183). But a clear distinction should be made between the two decades, for no capitalist 'take-off' occurred until the 1960s according to Gallagher (1983).

In 1960 a large share of the active population remained in the primary sector and the degree of urbanization was quite low. According to the census of that year, 44 percent of the workers were in the primary sector, 29 percent in the secondary sector and 27 percent in the tertiary sector. Besides Lisbon and Oporto, only four urban centres on the mainland (Setúbal, Coimbra, Braga and Vila Nova de Gaia) had more than 40 000 inhabitants and the percentage of the population living in urban centres (over 10 000 people) was only 23.1 percent. The standard of living of those dependent on agriculture – which produced 26 percent of computed GNP compared to 36 percent in the secondary sector and 38 percent in the tertiary sector – was particularly low in absolute and in relative terms. The per capita production of agriculture was only 59 percent of the average domestic level, compared with 126 percent in industry and 136 percent in services (Pina, 1979, p41). In the whole of the country, but particularly in rural areas, social conditions of life and cultural standards were also very low. A high percentage of villages had no electricity and domestic water supply, accessibility and communications were in many cases difficult or nonexistent. In the country as a whole, the number of inhabitants per doctor was very high (1298.8) and the percentage of illiteracy extremely high (38 percent). During the dictatorship people were also deprived of basic political rights, namely free association, free expression and free access to information. These restrictions were enforced by the political police (PIDE – International Police for the Defense of the State), censorship and other methods of political control. In particular, until the 1960s it was possible to minimize connections with other countries by restricting the sales of books, journals and films, and limiting the right to participate in political and cultural meetings.

The inflow of foreign capital was also still very limited, being equal to only 1 percent of gross capital formation in 1959. This can be explained by the difficulties of capital transfer, a condition that was progressively removed later, with the encouragement of recently-created international monetary institutions: the European Payments Union (EPU), the European Monetary Agreement (EMA) and the International Monetary Fund (IMF). Salazar had a clear design, wishing to avoid large, indiscriminate inflows of foreign capital. This policy was especially implemented through the Nationalization of Capitals Act (Lei da Nacionalização dos Capitais: Lei 1994, from 13.4.1943). In practice it was not quite as drastic as the title suggested, but it had the effect of reducing the role of foreign investment in Portugal.

Finally, throughout this period Portugal retained her large 'overseas territories' stretching from Cabo Verde to Timor (with a total area of 2 089 948 sq km, that is, 23 times the Metropolitan area) virtually without resistance and therefore without great costs. These territories were thinly populated with only about 13.5 million inhabitants, mostly illiterate and lacking the necessary experience for political organization. In addition, because the interests of the world powers in these territories were comparatively weak as yet, the Portuguese 'empire' could be quietly maintained, with a small number of regular forces and military conscripts.

2. The 1960s: European integration, emigration and colonial wars

In the beginning of the 1960s three events led to important changes in Portugal: the integration of the country in the European Free Trade Association (EFTA); the outbreak of wars for the independence of the African territories; and a new chain of emigration towards the more industrialized countries of Europe. Taking into account these changes, Saraiva (1974, p57) has argued that '. . . what in history became known as the "New State", and particularly what can be called "consequent Salazarism" . . .' should be reduced to the period from about 1936 until 1960–1961.

European integration

When, at the end of the 1950s, European countries sought international integration, it seemed clear that Portugal could not become a member of the European Economic Community (EEC). The founding members would not accept a country without a democratic political system, and for the Portuguese authorities, it would not be acceptable to be included in an organization with supranational powers, wherein Portugal could not retain any preferential system with the colonies. However, to stay outside of all European movements (as, for example, did Spain) would probably have led to the loss of existing markets, in particular the British one which then took more than 12 percent of Portuguese exports. There were good economic reasons then for membership of EFTA while politically it was '. . . a choice for noncommitment in European affairs' (Tsoukalis, 1981, p51; see also Moura 1973 and Cravinho 1979).

By joining EFTA, Portugal was able to retain markets and maintain exports, which were to be relevant factors leading to high rates of growth in production in the 1960s (see for example ILO 1978; Tsoukalis 1981; Cravinho 1982 and Lopes 1983). The negative effects of membership were avoided because the special regimes of Annexe G of the Stockholm Convention allowed Portugal to retain protection measures for several years against imports from other, stronger EFTA countries and even to increase

Table 4.1   Geographical distribution of Portuguese trade

Trading partner	Exports %		Imports %	
	1960	1972	1960	1972
Overseas territories	25.5	14.7	14.4	11.6
EFTA (7)	20.3	38.8	19.5	23.5
EEC (6)	21.6	20.5	38.2	31.5
Other Western European	2.6	5.1	1.8	7.0
United States and Canada	12.3	12.4	7.9	9.6
Rest of world	17.7	8.5	18.2	16.8
Total	100.0	100.0	100.0	100.0

Source: Instituto Nacional de Estatística (INE), Estatísticas do Comércio Externo, Lisbon.

import duties to protect infant industries. Finally, by joining EFTA, Portugal was able to occupy a much stronger negotiating position in future discussions with the EEC (Oliveira 1963; Cunha 1965; Xavier 1970). The increasing role of EFTA countries in the value of Portuguese trade can be seen in Table 4.1. Imports from other EFTA countries increased by four percentage points but the increase in the share of exports (by 18.5 points) was more important. The changing relative position of the Western economy as a whole vis-a-vis the overseas territories and 'the rest of the world' was also significant. The West European market, which in 1960 took 44.5 percent of Portuguese exports and sent 59.9 percent of Portuguese imports, was far more important by 1972, not only for imports (62 percent) but also for exports (64.4 percent). These developments partly explain changes in attitudes, in the middle of the 1970s towards the geographical role of Portugal.

Together with these changes in the geographical composition of Portuguese trade during the 1960s, there were also very important changes in the roles of different export sectors. Traditional exports, which in 1960 represented 75.1 percent of the total, in 1970 represented only 58.3 percent. A marked decline occurred in canned fish, wood and cork, resins and mineral products which dropped from 46 percent to 22.7 percent. An important role in increased exports was played by the traditional products of textiles and clothing, but more important were new exports, such as tomato paste, chemicals, paper, nonmetallic minerals and electrical and nonelectrical machinery, with an annual increase of about 20 percent (Alvares and Fernandes 1980).

Table 4.2 Sectoral composition of manufacturing in Portugal

Branch	(10⁹ Escudos – 1963 prices)							
	1963		1973		Annual increase 1963–1973	1981		Annual increase 1973–1981
	No.	%	No.	%		No.	%	
Food, beverages and tobacco	3.1	13.0	6.4	10.0	9.6	8.4	10.0	3.5
Textiles, clothing and footwear	5.6	22.5	15.9	24.0	16.7	21.0	26.0	3.6
Wood and cork products	2.2	9.0	3.7	6.0	6.2	2.9	3.0	-2.4
Paper products and printing	1.3	5.2	3.0	4.6	11.9	3.5	4.4	1.8
Chemicals and related products	2.7	10.8	7.9	12.0	17.5	9.2	11.0	1.8
Nonmetallic mineral products	1.8	7.2	4.6	7.1	14.2	6.8	8.5	5.3
Basic metal industries	0.9	4.0	2.3	3.5	14.2	1.6	2.0	3.4
Metal products, machinery and transportation equipment	5.9	24.0	18.6	28.5	19.5	23.9	30.0	3.1
Other manufacturing	1.1	4.3	2.8	4.3	14.0	4.2	5.1	5.6
Total manufacturing	24.8	100.0	65.2	100.0	14.8	79.3	100.0	2.4

Source: Monteiro and Malheiro (1983).

Finally, export opportunities contributed to changes that occurred in the structure of Portuguese industrial production shown in Table 4.2 (although of course other factors were also important). In general terms, the highest increases in production occurred mainly in sectors that also had the highest increases in export performances.

Emigration

Another important source of economic and social change was the unprecedented emigration which occurred during the 1960s. Portugal has traditionally been a country of emigration, and this has been referred to as a 'structural feature' of Portuguese society (Serrão 1972), but an extraordinary increase occurred in the 1960s (see Chapter 6, Tables 6.1 and 6.2). The average annual number of emigrants, which had been about 30 000 from the beginning of the century until 1949, increased to more than 35 000 between 1951 and 1960 and rose substantially after the beginning of the 1960s. The number of emigrants peaked at an estimated 173 000 in 1970 and total emigration was over one million in the decade, representing about a sixth of the total population in 1960 (Franco 1971; Porto 1977 and 1979).

There was an important shift in the destinations of the emigrants: between 1951 and 1960, 95 percent of emigrants went to other continents (69 percent to Brazil) whilst from 1961 to 1973, 64 percent are reported to have emigrated legally to Europe. There was also a drastic increase in clandestine emigration; whereas this represented less than 3 percent of the total between 1951 and 1960, it had risen to more than 37 percent between 1961 and 1973. Clandestine emigration was probably particularly important in the flows towards European countries, especially France.

Emigration had extremely important effects on the whole of the country. Besides the impact of remittances (which will be stressed later), it had effects on the labour force – especially in the poorest regions of the country – and on the cultural standards of the people. The new preference for Europe was itself particularly significant, increasing the probability of return and the frequency of visits to Portugal: for these reasons, there was a greater inducement to send money home, there was more cultural influence from abroad, and emigrants retained closer connections with their families.

Emigration was one of the main factors leading to the unprecedented loss of population that occurred during the 1960s. According to the census of 1960 and of 1970, the total population of mainland Portugal decreased from 8 293 000 to 8 123 000. Of the 274 *concelhos* (local authorities) on the mainland, only in 51 was there a population increase (Gaspar 1979), thus aggravating further the sharp disequilibrium that already existed between the littoral and the interior of the country. The continuation of this trend in relative terms has been confirmed for 1970 to 1981 (Lewis and Williams 1982).

Colonial wars

The outbreak of the wars of independence in the Portuguese colonies in Africa were very significant. These wars were preceded by India's struggle to integrate the territories of Goa, Damão and Diu in India. Salazar did not want to achieve a negotiated solution with India, as this might have set a precedent which would affect relationships with the African territories. Finally, however, integration was imposed through military action by India on December 18 1961. At the outbreak of the wars in Africa, in Angola in February 1961, the liberation movement was supported by the United States. Later, liberation movements in Portuguese Africa were supported by others, in particular the USSR and the Popular Republic of China, not only in Angola but also in Guinea, after 1963, and Mozambique after 1964.

One of the first effects of the war was to increase the numbers of regular soldiers and conscripts, which rose rapidly to about 200 000. Usually, the latter had to provide at least three years of military service, while many soldiers, mainly from the regular forces, had to undertake repeated missions with a high incidence of death or injury. This situation greatly influenced job expectations in the Portuguese labour market, cultural values, marriage and life-chance prospects. It was an overwhelming influence, because almost all Portuguese families, in the years to 1974, had some relatives involved in the wars. According to Maxwell (1974), in the late 1960s the armed forces represented a proportion per thousand of the population (30.83), exceeded only by South Vietnam (55.36), Israel (40.9) and North Vietnam (31.66); this was five times the ratio in the USA and three times that in Britain and Spain. One in four men of military age was in the armed services.

The war also led to a huge increase in public expenditure (for example, by 44 percent from 1961 to 1962) and military expenditure represented almost one half of total public expenditure in most years during this period. Moreover, there was a great increase in public investment, because the Portuguese authorities felt that the war effort had to be accompanied by a strong development effort at home, for political and social reasons. In order to achieve this goal, it became necessary to permit and attract a greater inflow of foreign investment. Only in this way was it possible to leave sufficient domestic resources for the war effort. In addition, the involvement of foreign investors was a way of attracting the general sympathy of their governments. From 1961 to 1967 the inflow of long-term foreign capital was 10 times larger than from 1943 to 1960 and, in 1971 alone, was almost three times greater than during the 18 years of 'economic nationalism' (Matos 1973; see also Almeida and Barreto 1970). Therefore, while in 1959 foreign direct investment accounted for less than one percent of gross capital formation, by 1970 it had risen to over 27 percent, and was used both for private and public purposes. The need to increase public investment led Salazar, however, reluctantly to seek financial assistance abroad including a bond issue in London, an IBDR credit for the Douro hydro-electric project and Export–Import financing for the Lisbon bridge. For the sectoral distribution of investment in manufacturing see Donges (1979), Macedo (1980a) and Lewis and Williams (1982).

Finally, a rapid growth in tourism was seen as another means of acquiring foreign exchange as well as the sympathy of public opinion abroad. Of course, this growth was largely induced by conditions in the countries of origin, where the nationals had increasing real incomes and were allowed to go abroad without or with few foreign exchange restrictions. But it was also a result of deliberate policy by the Portuguese authorities who, for example invested in advertising campaigns and promoted hotel construction. Overall, the annual number of foreign tourists grew from 353 000 in 1960 to over 4 million in 1972.

The development effort induced by the war was particularly strong in the overseas territories, although it has been argued that these would have developed anyway (Newitt 1981). In the words of Gallagher (1983, p175) '. . . during the final 13 years of Portuguese rule Angola and Mozambique may have witnessed more economic expansion than in the previous 100 years'. To promote economic growth and closer connections with the mainland, *decreto lei* (decree law) 44 016 of 3.11.1961 aimed to create a single economic and monetary area but it was, however, predictable that this would be an impossible goal (Franco 1970). There were also incentives for settlement and the number of Portuguese white settlers in Angola increased from about 172 500 in 1960 to about 400 000 in 1974, composing 8 percent of the territory's population.

Consequences

As well as the positive and negative effects already discussed, integration into EFTA, the new emigration trend and the wars in Africa also led to a remarkable increase in the demand facing Portuguese producers. The opening of important foreign markets, the increase in private transfers, the growth of public expenditure and the inflow of tourists had a significant impact on a small economy that had previously suffered from the limitations of a very small internal market (Cravinho 1982).

Moreover, the changes of the 1960s took place without the problems of short-run economic constraints. On the contrary, in some cases short-run supply conditions were the main factors contributing to the performance of the Portuguese economy. The outflow of labour, mainly through emigration but also to some extent through military service, did not reduce substantially the capacity for market-oriented production. Among those who emigrated during the 1960s, more than 46 percent were 'noneconomically active' (mainly housewives who had not contributed to the computed GNP), while about 27 percent were workers from the primary sector, where there was overemployment and low productivity. There was, therefore, a surplus of labour that could be used in the expansion of the economy and emigration could be seen as a strategy to avoid the problem of unemployment, and the social and political unrest which this could generate. Price increases were also quite small. During the first half of the decade, price rises rarely exceeded 5 percent and, during the second half, hardly ever exceeded 10 percent. The lack of inflationary pressures encouraged entrepreneurs to increase investment.

During this entire period Portugal had no balance of payments difficulties, 1962 being the last year in which a current account deficit was registered. After that the country always had surpluses, mainly due to the high levels of emigrant remittances which compensated for chronic trade deficits. It was, therefore, possible to import without restrictions the equipment and the raw materials which were required in some of the more rapidly expanding sectors of the Portuguese economy. Finally, it was also possible to keep the state budget in 'equilibrium', with receipts covering expenditure (Ribeiro 1977).

Given the favourable economic context, Portugal had an annual increase in GNP of 6.1 percent from 1961 to 1970. Growth was particularly high in the secondary sector (9.1 percent) and in the tertiary sector (5.9 percent) but in the primary sector was only 1.5 percent. This led to important changes in the structure of production so that, in 1970, 33 percent of the active population were in the primary sector, 35.8 percent in the secondary sector and 31.2 percent in the tertiary sector. The respective shares in production were 15.6, 45.9 and 38.5 percent.

There were also a number of social changes linked to these economic developments. Important improvements were achieved in the system of social security which was extended to a broader stratum of population in most fields, and the number of inhabitants per doctor decreased to the more acceptable level of 1056. The percentage of illiteracy also decreased, although only to the still appallingly high level of 25.8 percent, but some cultural opportunities were broadened, especially through widespread access to TV (introduced in 1957). The level of urbanization also increased markedly (see Chapter 8).

However, an alternative view of developments is that '. . . the rapid economic growth achieved in the 1960s could coexist with increased disparities in income distribution, with unemployment created by changes in technology, an increase in the size of underprivileged groups and a worsening of their conditions, with glaringly inadequate levels of basic services in the growing urban areas, with the drift from the land and emigration, with pollution and deterioration of the environment – in short with an unsatisfactory quality of life' (ILO 1979, p189). These negative effects were largely the consequence of the rapid, uncontrolled growth of the Portuguese economy. Of particular importance were the increases in regional inequalities (see Chapter 8). Despite the emigration outflows from the poorest regions of the country, even per capita inequalities were strongly aggravated during the 1960s. The ratio of GDP per capita in the poorest *distrito* – Viana do Castelo – relative to the richest one – Lisbon – decreased from 0.33 in 1953 to 0.29 in 1964 and 0.23 in 1970. Equality had certainly not followed growth.

3. The Caetano years

In September 1968 Salazar suffered a paralyzing stroke that put an end to a premiership which had lasted almost 40 years. Marcelo Caetano, as expected, then took office for a period that was to last five and a half years until April 25 1974. At the beginning of his premiership, Caetano took some steps to liberalize and modernize Portuguese society but he was apparently unable to overcome conservative interests and had to abandon his original aims.

Some steps were indeed taken to liberalize political life. Individuals who had been in exile, like Mario Soares and the Bishop of Oporto, Dom António Ferreira Gomes, was able to return home. Censorship was reduced in both the production and importation of books, journals and films. The weekly newspaper *Expresso*, founded by Pinto Balsemão in 1969, was permitted to express a liberal and critical view of the political establishment and became particularly influential. Another relevant event was the foundation of SEDES (Social Development Study Group), an association of intellectuals which became an important pressure group, whilst some catholic groups and movements also became active. The political police (PIDE) underwent a change of name (to DGS – General Directorate of Security), and, at least initially, had their activities reduced. The political movement which supported the regime, the National Union (UN), was also 'liberalized' after 1968 under the leadership of Melo e Castro and the introduction of some younger elements. Its name was changed in 1973 to National Popular Action (ANP) mainly to reflect the 'liberalization' that had been introduced. Finally, there was an unexpected reform of the education system when Veiga Simão was Minister of Education.

The elections of 1969 provided an opportunity for relatively broad political participation. These were not free elections, for the number of people entitled to vote was extremely small (only about 1.8 million compared with the 6.2 million that could vote in 1975) and the opposition was not able to control all polls and all steps in the electoral process. But three opposition movements, the CDE (Electoral Democratic Commission), the CEUD (Electoral Commission of Democratic Unity) and the Popular Monarchists were allowed to participate. In addition, some more independent and open-minded individuals were included in the progovernment UN lists. The UN polled 88 percent of the votes, as against 10.5 percent for the CDE and 1.6 percent for the CEUD. However, the opposition was unable to win any seats in Parliament given the rules of the electoral system – plurinominal closed lists. Nevertheless, the group of 'liberals' was very active in the Assembly. Some 'liberals', like Sá Carneiro, Mota Amaral, Pinto Balsemão, Miller Guerra and Magalhães Mota, who began their political careers in this way, later played an important role after April 25 1974.

Caetano also took steps to liberalize and modernize the economy, by appointing young 'technocrats' such as Rogério Martins, João Salgueiro and Xavier Pintado as Secretaries of State. The Industrial Development Act (*Lei do Fomento Industrial: lei* 3/72 from 27.5. 1972), the outline of which was presented by Rogério Martins in a speech in February 1970, was particularly important as it replaced the old system of industrial control with a new system of industrial incentives. Important steps were also taken in the planning system, the *III Plano de Fomento* (Development Plan) for 1968–1973, representing a major advance over previous plans. In particular, for the first time, substantial attention was given to regional planning and four planning regions were established on the Portuguese mainland. Improvements were also introduced in the institutional framework and in planning methods from which the *IV Plano de Fomento*, for 1974–1979, benefited.

A number of important projects were also agreed in principle or were implemented, in particular the deep-water port and industrial complex of Sines, the programme for the construction of the motorway between Lisbon and Oporto and the expansion of selected industrial sectors. Finally, special attention should be paid to the trade agreement with the EEC, signed in 1972. It was only a trade-liberalizing agreement, with some clauses protecting both Portugal and the EEC with respect to some so-called 'sensitive products'. But it was understood as a step towards full integration as Mota Campos, Minister of State, clearly stressed; '. . . we should . . . acknowledge and proclaim our European vocation, reflected in irreversible actions, in particular accepting the evolution of our Agreement with the European Community in such a way that we can someday overcome present impediments and occupy the place that we are entitled to have among the people of western Europe'.

The Portuguese economy kept on growing during the period 1971 to 1973 at a rate of 7 percent, which was even higher than that experienced in the previous decade. The relative changes in the different sectors varied: compared to the 1960s, in the primary sector the rate of annual increase was lower, at only 0.7 percent, but in the secondary sector it was similar, at 9 percent, while it was much higher in the tertiary sector, at 7.1 percent. As Baklanoff stresses (1981, px), '. . . significantly, during the Caetano regime the Portuguese economic growth rate matched that of Spain'.

However, Caetano either did not want to or could not proceed with the policies of liberalization and economic improvement. In the political area there were signs of a return to old practices, with increased activity by the political police and greater censorship (after the 1969 elections Soares had once again been forced into exile). Even the 'liberal' deputies experienced increasing difficulties and, in 1973, after the reappointment of Américo Tomás as President of the Republic (already 78 years old and known as an influential conservative hard-liner), they abandoned the *Assembleia Nacional* (National Assembly). Political reasons also led to the young 'technocrats' leaving the economic ministeries. Finally, the election for the *Assembleia Nacional* in 1973 saw a return to old ways, both in the choice of ANP candidates and in the conditions under which the opposition operated. Opposition candidates refused to contest and the election lost all democratic significance.

A peculiar event occurred early in 1974. This was the granting of permission for the publication of Spinola's book *Portugal e o Futuro*, which appeared on February 22 1974, defending a federalist solution for the African 'problems'. The authorization was given by one of Caetano's closest confidants, the Minister of Defence, Silva Cunha, therefore it is probable that Caetano wanted to have the door opened to an alternative solution because he was no longer convinced that the overseas territories could be maintained by military means (Saraiva 1974). Nevertheless, some days later he gave a speech in the *Assembleia Nacional*, arguing against the book, and he sacked both Spinola and his colleague Costa Gomes because they refused to pledge their loyalty to the existing policy for Africa. Faced with increasing difficulties, and probably under pressure from the more hard-line military officers, Caetano retracted from a number of his new policies.

Meanwhile, economic conditions in the country were deteriorating. Largely as a result of the oil crisis and the onset of the world recession (see Macedo 1979, 1980a), Portugal was already suffering from high inflation, unemployment (with increasing barriers to emigration to the usual destination countries) and balance of payments deficits by the end of 1973. Some groups enjoyed the euphoria of stock exchange speculation, queuing for issues of new assets, but productive investment was actually falling. Political, economic and social pressures on the regime were therefore increasing.

4. The coup, April 1974 and the transition to democracy

The Armed Forces Movement and the coup

The internal difficulties faced by Caetano during his premiership reflected the conflict between two main forces in Portugal. One of these was composed of individuals who, like President Tomás, tried to bring the regime back to previous practices and philosophy (in particular with respect to the African territories) and the other included an increasing number of people who thought that alternative policies had to be followed. Within this latter group there were individuals with quite different views and economic interests. At the beginning of the War, probably only left-wing political groups opposed Portuguese intervention but, later, even more conservative groups were against it; either because they thought that an alternative solution could preserve Portuguese interests in Africa or simply because they were tired of war and realized that a military solution was impossible. The increasing role of European trade, relative to trade with the colonies (see Table 4.1), had the effect of convincing many that these territories were no longer vital to Portuguese interests.

The Movement of the Captains (*Movimento dos Capitães*), which led to the Armed Forces Movement (*Movimento das Forças Armadas*) that carried out the coup on April 25 1974, began with the resentment of full-time officers against a new act (*lei* 353/73 from 13.7.1973) giving similar career conditions to conscript officers. However, this was only the immediate cause of their action for the whole professional officer group, after repeated expeditions in Africa, was tired of a war without apparent end. By 1974, ending the war was the one objective that had the support of a large part of the Portuguese people, including those who wanted preservation of some features of the old regime, or at least of its economic system.

The old regime therefore was probably not as weak as it appeared from the rapid success of the coup of April 25, or the partial success of the earlier attempted coup on March 16 (see Rodrigues et al 1974). It was only due to the combined support of groups with different economic and political interests that the coup was so readily successful, overthrowing with a few shots and no deaths, a 40-year-old regime behind which many powerful interests had been created.

The Programme of the Armed Forces Movement (published in *lei* 3/74, from 14.5.1973) clearly stressed the importance of ending the wars; it stated at the beginning that '. . . after 13 years of fighting overseas the existing political system had failed to define, in a concrete and objective way, an overseas policy leading to peace among Portuguese of all races and creeds'. The need to '. . . clear internal policies and institutions, transforming them by democratic means into institutions truly representative of the Portuguese People', was then referred to as a prerequisite to that overseas policy. In the very sensitive areas of the economy, the Programme had as its main and almost single concern, '. . . the fight against inflation and the excessively high cost of living, including an antimonopolist strategy'. The succession of events that followed confirmed that groups with contradictory economic and political perspectives had supported the coup. All agreed on the need to end the wars, but conflicts were sharpened over the shape that the new political system was to assume.

The movement to parliamentary democracy

The first stage of the postcoup process, from April 1974 until the middle of

1975, can be summarized in terms of there being a progressive shift of political leadership towards the Communist Party (PCP). The President of the Junta of National Salvation (to which the Armed Forces Movement had attributed power) and first president of the Republic after the revolution, the moderate General Spinola, felt increasing difficulties in view of this shift. The first great political crisis in July 1974 led to the dismissal of the moderate Prime Minister Palma Carlos and his replacement by Vasco Gonçalves who had close connections with the PCP. As a result Spinola felt himself to be under even more pressure and in September, after a dramatic speech which stressed his concern about the feasibility of instituting democracy and improving economic conditions in the country, he resigned and was replaced by Costa Gomes. The next significant political event happened on March 11 1975 when, supposedly, after an attempted coup, Spinola and some of his followers fled to Spain (see Porch 1977). Therefore, the potential leader of centre-right forces had been removed from the political scene.

After this there was a further leftwards shift in political power: the Revolutionary Council (*Conselho da Revolução*) was formed and moved to nationalize some major sectors of the Portuguese economy, including banking, insurance, shipbuilding, air and road transport, cement and beer production. This increased the share of direct intervention by the Portuguese State in the economy (previously relatively small) to 19.3 percent of employment, 24.4 percent of gross value added and 45.5 percent of gross investment[1] (Valadas and Murteira 1976). Also during 1975 most of the large farms which were dominant in the Alentejo (the South) were occupied by their labour forces (Rosa 1976); this is discussed further in Chapter 9. In political terms it would help consolidate the hold of the PCP on the region.

A decisive event in the institution of democracy in Portugal was the election of the Constitutional Assembly (to draw up a new Constitution and prepare for general elections) on April 25 1975. The Armed Forces Movement had urged that ballot papers be left blank, implying a preference for the leadership of the Movement rather than for the transfer of power to civilian political parties. However, despite the difficulites some parties experienced during the electoral campaign, there was a 91 percent poll and only 7 percent cast blank votes (see Table 4.3). Of the valid votes, 37.9

---

[1] These values include the traditional public sector but do not include forms of minority participation.

Table 4.3   Assembly and municipality electoral results in Portugal, 1975–1983

Parties	Percentage of vote							
	AC 75	AR 76	CM 76	AR 79	CM 79	AR 80	CM 82	AR 83
	91.7	83.3	64.4	87.5	73.8	85.4	71.4	78.6
Blank and null votes	6.9	4.6	4.4	2.8	2.6	2.4	3.8	2.6
PS	37.9	35.0	33.2	27.4	27.7	*0.9	31.8	36.3
FRS (coalition based on PS)						27.1		
PSD	26.4	24.0	24.3	*2.4	14.7	*2.5	14.6	27.0
CDS	7.6	15.9	16.6	*0.4	6.9	*0.2	7.5	12.4
AD (coalition based on PSD and CDS)				42.2	25.5	44.4	19.6	
PCP	12.5	14.6						
FEPU (coalition based on PCP)			17.7					
APU (coalition based on PCP)				19.0	20.5	16.9	20.7	18.2
Others	8.7	5.9	3.8	5.8	2.1	5.6	2.0	3.5

* Votes in the Azores and Maderia, which the CDS and PSD contested separately rather than as the AD coalition, and which the PS also contested seperately rather than as part of the FRS coalition.

AC = Constitutional Assembly (*Assembleia Constitucional*), *AR* = Assembly of the Republic (*Assembleia da República*) and CM = Municipal Executives, (*Câmeras Municipais*).

percent were in favour of the Socialist Party (PS), 26.4 percent for the Popular Democratic Party (PPD), 12.5 percent for the PCP and 7.7 percent for the Social Democratic Centre Party (CDS).

However, while Members of Parliament discussed the formulation of a new Constitution during the 'hot summer' of 1975, the future of parliamentary democracy was being disrupted by the PCP and far left-wing groups. An example of literally extraparliamentary activities is that in September, a mob supporting these forces surrounded Parliament for a whole night, denying food to all but the Communist representatives. In June, in an interview given to the Italian journalist Oriana Fallaci, the leader of the Communist Party, Alvaro Cunhal, actually declared that Portugal would not have a parliamentary democracy, '. . . there is no possibility of a democracy like the one you have in western Europe . . .

Portugal will not be a country with democratic freedoms and monopolies. It will not allow it'.

During 1975 the PCP strengthened its power base in the industrial suburbs of Lisbon and in the Alentejo (organized around the collective farms) while the parties of the right improved their position in the centre and in the north of the country, traditionally more conservative regions where the Catholic Church retained a strong influence. These are regions with a highly fractured property structure, where most farmers are land-owners. In the northern littoral there is also a dynamic small and medium sized industrial sector in which most entrepreneurs are former workers, and where the workers may supplement their income from working small plots of land: such groups tend to be more conservative. In some cities and villages the population violently rejected the influence of the PCP on the government and burned down its offices.

Following the apparent change in the strength of the different political groups, more moderate elements were included in the Sixth Provisional Government, formed in September 1975, with Pinheiro de Azevedo taking over as Prime Minister from Vasco Gonçalves. At that time, a leading role was played by Otelo Saraiva de Carvalho, former commander of both the elite COPCON force and of the Lisbon military region. He was linked with far left-wing movements which opposed a political outcome that would have given definitive control of the Country to the PCP, and was in a position to restrain the ambitions of the latter. It was clear that divisions within the left would fundamentally weaken their attempts to gain power. Finally, on November 25 1975, after one more attempt at a coup by left-wing military officers, there was a decisive defensive action by moderate officers which effectively consolidated parliamentary democracy. Ramalho Eanes played an important role in this movement, obtaining considerable prestige which contributed to his clear victory in the presidential election in the following year. Once the Constitution was approved and published, a general election was held on April 25 1976, and this marked the end of the transitional period. Since then, the results of the elections, contested freely (with a few exceptions in some parts of the country), have been the main feature of political life.

Another important event in 1975 was the granting of indepedence to the old colonies, which was to have political implications, particularly through the role of the *retornados* (returnees). As a result of the struggle for power between different liberation movements in Angola and the difficult condi-tions that the new ruling authorities were creating for the Portuguese who stayed in the African ex-overseas territories, more than 600 000 people (estimates vary) fled to Portugal. They did not form a specific political movement but had their own pressure groups which, reputedly, had mainly right-wing leanings. It has, in fact, been argued (see Robinson 1979) that the PCP was more concerned to hand over power to friendly liberation groups in the colonies than it was with domestic politics at this time.

Economic changes 1974–6

Turning to the economy, it will be recalled that conditions began to be sharply aggravated at the end of 1973, mainly for exogenous reasons. The succession of political events in 1974–75 also had important economic repercussions. The discovery of freedom, after so many years of dictatorship, was a spark which released workers' long frustrated demands for wage increases and for increases in consumption. Rapid improvements were achieved in the distribution of income (see Carvalho 1976) and from 1974 to 1975 private consumption increased 3.1 percent and public consumption by 15.3 percent. Furthermore, there was a lower rate of inflation (16.4 percent in 1975 compared with 25.8 percent in 1974) as a result of many prices being frozen by State decrees. However, there were also negative developments. Imports increased 24.6 percent and, as a result of social unrest and a climate of uncertainty, investment fell so that GDP decreased 4.4 percent, with a decrease of 5.4 percent in industrial production. Exports also decreased, by −20.8 percent, and fixed capital formation fell by −38.6 percent. From 1975 to 1976 private and public consumption increased 3.3 and 14.1 percent respectively, but inflation had already risen to 20.2 percent because it was impossible to maintain the artificial controls on prices. Gross capital investment further decreased by −3.4 percent but there was a clear increase of 8.1 percent in GDP (partly due to recovery of 1974 levels) while exports increased by 1.3 percent.

The independence of the old colonies created additional problems. In many cases those who came from Africa were not really *retornados*, because they had been born overseas, sometimes from families that had emigrated several generations earlier. They were also a very large number to absorb in comparison with both the total Portuguese population and a total labour force of less than 4 million, in a period when Portugal already was experiencing high unemployment and when there were reduced opportunities for emigration to other countries. Furthermore, despite the decreasing role of colonial markets in the 1960s (Table 4.1), these had remained important for several key sectors for which the disruption of colonial ties was disastrous; by 1976 the ex-colonies took only 6 percent of all exports and 2.5 percent of imports. This, of course, had repercussions for the performance of the Portuguese economy as a whole.

5. Post 1976, the era of parliamentary democracy

Early Socialist governments

From 1976 free elections were the major platform for political debate and the critical means for the formation of governments. As Lopes (1983, p480) stresses '. . . after the presidential and parliamentary elections of that year, the democratic regime became fully normalized'. However, the 'new' democratic era has not been without its problems: until the present time, no party has been able to obtain an absolute majority in parliament (because there are four quite strong parties), and there has also been tension between governments and the President of the Republic.

The results of the different elections – for the assembly, the presidency and local authorities – can be seen in Tables 4.3 and 4.4 (for a detailed interpretation of the results, see Gallagher 1983 and Gaspar 1983). In 1976, with 35 percent of the vote, the PS (Socialist Party) formed a minority government, the first constitutional government, which was sworn in on July 16. There were constant difficulties, including struggles within the party (which encompassed a broad political spectrum), but this government remained in office until the beginning of 1978. Then the second constitutional government was formed, a coalition between the PS and the relatively right-wing CDS. However, there were important differences between the parties, especially concerning agricultural policy, and the coalition was dissolved in July 1978. Soares then tried to form his third government, a new minority PS government, but President Eanes would not agree to this. Instead, using his constitutional powers, he invited Nobre da Costa to form the first 'presidential' government. However, parliament opposed this move and the government failed to get its programme approved, as a result of the joint opposition of the PS and CDS. President Eanes still persisted with this solution and, in October, Mota Pinto was invited to, and succeeded in forming a new 'presidential' government – supposedly nonparty aligned. He experienced a number of difficulties both in his relationships with Eanes and with Sá Carneiro (the PSD blocked his first budget). In August 1979 he resigned and President Eanes then decided to call a general election in an attempt to resolve the crisis. These were only interim elections for, under the constitution, general elections had to be held every four years.

Gallagher (1979, p213) has provided an interesting assessment of the first Socialist governments, writing that '. . . the Socialist Party's experience in government is somewhat akin to the MFAs. Having been united in resistance to dictatorship, the pressures and responsibilities of office quickly combined to erode party unity. Within months of entering government, the PS showed itself to be a polyglot party badly split on a whole range of economic and social issues'. Above all, the party was unable to come to grips with the country's economic slide (the right-wing favoured deflation, the left favoured growth) and this badly dented its national reputation. The government was not without achievements – notably in absorbtion of *retornados*, applying to join the EEC, and in steering a relatively stable course through the first two years of the democratic era – but it went into the 1979 election with its image tarnished and its support wavering.

Table 4.4   Voting for the President of the Republic in Portugal, 1976 and 1980

Parties	(Percentages)	
	1976	1980
Votes cast	75.5	84.2
Ramalho Eanes	61.5	56.5
Otelo Saraiva de Carvalho	16.5	1.5
Pinheiro de Azevedo	14.4	
Octávio Pato	7.6	
Soares Carneiro		40.2
Galvão de Melo		0.8
Pires Veloso		0.8
Aires Rodrigues		0.2

The Democratic Alliance

In a decision that was to have profound electoral effects, the PSD, the CDS and the Popular Monarchists (PPM) formed a centre-right electoral coalition, called the Democratic Alliance (AD), led by the charistmatic Sá Carneiro. This alliance obtained 45 percent of the vote in the December elections a large enough proportion (given the Portuguese electoral system, with the de Hondt rule) to secure an absolute majority of MPs (128 out of 250) and, therefore, to form a majority government. In the general elections of October 1980 (held as a constitutional requirement), the AD increased its share of the vote to 47.1 percent which reinforced its majority (with 134 MPs). These were the only times that elections directly produced clear majorities for one party or an electoral coalition in the post-1974 period.

The leadership of the AD, strongly influenced by Sá Carneiro, considered that President Eanes, the Revolutionary Council and some articles of the Constitution (formulated in a more radical era) were major obstacles to implementation of its policies: certainly they found a number of their more contentious policies blocked. Therefore, they proposed their own candidate, Soares Carneiro as an alternative to Eanes in the 1980 presidential election. However, despite considerable campaigning efforts by the AD leaders, in particular Sá Carneiro, Soares Carneiro always trailed Eanes in popularity and failed to be elected.

Soares Carneiro's electoral failure faded into political insignificance compared to another event in early December: on the evening of December 3, Sá Carneiro died in an aircrash and immediately the AD coalition seemed very fragile. Less publicized, but politically important, was the death in the same accident of Amaro da Costa, Vice-President of the CDS. Both these men had played key roles in cementing the alliance between their parties. The failure to get Soares Carneiro elected also added to tension between the uneasy coalition partners.

Sá Carneiro's successor, Pinto Balsemão, tried to hold together the leadership of the AD, but its eventual demise was perhaps inevitable as a result of difficulties stemming both from within and between the PSD and the CDS and, on a lesser scale, the PPM. He was actually able to stay in office for longer than any other Prime Minister since 1974, but with little enthusiastic support. On two occasions there were unsuccessful attacks on Balsemão's position by rival factions from within his own party, but he was able to resist these. Then, in the first elections that he contested as leader of the AD – for the municipalities in December 1982 – the alliance, although retaining a high proportion of the vote (42 percent) performed less well than it had previously under Sá Carneiro. In an unexpected decision, after returning from an official trip to the United States, Balsemão resigned as Prime Minister. There was an attempt to get Victor Crespo of the PSD appointed Prime Minister of a new AD government but this was refused by Eanes who, instead, announced interim general elections for April 25, 1983;

once again differences between the President and the political parties were evident.

The AD did not survive much more than two years after the death of Sá Carneiro, and the 1983 election was contested separately by the PSD, the CDS and the PS. However, constant disputes while in government had weakened the parties and there had also been a clear increase in the personal popularity of Mario Soares. The PS, recovering some of the ground it had lost since 1976, obtained the largest share of the vote, 36.3 percent, followed by the PSD with 27 percent, the PCP (APU) with 18.2 percent, and the CDS with 12.4 percent. The lessons of 1976 had been learnt and, this time, the PS would not consider governing alone. Its choice of coalition partners was limited – the PCP was unacceptable because of its dictatorial policy and ideology and links with the CDS had already proven difficult. The only remaining and indeed more logical permutation was a coalition between the PS and PSD, forming the *bloco central* (central block) with 63.3 percent of the votes (and 175 MPs). The AD, like the Socialists before them, had found reversing economic decline while balancing the interests of different political factions to be an almost insurmountable problem.

Recent economic changes

Political uncertainties since 1974 have not provided a favourable background for the development of social and economic policies. However, the increased roles of State social services departments and of local authorities has helped to provide for some of the basic needs of the population. The large scale nationalizations of 1975 had transferred some major corporations to the State and the increasing pressure of demand had led to considerable extension of the services provided (albeit, frequently without concern for economic rationality). The local authorities, freely elected in 1976 for the first time in half a century, had their powers increased, mainly through the Attributions and Competences Act (*Lei das Atribuições e Competências: lei* n 79/77, from 28.10.1977) and the Local Taxation Act (*Lei das Finanças Locais, lei* n 1/79 from 2.1.1979). Previously local authorities had possessed a very weak resource base (having only 6.7 percent of total public expenditure in 1976), but the new legislation strengthened their financial autonomy. Together, the increased roles of State departments, of public enterprises and of local authorities led to important improvements in some services, notably health and education, electricity supply and telephones, sewage and water supply. Moreover, the improvements in income distribution and in consumption that occurred immediately after 1974 also contributed to important advances in social and cultural conditions.

The reverse side of the coin was that increasing intervention led to growing deficits in the State budget (see, for example, EFTA 1980). In addition, losses were recorded by some corporations that had been profitable prior to nationalization. Another negative factor was that, after nationalization, the banks lost the initiative to promote new investments (despite the large surpluses that were available to them). Therefore, at a time when obtaining investment funds was becoming difficult at the world scale, in Portugal important institutions exchanged an active for a passive role in this field. Finally, the channelling of capital flows remained restricted without the reactivation of the stock exchange, which had been abolished soon after April 1974.

In addition to internal difficulties, the Portuguese transition to democracy occurred in a context of grave international economic difficulties which made it necessary to follow very stringent short-run policies. External imbalances were often the most critical problem, compelling the authorities to follow a restrictionist policy (formalized in an agreement signed with the IMF in June 1978). The costs of this policy were reductions in real wages (see Barbosa and Beleza 1979; Cardoso 1979; Krugmann and Macedo 1979; Macedo 1980a; Schmitt 1981; Lopes 1983) but it was possible to recover the current account deficit from a level of $1,490 million in 1977 (equivalent to 9 percent of GDP) to $52 million in 1979 (Lopes 1983). In 1980, under the first AD government, there was some success in reducing inflation (from 24.2 to 16.6 percent) and increasing the rate of gross capital formation (from −1.6 to +9 percent). However, in that year there was again a considerable deficit in the current account ($1,250 million) which was aggravated in following years (reaching $3,200 million in 1982). External disequilibrium continued to be the most critical problem for the Portuguese economy, leading to negotiation of a new agreement with the IMF.

In this context of short-run economic concerns and, for some time, of political unrest, substantial changes in the structure of the Portuguese economy were not to be expected: rates of capital formation were very low or even negative (partly because of the need to retain employment in labour-intensive sectors). In 1981 the distribution of the active population was estimated as being 27.3 percent in the primary sector, 36.8 percent in the secondary sector and 35.9 percent in the tertiary sector. Within the secondary sector, as can be seen in Table 4.2, smaller changes occurred between 1973 and 1981 than between 1963 and 1973. By any measure, therefore, there was less economic change in the 1970s than the 1960s.

In recent years the importance of western Europe for the Portuguese economy has also been accentuated. It now accounts for 69.7 percent of the country's imports and 72.9 percent of the country's exports (Table 4.1). This has increased the conviction of some groups that Portugal must find its place in Europe and, in particular, within the EEC. Nevertheless, close contacts have been retained with the old colonies. Once they became independent, it was clear that Portugal was not strong enough to harbour imperialistic designs over the ex-overseas territories while, for linguistic and cultural reasons, it was in a privileged position to strengthen co-operation.

6. Conclusion

Those who have had the good fortune of having been participants in or observers of the events of the last 20 years in Portugal, in retrospect must recognize that, although there are some permanent features of the socio-economic system, there have been important changes in economic, social and political affairs. Since the 1960s, advances have occurred in social conditions for economic growth has permitted improved general conditions for the population. Emigration may have impoverished some regions but remittances (and other monetary inflows) and increasing urbanization have improved standards of living for some and have changed cultural and family patterns. Despite remaining the most backward country of western Europe, Portugal is no longer a rural society as it was in 1960.

The economic growth of the 1960s, largely export-led, resulted in a marked change in the structure of employment and production, increasing the relative importance of the secondary and tertiary sectors and altering the production shares of the different industrial sectors. As a result of the crisis, both in the country and abroad, there were only limited structural changes in the 1970s. During the two decades the main concerns and goals of economic policies have completely changed. Since the beginning of the 1960s, when the pressures of events in Africa led Salazar to change his attitude to the preservation of traditionalist features of society, the main objective was the achievement of higher rates of economic growth. This was possible in a period when Portugal did not suffer from short-run economic constraints: the country had neither shortage of labour, nor inflation, nor external (or internal) deficits. Since 1973, external and internal factors created extremely difficult short-run problems, the solution of which became the major concern for the Portuguese State. Mainly due to critical problems in the balance of payments, the authorities followed austerity policies which jeopardized growth and employment prospects in the following years.

Political events after March 11 1975 had extremely important economic repercussions, changing some central features of Portuguese economic structures. Until then the economy had been characterized by an oligarchy which dominated the banks, insurance companies, shipbuilding and repair, basic transport and some major manufacturing sectors. In the south, agriculture was dominated by a small number of landowners who controlled the vast majority of the land. The transfer of property to the State in 1975 (despite some reversals in the following years) led to a drastic change in the centre of power in the Portuguese economy. Since then, the State has had responsibility for most of the major sectors of the economy. Problems have arisen, however, with management difficulties in the corporations and agricultural enterprises: there has been a lack of initiative and large deficits have been mounting. In addition, the banking system has lacked the initiative to finance industrial investment.

A complete change has also occurred in political institutions and in participation. From a dictatorial regime in which it was impossible to write freely, meet freely or hold free elections, Portugal has moved to a situation where, despite some difficulties, people can freely participate in political organizations and elect their representatives. The only organ of sovereignty that, after 1976, did not depend on a popular vote was the Revoutionary Council, and this was abolished in 1982 following revision of the Constitution. Political democracy is now implanted in Portugal, at the national, the local and the associational levels.

Finally, Portugal has ceased to be an 'empire' that, as we were taught in school, stretched from the Minho, in the north west of the mainland, to Timor in Oceania. With the exception of Macau, the country is now confined to a narrow quadrangle in the extreme south west of Europe and the archipelagos of the Azores and Madeira. Any doubt about the 'European' nature of the country have disappeared. For these reasons and also, of course, for economic reasons, it is clear for most groups that for Portugal there is no alternative to a European future. The negotiations with the EEC and the prospects of integration therefore will be basic problems for Portugal. Meanwhile, there have also been moves to promote a special relationship with the old colonies, based on close cultural and technical links.

For the remainder of the 1980s a number of uncertainties face Portugal.

President Eanes has played a central and, arguably, a stabilizing role in political life but, under the Constitution, is not allowed to stand for a third term of office. It is not yet clear who, if anyone, will have sufficient authority to replace him successfully. The search for a workable government will also continue as the *block central* tries to agree and implement joint policies. This is already the fourteenth government to hold office since 1974. These political changes will have to be worked out against a background of short-run economic constraints and continuing difficult negotiations with the EEC.

References

Almeida, C. and Barreto, A. (1970) *Capitalismo e Emigração em Portugal*, Lisbon, Prelo Editora.
Álvares, P. and Fernandes, C.R. (1980) *Portugal e o Mercado Comum, da EFTA aos Acordos de 1972 Vol. I*, Lisbon, Editorial Pórtico.
Antunes, M.L.M. (1973) *A Emigração Portuguesa desde 1950. Dados e Comentários*, Lisbon, Gabinete de Investigaçães Sociais.
Banlanoff, E.N. (1978) *The Economic Transformation of Spain and Portugal*, New York, Praeger.
Barbosa, M.P. and Beleza, L.M. (1979) External disequilibrium in Portugal: 1975–78, in Fundação Calouste Gulbenkian and The German Marshal Fund of the United States (ed), *Segunda Conferência Internacional sobre Economia Portuguesa*, Vol. I, Lisbon.
Cardoso, M.T. (1979) Política monetária e a balança dos pagamentos: 1976–78, in Fundação Calouste Gulbenkian and the German Marshal Fund of the United States (ed). *Segunda Conferência Internacional sobre Economia Porguguesa*, Vol. I, Lisbon.
Carvalho, O.E. de (1976) Alguns indicadores de desigualdades na distribuição do rendimento em Portugal nos últimos anos, in Fundação Calouste Gulbenkian and The German Marshal Fund of the United States (ed). *Conferência Internacional sobre Economia Portuguesa*, Vol. II, Lisbon.
Cravinho, J. (1979) Motives and Problems of the Second Enlargement: The Case of Portugal, paper presented at the Second Conference on Integration and Unequal Development, Madrid.
Cravinho, J. (1982) Sources of output growth in the Portuguese economy, (1959–1974). *Estudos de Economia*, Vol. II, pp271–89.
Cunha, P. P o (1965) A integração economica da Europa Ocidental, *Cadernos de Ciência e Téchnica Fiscal* série A, 77.
Dias, Júnior, J.F. (1945) *Linha de Rumo: Notas de Economia Portuguesa*, Lisbon, Clássica Editora.
Donges, J.B. (1979) Foreign investment in Portugal, in Fundação Calouste Gulbenkian and the German Marshal Fund of the United States (ed), *Segunda Conferência Internacional sobre Economia Portuguesa*, Vol. I, Lisbon.

EFTA (1980) *Main Developments in the Portuguese Economy 1973–1980*, Forty-third meeting of the Consultative Committee, Lisbon 8th and 9th September, note by the Secretariat (EFTA/CSC 10/80).

Franco, A.L.S. (1970) *A Integração Económica do Espaço Português*, Évora, Instituto Superior Económico e Social.

Franco, A.L.S. (1971) *A Emigração Portuguesa no Último Decénio — Causas, Problemas, Soluções*, Guimarães, Edição da Assembleia de Guimarães.

Gallagher, T. (1979) Portugal's bid for democracy: the role of the Socialist Party, *West European Politics*, Vol. 2, pp198–217.

Gallagher, T. (1983) *Portugal: A Twentieth Century Interpretation*, Manchester, Manchester University Press.

Gaspar, J. (1979) *Portugal em Mapas e Números*, Lisbon, Livros Horizonte.

Gaspar, J. (1983) As eleições de Portugal de Abril, in J. Medina (ed), *História Contemporânea de Portugal*, Lisbon, Amigos do Livro.

Holland, S. (1979) Dependent development: Portugal as periphery, in D. Seers, B. Schaffer and M.L. Kiljunen (eds) *Underdeveloped Europe*, Sussex, Harvester Press.

ILO (International Labour Office) (1979) *Employment and Basic Needs in Portugal*, Geneva, ILO.

Krugman, P. and Macedo, J.B. de (1979) The economic consequences of the April 25th Revolution, *Economia*, Vol. III, pp455–483.

Lewis, J.R. and Williams, A.M. (1982) Desenvolvimento regional desequilibrado em Portugal: situação actual e impacto provavel do adesão a CEE, *Desenvolvimento Regional*, Vols. 14/15, pp79–139.

Lopes, J. da S. (1983) IMF conditionality: the stand-by arrangement with Portugal, 1978, in J. Williamson (ed) *IMF Conditionality*, Washington, MIT Press.

Macedo, J.B. de (1979) Portuguese currency experience: An historical perspective, Special Issue of the *Boletim da Faculdade de Direito de Coimbra, Estudos em Homenagem ae Prof. Doutor José Joaquim Teixeira Ribeiro*, Coimbra, University of Coimbra.

Macedo, J.B. de (1980a) Portugal and Europe: The Channels of Structural Interdependence, New Jersey, *Discussion paper n. 88, Research Program in Development Studies*, Woodrow School, University of Princeton.

Macedo, J.B. de (1980b) Portugal e a Europa: Deslizar ou Flutuar?, in Intereuropa (ed), *Portugal e o Alargamento das Comunidades Europeias*, Lisbon, Conferência Internacional.

Marques, A. (1980) *La Politique Économique Portugaise dans le Periode de la Dictature* (1926–1974), Analyse de Trois Stratégies de l'État, Thése de Doctorat de Troisième Cycle, Grenoble.

Matos, L.S. de (1973) *Investimentos Estrangeiros em Portugal*, Lisbon, Seara Nova.

Maxwell, K. (1974) Portugal: a neat revolution, *New York Review of Books* 13.6.1974.

Monteiro, J.C. and Malheiro, H. (1983) O ambiente económico e a sua repercurssão na actividade empresarial: o Caso Português *Jornadas de Gestão*, Faculdade de Economia, Coimbra.

Moura, F.P. de (1973) *Para onde vai a economia Portuguesa*, Lisbon, Seara Nova.

Newitt, M. (1981) *Portugal in Africa. The Last Hundred Years*, London, Hurst.

Oliveira, J.G.C. de (1963) *Portugal e o Mercado Comum*, comunicação do Ministro de Estado à Imprensa, 19.9.1963, SNI, Lisbon.

Pina, A. (1979) *Some Aspects of the Portuguese Economy*, KMI General Assembly, Portugal.

Porch, D. (1977) *The Portuguese Armed Forces and the Revolution*, London, Croom Helm.

Porto, M.C.L. (1977) Emigration and regional development in Portugal, paper presented in the *Seminário sobre Problemas de Emigración en el Area Mediterranea*, University of Granada, Published also by Comissão de Planeamento da Região Centro, Boletim 5.

Porto, M.C.L. (1978) *Desequilibrios Regionais e Emigração, Prospectivas* Jan.–Feb.– March.

Ribeiro, J.J.T. (1977) O abandono do equilíbrio do orçamento ordinário, faculdade de direito de coimbra, *Boletim de Ciências Económicas*, Vol. XIX.

Robinson, R.A.H. (1979) *Contemporary Portugal: A History*, London, George Allen and Unwin.

Rodrigues, A., Borga, C. and Cardoso, M. (1974) *O Movimento dos Capitães e o 25 de Abril*, Lisbon, Morães Editora.

Rosa, E. (1976) *Portugal: Dois Anos de Revolunção na Economia*, Lisbon, Diabril.

Saraiva, J.A. (1974) *Do Estado Novo à Segunda República*, Lisbon, Livraria Bertrand.

Schmitt, H.O. (1981) *Economic Stabilization and Growth in Portugal*, Washington, International Monetary Fund.

Serrão, J. (1972) *A Emigração Portuguesa*, Lisbon, Livraria Horizonte.

Spinola, A. de (1974) *Portugal e o Futuro*, Lisbon, Arcádia.

Tsoukalis, L. (1981) *The European Community and its Mediterranean Enlargement*, London, Allen & Unwin.

Valadas, M. and Murteira, B. (1976) A gestão do sector público produtivo, in Fundação Calouste Gulbenkian and The German Marshal Fund of the United States (ed), *Conferência Internacional sobre Economia Portuguesa*, Vol. II, Lisbon.

Xavier, A.P. (1970) *Portugal e a Integração Económica Europeia*, Coimbra, Livraria Almedina.

CHAPTER FIVE

SPAIN: FROM CORPORATISM TO CORPORATISM

S. Giner
and
E. Sevilla

1. Introduction

The transition from dictatorship to constitutional, parliamentarian rule in
Spain has been a remarkable event. A large western European country has
freed itself from the shackles of arbitrary and despotic rule and has established the basic freedoms enjoyed by some advanced nations. Successful
processes of liberalization and democratization are infrequent. When they
occur, they are often a consequence of violent external forces which first
bring about the downfall of a tyrranical state. Such were the cases of
Germany, Italy and Japan at the end of World War II. No wonder then that
there has been such intense and widespread attention given to what has
occurred in Spain since 1976.

Some assumptions about the Spanish situation deserve closer scrutiny.
The image conveyed by most analyses is that of a Spain that has evolved,
peacefully and in an orderly manner, into a pluralist, liberal, if fledgling,
democracy. This democracy is seen as precarious because it is recent and
therefore lacks deep roots in the political culture of the Spanish people.
Forces lurking in the shadows – for the most part, extremists, terrorists and
military plotters – add to its fragility. This popular image may not be
altogether inaccurate. Yet, understandably, it fails to do justice to the
intricacies of the situation. Much in the Spanish political transition from
dictatorship to democracy still remains to be related by contemporary
witnesses and historians. Much, too, remains to be interpreted in a theoretically more informed manner. Not a few accounts of the Spanish transition, while claiming to be grounded in the field of political sociology, suffer

from a too casual approach to the issue. They tend to be sprinkled with ad hoc references to concepts and hypotheses but do not reflect an identifiable theoretical position. At the other end of the spectrum there have been a few notorious cases of theoretical overkill, where the problems at hand have been sacrificed on the treacherous altar of ideology.

It is our intention to avoid such pitfalls. We shall simply attempt to look at the entire political process from the standpoint of a relatively cogent theoretical perspective, that is, from one single set of general assumptions about the Francoist dictatorship, its consequences for the transition, and the nature of the ensuing political order. What we have in mind is quite simple and straightforward; we think that the entire complex sequence at hand can best be grasped with the help of a wider interpretation, based upon certain concepts which relate to domination, class and class conflict, corporate power, centre-periphery tensions, advanced capitalism, and changes in the legitimation of public authority. As this is not the place to burden the reader with sheer speculation, we simply hope that the perspective that underpins our analysis will become apparent in the course of the discussion, and that it will be interesting and fruitful.

The main thrust of the argument rests on a metaphor, that of corporatism. It is assumed that the Spanish polity has experienced a transition from a form of *fascistisant* corporatism (or 'corporativism') to a newer form of corporatism, this time linked to a notable degree of democratic representation but nevertheless poliarchic, oligopolistic and class based. It is a misnomer because we believe neither that Francoism was really corporatist nor that the country now fits the corporatist mould as described by some theorists of advanced industrial societies. For one thing, corporatism is mediated in Spain by ethnic nationalism, while the power of traditional corporations, such as the army, give it a very particular slant. The two 'corporatisms' are only two terms of reference – we hesitate to say models – which we hope will prove useful as a guiding thread for the analysis.

Within this frame of reference we attempt to describe how a dictatorial regime essentially based on a reactionary coalition, dismantled itself, albeit under powerful external democratic pressures, and how parliamentary democracy emerged without a break in continuity at any point, not even at the level of ideology and legitimation – for the monarchy itself remained untouched. We shall then examine the partial rearticulation of the state in terms of home rule and regional devolution of power, that is, the slow transformation of traditional centre-periphery patterns in Spain. We will refer, in this context, to its consequences for greater corporatization. The military tutelage of the political order will then receive the attention it deserves. All this, we hope, will provide an explanation for the relative displacement which has occurred within established 'radical' forces in Spain towards moralistic and educational rather than economic and structural reforms. We finish with some thoughts about the likely future evolution of Spanish society, given its present position in the world economy and its relationship with its western political environment.

2. Francoism

The nature of Francoism

The political metamorphosis of Spain must be explained with reference to the nature of the regime which made it possible. Francoism was, however, more than a regime; it was also a complex political order, with deep historical, cultural and social roots in the country upon which it was violently imposed, and where it lasted for nearly four decades. It was endowed with remarkable powers of adaptation. Under its resilient crust, massive changes of all kinds occurred in Spanish society, and from 1936 to 1976 the face of Spain was transformed. Her demography, industry, agriculture, cities and social classes changed profoundly, in some cases beyond recognition and nearly always in the direction of 'modernization'. Some of these modifications were initiated by the regime and practically all were in one way or another influenced by it (see Appendix). Indeed, Francoism itself, once constituted, became a structuring factor in the life and destiny of the Spanish people. It was not just another dictatorship in a country endemically suffering from autocracy and arbitrary rule.

Francoism was, of course, an historical entity and, as such, varied in the composition of its elites, the economic policies which prevailed during each period, the ideologies that were upheld by its representatives and the government, and the several forces that it represented. In the effort to get to the period of major concern – the post Franco years – it will be necessary to ignore such fluctuations and changes. At any rate, Francoism displayed a remarkable degree of internal coherence and continuity, which was certainly not confined to the continuous presence of the dictator himself.[1]

[1] The authors have published a number of studies of Francoism. Most recently Giner and Sevilla (1980), and the present essay can be seen as a continuation of that one. For a detailed account of the concepts referred to in the following paragraphs the reader should consult this source.

Francoism was a form of modern despotism that reflected the interests of a reactionary coalition of social classes and political, ideological and military forces. It was embodied in the supreme rule of one dictator, General Franco. Throughout his long rule as chief of state he was the imperative arbiter of the regime which now bears his name. He was accountable to no one, save to God and History, as he himself stated.

The several Francoist governments faithfully reflected the reactionary coalition they served. Though there were fluctuations in their composition, these were far from random, for they responded to the economic and political demands of the moment as well as to concealed factional struggles within the regime (see Ferez (1982) on elites in the early and middle stages of the regime). The power elites were made up of law-and-order generals, fascist middle class *arrivistes* and demagogues, right-wing monarchists, traditional Carlists (also monarchists), and members of two extremely conservative and secretive Catholic associations, the Asociación Catolica Nacional de Propagandistes (ACNP), from the start, and the Opus Dei at a later stage. Together all these groups made up a political class representing the interests of the industrial, financial, and land-owning oligarchy as well as those of conservative sections of the middle classes. The long duration of the regime allowed for the slow coalescence of the several ruling classes of Spain (often regionally based) into one single, 'national' ruling class.

This coalescing ruling class was essentially a 'distributional coalition', engaging in 'rent-seeking' rather than in the general well-being of society and in increasing collective wealth and prosperity. It was a reactionary, distributional coalition of special interest groups which, in the manner of such social entities, practiced exclusive policies against all other, non-organized classes and strata. Systematic political exclusion (and selective repression when needed) was exercised against the subordinate sections of society. Like all distributional coalitions, their decisions (and the decisions of the dictator) were slow, cautious and only brought about by the force of events (Olson 1982). It is therefore a mistake to attribute economic development (after 1959) and social mobility to the intentions and designs of Francoism. These occurred under the pressure of exogenous factors and were largely unintended consequences. The rhetoric of national aggrandizement during the early phases of the regime, and that of economic development in its later ones, ought not to disguise this important feature of Francoism.

The ruling classes of Francoism were always in full control of the state apparatus: their service classes and the bureaucracies held only delegated power. This is why, when the final crisis of the regime began to loom on the horizon, the service classes were unable to put up any serious resistance against the change of will of the hegemonic classes. Only a fraction of the service classes – and a very important one at that – realized the hopelessness of the situation and began to move over to a new ideology. By becoming democratic or actively favouring a change towards constitutionalism and democracy, they not only saved their positions as high civil servants, political dignitaries, and so on, but even reached the highest offices in the early and middle stages of the transition.

Domination was implemented through a series of institutions of political repression which, once the aftermath of the Civil War was over, concentrated selectively on potential or real enemies; since the political formula of Francoism was not based on mobilization but on passive obedience, 'apoliticism' and internal peace. It was also implemented through a series of institutions of economic control for the necessary violent accumulation of capital. Labour repressive methods characterized the regime. It also set up an efficient network of institutions of ideological legitimation and the legal and political façade necessary to a modern despotic regime. All this provided a considerable amount of parasitical resources for great numbers of people, and inflated some institutions, such as the army officer corps. Such inflation of personnel would have interesting consequences in the years following the demise of the regime.

Francoist Corporatism

Though Francoism was more fascist than some commentators have suggested, Spanish fascist corporatism was largely a sham. Apart from a few isolated ideologues no one within the regime seriously held that Spain was a wholly (fascist) 'corporatist state'. Yet, to its dying day, a number of fascist-corporatist features were held to be necessary and were, as such, incorporated into the regime's constitution. Three were exceedingly important:

(a) All representative trade-unions were banned and a massive, complicated, and thoroughly parasitical bureaucracy, that went under the name of 'vertical syndicates', was set up in their stead. In the allocation of resources this bureaucracy was entrusted to Falange party members, and it became a source of sinecures or part-time employment for a potentially disaffected sector of the ruling coalition.

(b) A second corporatist element was the Cortes, or rubber-stamp parliament, whose functions as 'sounding box' for dictator and government alike and international legitimator of a (corporatist) 'organic democracy', need no further explanation.

(c) The ideology that class conflict had been overcome by Francoism, and that a harmonious pyramidal structure (state, province, municipality, family) had been substituted for older confrontations, was actively propounded. In so far as this was enforced through administrative and local government structures as well as the occasional, rigged referendum, corporatism of the fascist kind did exist.

Francoism also inherited a Catholic tradition which advocated a hierarchical, patrimonial, deferential social order capable of coping with the social dislocations and cultural corrosions of modernity. In this, of course, it was not unique, since a number of Catholic countries, from Austria to Portugal, saw the rise of political movements whose aims were to confront and fight atheism, secularization, and revolution. Their ideal was to rescue the faith of the Church from its dire plight through some sort of guild-like social order.

Under the strains of acute political tension, these movements and their ideas were taken up by considerable sections of a bourgeoisie which had suffered the shock of a proletarian uprising, or its imminence, through Popular Front politics and had then confronted it in a long and deadly quarrel. However, the realities of modern capitalism, and the political consequences of the Civil War stood in the way of any neat corporative organization of Spain along the lines of Catholic neomediaevalism.

The institutionalization of interest groups (ideological, partisan, and class groups) had been precarious before the conflagration. As a consequence, outright confrontations were more common than interest groups disputes and negotiations. Interest groups had been unsuccessfully articulated, so that a great many conflicts could not be cushioned or mediated by them. This had made *pronunciamentos*, abrupt regime changes and even civil wars all the easier. With important regional exceptions and differences Spain had had a weak civil society (see Linz 1981). With the outcome of the Francoist victory the weakness of the civil society had been increased (it was now at the mercy of the ruler) but an important new phenomenon had taken place. Although weak, the corporate and interest groups linked to the victorious side were granted generous protection and, in some cases, impunity. Given the nature of the 'corporatist' regime some groups, such as employers' organizations, became theoretically integrated into the 'vertical unions', but they were able to retain their identity and prominence in every way. Yet, these conservative groups had for the moment lost one of their chief *raisons d'être* — interest – group protection from working class and other threats to their integrity. The government most successfully had taken over that task. This is the reason why some of them languished until the coming of democracy after 1976 brought them back to life. Other groups, such as professional associations fared very well under the new circumstances. Each professional body or *cuerpo* (mining, industrial, or highways engineers; lawyers, doctors, architects, and others) attempted to carve out a slice of the posts (*cargos* and *altos cargos*) available in the State. The phenomenon was not new: in fact Francoism can be seen as the successful outcome, among other things, of widespread efforts among the professional groups of Spain towards a monopolistic distribution of resources. The dictatorship, therefore, wholly incorporated into itself older forms of corporatism and interest-group representation.

There was a high degree of ideological congruence between the latent mentality of these professional groups (as well as managerial and land owners' associations) and that of the Catholic upper and middle class movements that were allowed to thrive under Francoism. Thus both the already mentioned ACNP and, much more so, the Opus Dei, advocated an 'apolitical' stance, and emphasized economic development (without democracy), corporatist articulation (without negotiation) and the unquestioning subordination of the many to the professional and competent few. It seems sensible, therefore, to accept that Franco's Spain was in a specific and nonconventional, nonfascist way, a traditional corporatist universe, a corporatism of exclusion rather than inclusion, of subordination rather than mobilization. Once more, it was not corporatist in any of the senses proclaimed by the doctrinaire advocates of early corporatism.

To sum up: in Spain corporate groups and organized interests had been traditionally weak. After the Civil War, those which were rooted within the acceptable and legitimate sphere (employers' associations, Catholic organizations, professional colleges, and such like) were given special protection, though some were subject to a considerable degree of political surveillance. They then became 'strong' in that they were unchallenged and unmolested by rival groups in the distributional struggle for resources, influence and privilege. Despite an increase in bureaucratic parasitism and certain large scale cleptocratic practices, there was, on the whole, a marked diminution of organizational density in many areas. Thus, the subordinate classes (principally workers and peasants) were totally bereft of their unions and political movements and parties. It was to a large extent the sham character of (fascist) corporatism that became one factor in the later economic take-off of the country, by providing a low-paid and politically domesticated work-force. Other factors – such as very low fiscal pressure upon the rich overspill effects of the postwar European and American prosperity, the rise of state capitalism, a state unburdened by large welfare commitments – completed the picture. The areas of society controlled by the *fascistisant*, despotic regime, and left devoid of real interest representation and organization, were vast. Paradoxically, therefore, Francoist corporatism meant the de facto decorporatization of a large and subordinate part of Spanish society.

3. The defeat of dictatorship

The myth of Francoist reformism

The nature of the Francoist dictatorship made possible the smoothness of the political transition, but that transition itself occurred against the will of the regime's principal supporters. The absence of a solution of continuity in the passage from despotic to democratic rule has led many observers to see intentions and strategies for change where there were hardly any. The last years of the regime were characterized by a very effective resistance to liberalization and democratization.

The fact that, according to all appearances, the regime transformed itself into something different has been a very powerful factor in shaping the prevalent belief that it did so of its own accord. Obviously, keen analysts stress the role of the clandestine opposition, the workers' movement, the climate of public opinion, and the growing hostility of many Catholics, students, ethnic nationalists and other groups as forces contributing to the final outcome. Yet, these forces tend to be seen as playing a relatively minor role, when compared to the internal dynamics of the government and the official establishment. The reasons for this ideological bias lie beyond the scope of these reflections. Suffice it to say that they may be found in a certain prevalent reluctance to admit the success of a popular movement towards democracy especially, and this seems to be crucial, when the final result of the transition process had not produced a radical social political order, but a stable, cautiously reformist, liberal, constitutional monarchy.

The continuation and perpetuation of the regime was the central, guiding idea of its men of power, both before and after the death of their leader. *Continuismo* (immobilism and 'continuism') was not an ideology among several: it was the chief one and also the official one. Historians who, like most other analysts, subscribe to the endogenous view of the transition rather than to a more exogenous interpretation such as ours, do stress the massive resistance to change displayed by the last governments of the regime (headed by Prime Ministers Carrero and Arias) throughout the early 1970s. They correctly emphasize the sham character of all projects for political reform emanating from them as well as the utterly undemocratic nature of the government's proposal for the creation of so-called 'political associations' within the Francoist legality. (The remote possibility that such associations may one day become anything resembling a political party, was explicitly excluded. None of them survived the regime. Carr and Fusi (1979) is a prime example of the endogenous analysis of political change. However the authors themselves insist time and again on the 'immobilism' of Francoists in power until the last day of Arias' last government and on the essentially antidemocratic nature of all schemes for political innovation stemming from it. It is therefore surprising to see how some observers are prepared to detect real attempts at reform and liberalization as far back as the mid-1960s. If anything, such very minor attempts were tactical moves to adapt the situation to growing pressure from below and from outside, in order to consolidate the hold of the regime upon a rapidly changing society and to minimize the ever growing costs of repressive control (de Miguel; 1975 on *populismo aperturista*).

A survey of events from the late 1960s onwards shows an acceleration and intensification of opposition activities until they became quite unmanageable for the authorities. The distant roots of this trend stretch as far back as 1962, with the Asturian miners' strikes and the opposition leaders' meeting at Munich, or even to the Barcelona general strike of 1951. However, only by 1969 (national state of emergency) and 1970 (Burgos court martial of Basque separatists) can it be said that the democratic movement began to reach threatening proportions for the regime. Only then did the repressive activities of the government (including selective torture, occasional deportations, arrests, exiles, trials of striking workers, blind counterterrorist measures, and the death of peaceful demonstrators) begin to endanger its own chances to survive unreformed. What is important in all this is that, from about that date, the opposition took over the political initiative, and the government was confined to reacting and responding. Obviously what can be termed for convenience the 'opposition' was far from united. Its different components had very different ideas of what had to be done; but, thanks to Francoism, the minds of its numerous supporters were wonderfully concentrated. A high degree of consensus arose amongst them which was to prove decisive in the following years. Even those small groups which advocated violence or terrorism, in so far as they did not use these indiscriminately, enjoyed an undeniable measure of popularity at the time. They were also useful in making orderly left-wing movements and organizations – such as the communists, the free trade-unions, the socialists and the Christian left-wing – appear as moderate and sensible, despite continuous official propaganda to the contrary.

Taking into consideration the strength of the illegal opposition in combination with the government's persistent unwillingness to reform and yield to its moderate demands until totally overwhelmed, one is bound to conclude that, in essence, the regime was defeated. Its final transformation and self-liquidation was the only option left to it by an ever stronger democratic opposition. During the very last years of its life the opposition also encompassed many defectors from the Francoist ranks, as well as numerous journalists in the crucially important mass media. Widespread disaffection and derision, together with a popular willingness to demonstrate and face the riot police, finally gave the organized political opposition the weapons it needed to force change and reform upon the government. One of the mistakes made by the prevalent 'endogenous school of thought' is to consider ex-Francoist defectors as part and parcel of the regime. Whatever their political past, defectors are defectors, and 'going over to the enemy' is a well-known phenomenon, not only in revolutionary processes, but also in less dramatic political changes through history. Moreover, if political elites cross the lines of the government they had hitherto supported to the opposition, it is because the latter have managed to become a plausible alternative to a deteriorating situation. Therefore, if conservative observers are partly wrong in their analysis of the Spanish transition, but radical ones are equally wrong and certainly moralistic and naive in their description of the latter-day reformists of the Francoist establishment as 'opportunists' and 'pseudo-democrats'. But for this group, the transition would not have taken place as it did.

The collapse of the regime

From the death of General Franco in 1975 until the end of 1976, when there was a referendum on political reform, the pent up forces of democratic change burst open in a series of public demands which constantly overcame and outflanked the dictatorial government. The divorce between government and civil society reached unprecedented proportions. In some parts of the country a new legitimacy began to emerge alongside that of the government. This was particularly the case in Catalonia, where an entirely illegal Democratic Assembly – a gathering of the most disparate political forces – appeared to the Catalan people as wholly representative. It was able, from the moment of its inception in 1972, to achieve remarkable degrees of popular mobilization. On the labour front, the Workers' Commissions (which were rapidly falling under communist control) succeeded in bringing about the final obsolescence of the fascist 'trade-unions'. Political forces which were grouped under two different alliances, one containing the communists (the Democratic Junta) and another the socialists (the Platform of Democratic Convergence) finally joined into a single Committee of Democratic Coordination (in May 1976). A month and a half later President Arias, totally incapable of controlling the situation, was dismissed by the King. He was then able to appoint a reformer from within the system, Adolfo Suárez, as Prime Minister.

The fact that reformers only came to power after the situation had become uncontrollable bears out the contention that it was this situation (created by the efforts of the democratic movement) that forced change upon the regime. This, of course, does not rule out the importance of the personal skills and statesmanship deployed during the political manoeuvring of the period by a number of responsible people, beginning with the King himself, and including several of his close advisers, such as the President of the Cortes. Together, they engineered the self-dissolution of the Francoist Cortes, preceded by the assent given to political reform by the National Council of the Movement. (These characteristically fascist-corporatist institutions which were part of the political façade of the regime had unexpectedly acquired a certain importance, albeit short-lived, by virtue of the power void left by the dictator's death).

Under the strains of impending change and mounting democratic pressure, the 'service classes' and political factions of Francoism regrouped into three different strands:

(a) An immobilist sector, which included the staunchest Francoists and sizeable sections of the officer corps, together with members of the judiciary, high civil servants and the police. They became the mainstay of acute resistance to parliamentary democracy. Their ideology soon degenerated into *golpismo*, a political programme which starts and probably ends with a *coup d'état* against democracy. Some of its advocates joined small neofascist or extreme right-wing parties on the fringe of the new political order.

(b)   A sector of moderate reformism. Its members gave half-hearted support to some form of political representation. They were reluctantly prepared to support the constitutional rules of the game if they ever became law, and presented themselves as the 'civilized right'. Some of its members, such as Manuel Fraga, with his reactionary passage through the Minister of the Interior in 1976 (characterized by violent police repression) had very flimsy democratic credentials. They formed the Popular Alliance Party.

(c)   The more 'radical' and adventurous reformers, with a typical *arriviste* past. They were willing to take chances and risk the responsibility of shouldering the transition. They were young, and were led by Adolfo Suárez, a recent Minister of the Movement (that is, the Falange apparatus) who suddenly converted to democracy. Their basis was direct access to high political office and they were mostly governed by pragmatic notions of political expediency. They were the least ideology-bound of all Francoists. For all these reasons, this group soon acquired a crucial importance in the process of transformation.

The last-minute appointment of the reformers finally made possible a dialogue between the government and the still illegal opposition. The democratic groundswell had grown out of all proportion and the opposition was beginning to come out into the open. From that moment the transition rapidly became a matter of negotiation and multilateral agreements. The fact that the negotiations were not circumscribed to constitutional matters but also included programmatic ones was to be decisive for the shape of future events. Negotiating parties gave each other assurances about their future conduct, thereby 'fixing' policies and setting limits to their respective demands. That was the precise meaning of the comprehensive *consenso pactado* (negotiated consensus) painstakingly achieved from the moment Suárez became Prime Minister in July 1976 until February 1977, when the Communist Party was legalized. The implications were twofold. First, there was a considerable degree of deradicalization on the part of the major political forces. The government (and especially Suárez's budding Centre Party) abandoned repression and accepted political freedom. In exchange, the opposition gave up its doctrine of a 'democratic break' with the past (*ruptura democrática*) and imposed moderation upon working class aims. Radicals (marxist-leninists in the Communist party and marxists in the Socialist party) were to be contained and neutralized. Only *golpistas* on the one hand and terrorists or separatists on the other refused to accept the complex multilateral deal, while peaceful radicals thought they could fight and win either within their parties or by forming smaller, more combative ones. They fought, and lost.

4. The making of contemporary corporatism in Spain

Spain and the varieties of corporatism

Corporatism in societies based upon a liberal political tradition, involves a high degree of interest-group representation both inside and outside the sphere of government. Agreements on a great variety of issues (from prices to incomes, from public works to educational policies) are reached by the interest groups concerned through a process of negotiation, very often bypassing the democratic institutions of popular representation, or manipulating these to implement agreements previously achieved. This involves considerable devolution of public policymaking to the organized interests of unions, employers, pressure groups and other bodies. This kind of corporatism is ultimately inimical to liberal democracy but, at its present level of development, neither has it entirely driven out effective political pluralism nor can it be confused with the hierarchical, exclusive, and totalitarian corporatism of fascism. The similarities between the two, if they exist, are merely formal and restricted only to some aspects of the polity, so that it is unfortunate that both forms of interest organization and control go by the same name (see Giner 1983; and Giner and Péez Yruela 1983).

Spain's passage from a semiperipheral position in the world economic system to a more central one preceded its political incorporation into the pluralist-corporatist order. This did not entail its complete convergence with other Western political systems. Spain is, of course, a democracy in the sense that she has political parties, free public opinion, constitutional politics, free trade-unions and freedom of assembly and association. Likewise, her society harbours a number of familiar modes of corporatist intermediation and interest representation. They are often weak, if compared with their counterparts elsewhere, since the advent of democracy has been recent, and voluntary organizations need time to coalesce and settle. Trade-union membership, for instance, is low, though there has been an unsteady growth since trade-unions were legalized. Some parties actually lost membership in the 'disenchantment' period which followed the early democratic euphoria, although this seemed to be arrested to a certain extent towards the end of 1982. Yet decline in party membership has not meant a decline in organization: the contrary may often have been the case. Employers' organizations have steadily consolidated and found their own voice. The growing degree of corporatization of the parastate and private sector of the economy may still be relatively weak, but what makes the new corporatism different in Spain is not this sphere, but other forces at work. They have set the limits of the possible within the political and economic life of the country.

Paramount among such forces, during the long aftermath of Francoism, was the military establishment. For a long time, it exercised its veto power upon many aspects of the political process and put democracy under indirect military tutelage (though the word 'tutelage' may not be very apposite, for a section of the military posed an active threat to the democratic order). The 'corporatist' rather than 'professional' attitudes (see Perlmutter 1977) of a large part of Spain's armed forces made the political order of the transition years different from that of other western democracies. Spaniards often referred to the several metaconstitutional powers that shaped politics and constrained the margins of political life in their country as the de facto powers, the *poderes fácticos*. More often than not, this expression was a euphemism for the armed forces. It tellingly echoed the dictatorial age when euphemisms were endemic in the language of politics. The army's mere existence largely explained the nature of the 'agreed consensus' achieved throughout the transition period, and the quickly acquired habit of achieving deals outside the Cortes, including agreements to pass a law in order to satisfy the needs of such de facto powers, or to allay their anxieties.

Negotiated consensus and indirect military tutelage

The Spanish Constitution of 1978 declares that the armed forces' mission is to guarantee the country's sovereignty and independence as well as her constitutional order (Article 7). It also declares that they must obey the civil authority of the government (Article 97). Yet, the indirect surveillance of the polity by the army appears to colour and, in some cases, determine, many crucial decisions made by early democratic governments as well as a number of corporatist agreements.

The style was set by President Suárez's 'previous consultation' with the army chiefs as he set in motion his first political reforms, especially, it is widely believed, on the eve of his legalization of the Communist Party.[1] Subsequently, either he or his successors, or the King, often seem to have consulted before acting. Indirect surveillance also extended quite clearly to corporatist pacts for which there is little or no evidence of consultation with the army chiefs. Thus the all-important Moncloa pacts of 1977 (which established a policy of mutual restraint between government, political parties, employers and, indirectly, trade-unions) were explicitly reached with the intention of 'consolidating democracy'. However, the avoidance of strikes and lock-outs and the imposition of wage restraints were also accepted by all concerned as the only way to allay the fears of the *golpista* element in the armed forces and elsewhere. Avoiding 'rocking the boat' or any behaviour that could be construed as a provocation to the *poderes fácticos* became obsessive in Spanish politics, especially as the military appeared to be impatient and tense under the strains imposed upon them by the terrorist crimes perpetrated by mysterious 'extreme left' groups such as GRAPO, not to speak of the continued armed activity of the Basque separatist ETA. By contrast, right-wing terrorism against civilians, though extremely grave on some occasions (Atocha massacre of January 1977, and similar events) provoked consternation and widespread apprehension but was not seen as provoking the democrats into their own brand of *golpismo* or revolution. The very idea seemed absurd.

The Moncloa Pacts, as well as other social peace and wage restraint agreements that followed, could easily be interpreted in standard corporatist terms. After all, very similar 'social compacts' were being worked out in other countries at the time. The same cannot be said though of the projected law for the 'Harmonization of the Autonomies' (1981–1983). This controversial proposal was intended to 'homogenize the powers of the several (regional) home rule governments, with the implicit intention of curtailing the faculties of potentially 'separatist' nationalities. It was jointly prepared by the government party and the main opposition socialists in order to appease the military after the attempted coup and assault on the Cortes palace in February 1981. It was in the light of such a blatant extraparliamentary

[1] In a long conversation with one of the authors (S. Giner.) on May 26 1983, ex-Prime Minister Adolfo Suárez explained to him that 'previous consultation' with the High Command of the Armed Forces or with influential military men had never taken place during the delicate moments of the transition to democracy. Asked about the case of the legalization of the Communist Party, Sr. Suárez stated that he had simply *informed* top military men of his decision.

pact between the two majority parties, that many expressed the view that, in one sense at least, the coup had been successful. This may be an extreme interpretation of the immediate sequels of the failed coup, but it is undeniable that the Harmonization Law project was launched in order to allay the fears in the army (let alone the *golpista* element within it) that democracy inevitably would bring with it the breakup of Spain (see Giner 1984).[1]

The armed forces and the political transition

A detailed account of the makeup and ideology of the Spanish army, along with its position and problems within society cannot be given here (instead see Paricio 1983 and Sepúlveda 1983). Suffice it to say that the Francoist regime had helped create a specific army 'subculture', highly isolated from the rest of society yet attributing to itself the quintessence of patriotism and ultimate interpretation of the national interest. Its ideology was tinged with political paranoia and what can only be described as a schizophrenic attitude towards politics and power: on the one hand the army had to be entirely apolitical and on the other it was profoundly steeped in the world of power. From 1939 until 1959, one out of four high office posts in government and the administration was held by the military. Only with the coming of democracy did the army cease to be one of the main launching pads for high office (Jerez 1982). Although there had been some decline in the role of the army as a channel of access to power during the 1960s and 1970s, the change after 1976 was very abrupt. Moreover, of all the traditional 'corporations' and sections of Spanish society, the army was the least prepared for the sudden advent of democracy. The church was, at least, deeply divided about it and large parts were militantly democratic and even radical. The army (including the young officers) had been systematically inculcated with prejudices, misapprehensions and doctrines which were overtly antidemocratic. Very small and, in the numerical sense, unimportant groups of democratic officers had attempted to change this state of affairs. They were to pay heavily for it in the name of apoliticism and neutrality. Years later, and under a socialist government, officers who had expressed a desire to build a more democratically and constitutionally minded army, still suffered greater discrimination than others who had carried out notoriously

---

[1] The Socialist government's fear that 'centralist' de facto powers may take serious exception to strong and healthy home rule regional administration, became clear when the Constitutional Court declared several key sections of the projected Law unconstitutional. (August, 1983). Yet they insisted in passing the rest of the legal text, with the appropriate deletions.

antidemocratic and *golpista* activities against the constitutional order (see Pitarch 1983a). Not only those who wished to appease the officer corps as a whole insisted that not all army officers were *golpista* and that only a small minority were prepared to carry out anticonstitutional activities. Liberal and reform-minded military men, such as Suárez's Vice-President, General Gutiérrez Mellado, were in power and steadfastly upheld the Constitution. Others, whatever their private views, chose to obey their King and the government in office out of a commendable sense of duty and discipline. Still others felt at ease from the start with the new socialist government, especially as it showed itself to be extremely sensitive to the army's needs for modernization as well as to its demands as a corporate body, while it was punctiliously respectful of the armed forces in every sense.

The fact remains, however, that serious threats to democracy did repeatedly stem from the military's ranks during the democratic consolidation period, from 1976 until the socialist electoral victory of October 1982. Such threats included not only the spectacular coup attempt of February 1981 but also several conspiracies against constitutional rule, such as the 'Galaxia Operation' plot of November 1978 and at least one other after the failed coup (see Morales and Celada 1981). The lightness of the sentences imposed on several occasions underscored, time and again, the strength of the de facto power of the armed forces and the immense caution with which any freely elected civilian government had to tread. In noting this, some observers of the period tended to overlook a much more remarkable phenomenon: the fact that every coup or conspiracy failed (and bloodlessly at that) and that there was vast popular support for democracy in Spain.

The path from military 'corporatism' to military 'professionalism' is a thorny and arduous one anywhere. There are signs, however, that it has been undertaken in Spain. From half-hearted entry into NATO in 1982 to slow implementation of technical and organizational reforms by the socialist civilian Minister of Defence, such signs are quite unmistakable. Thus, at the end of April 1983 the Supreme Court was able to uphold the maximum 30-year sentences imposed on senior army officers involved in the attempted coup of February 1981 and, more significantly, raised the sentence of the 'political' inspirer of conspiracy, another general, from six to 30 years. Fearlessly, the Court increased the sentences in 21 of the 33 cases brought before it. It would be untenable to conclude from all this, however, that 'professionalism' had been achieved (see Pitarch 1983b and Campo Vidal 1983). For one thing, the army continues to enjoy a special position in the political order of democracy in Spain: it exercises indirect surveillance of its own corporate interests and possesses veto power on a number of issues. For another, all armed forces in the contemporary world have, in varying degrees, considerable direct or indirect power in the 'societal corporatism' of the age. Spain, of all countries, could hardly be an exception. With the advent of democracy the military establishment forced moderation, by its sheer presence, upon all constitutional left-wing forces, including the notoriously cautious Eurocommunists. (Their spectacular electoral defeats were in part the price they had to pay for moderation and the disappointment it created among more radical supporters.) The military in Spain have had the effect of deradicalizing the left in general and the socialists in particular, whether in opposition or government.

Spanish corporatism

According to Linz (1981, 336–7) 'the most noteworthy' characteristic of interest politics in Spain 'is that politics takes precedence over interests'. And he adds:

> 'Partisan cleavages are more important than interest conflicts. The articulation of interests on a permanent and continuous basis is therefore delayed and in part unsuccessful. This does not mean that interest, economic and social groups do not exercise a decisive influence on the policy-making process but that their institutionalization and legitimation is less successful than in other countries. Perhaps the organization and legitimization of interests requires prolonged periods of political stability; they can be said to some extent to be incompatible with intense conflicts.'

This observation is supported by the historical facts. Endemic cleavages – industrial/agricultural, centre/periphery, hegemonic nationalism/minority nationalism, clericalism/anticlericalism, despotism/constitutionalism, and several others – have criss-crossed the ideological, class and political composition of Spain for a long time and, in such manner, that they have fragmented, undermined and imperilled the functioning and expansion of other forms of social cohesion and coalescence, especially those which foster the growth of organized interest groups. It was thus that modern Spain became a zero sum world of tawdry or heroic confrontations rather than of negotiations and compromise.

Developments after the dissolution of the dictatorship in 1976 must lead, however, to reconsideration of this verdict, which had seemed accurate enough for the past. To begin with, it would be risky to assume that in less than a decade of political freedom, full interest-group consolidation has taken place, or that it has gone apace with the process of democratic consolidation itself. In many ways the latter, with the freedoms it presupposed for the unhindered growth of voluntary associations of all kinds, must precede the former. Yet, by 1983 a number of factors have come to strengthen the possibility of a stable western-style, 'corporatist' societal structure of interest representation in the framework of constitutional democracy in Spain. One is the incipient professionalization of the armed forces, to which reference has just been made: this may eventually lead the military away from a position of interventionist corporatism into one of representational and bargaining corporatism, more in tune with the stance taken by other influential armed forces in the West. Several other factors also stand out and three must be mentioned: the decline of the religious-secular divide, together with the mitigation of ideological maximalism; prolonged, uninterrupted peace since 1939; and the rise of organized, nationwide economic interests. In detail:

1. After the 1960s Spain underwent one of the deepest changes in its entire cultural and religious history. The deepest, no less, since the Enlightenment period. Among other things, such change entailed the substitution of anticlericalism by religious indifference (Giner 1982a). Collective problems of all sorts ceased to be cast or sublimated in Catholic or anti-Catholic terms. (Messianism and general *gemeinschaftlich* allegiances may have been displaced and redefined, however, in the intense and mutually opposed 'all-Spanish' and 'ethnic' nationalisms of the period.) The rapid decline of traditional anarchism and the collapse of the radical parties which once thrived to the left of Socialists and Communists under Francoist persecution added to the atmosphere of nonmilitant secularism. Perhaps the – for many unexpected – absence of a substantial Christian Democratic party of some importance in the country as a whole has also helped to dampen the possible anticlerical ires of the left. Despite its connections with certain parties (some of them ethnic minority-bound) the uncoupling of Church and party in Spain has considerably weakened political polarization on religious, or antireligious grounds (compare this to Italy – see Chapter 3).

2. The Francoist order was too *fascistisant* to allow for the spontaneous formation of associational life. It had its own idea of which organizations could be allowed to exist and it also set up its own. In this it contrasted with other former dictatorships in Spain itself. However, its prolonged duration, its forced accommodation with a

western democratic world, its need to shed much of its fascist façade, and the imperatives of economic development, forced the regime to make small but highly significant concessions once the early period of high-scale repression began to recede into the past. After a period the regime grudgingly had to accept some accommodation with social movements which were able to escape its complete control. Official recognition of some forms of free collective bargaining between workers and employers in 1958 opened a process which – after many illegal and costly strikes – led to the 1966 legalization of 'economic' nonpolitical strikes. Apart from the beneficial effects of these developments for the market economy, they created more favourable conditions for the consolidation of free trade-unions, even if they continued to be clandestine or illegal. It was thus that the Communist-controlled Workers' Commissions (but also other unions such as the Socialist National Confederation of Workers – UGT – or the smaller independent Syndical Union – USO) pre-dated and indeed encouraged the coming of democracy. The same goes for the student democratic movement, the representative bodies of several professional associations and, of course, for political parties and democratic movements. The already mentioned lack of a solution of continuity between dictatorship and democracy in Spain accounts for the fact that, sociologically, many of the organized interest groups of the constitutional monarchy have already had a longer life than it may appear. Prolonged peace, under conditions of modernity, allows for increased organizational density within polities and civil societies. It may also eventually lead to congestion, but Spain is still far from reaching that situation. If anything, there is still a low degree of corporatization, to be detected not only in the low rate of working class unionization but in many other instances as well.

3. The upsurge in regionalization and ethnic nationalism (formally culminating with the May 1983 election for the 'autonomous' areas still without their regional assemblies) may give the impression of increased fragmentation and tension between centre and periphery in Spain. In fact, such developments have been made possible without any danger to the general unity of the country by a number of recent trends: the deregionalization of the upper classes, the industrialization of formerly nonindustrial areas, massive migrations across ethnically distinct regions, the growth of an efficient transport network (by air and motorways, especially) and, above all, the

transformation of the economy. The penetration of foreign capital and multinational corporations in Spain (see Chapter 7), combined with the rise of state capitalism and investment has largely disregarded the traditional economic structure of the country, with its high ethnic area correlations. Apart from the obvious economic effects of all these – and other factors, such as large scale tourism and labour migrations abroad (see Chapter 6) – there has arisen a new, much more integrated structure in the financial, industrial and services sectors. Its nationwide range tends to preclude societal fragmentation, save perhaps at the levels of ideology, cultural identity, and political representation. For these and other 'infrastructural' reasons, therefore, the creation of home-rule governments does not threaten the greater unity of the country as a whole: the breakup of Spain, much feared by extreme ideologues of unity – that is centralism – at all costs, is a chimera. What is not a chimera is the danger of administrative inflation and further corporatization, created by the persistence of provincial structures, with their central government – appointed prefects and local bureaucracies, despite the existence of regional assemblies and governments. The highly artificial provincial units are logically incompatible with the more 'natural' regions. They have not been abolished, and a new and expensive administrative layer has been created between the citizen and the state.

5. Conclusion: the rise of 'social forces'

On 9 May 1983, in the aftermath of the Socialist victory at the local and home-rule elections, the Prime Minister Felipe González expressed the view that now his party had also won at those polls, the government need not solve the pressing national economic problems in conjunction with the opposition parties – though, of course, the dialogue with these would continue – but rather could turn to 'social forces' for the elaboration of effective policies. He then explained that by 'social forces' he understood organized labour and organized management. They were now, he said, the 'true negotiating forces' for the government (*los verdaderos interlocutores del gobierno*). It was through these that a 'new social compact' (*pacto social*) would be achieved in order to confront the serious economic situation.

Taken in isolation, this statement of programmatic corporatism may give an unfair idea of the true character of the Socialist government in power. Its experience of opposition (illegal and otherwise) and its democratic credentials ought to be a guarantee that fears of a monopoly of power, the growth of a large power *latifundio* (Cebrián 1983) which would incline it to systematically bypass the institutions of democracy, may be ill-founded. But it is significant of a new trend, whose beginnings in the 1977 Moncloa Pacts have already been pointed out.

The democratic consolidation years have witnessed a hurried ferment of interest group formation, of which the foregoing pages have only given a partial idea. Professionals of all sorts – airline pilots, sportsmen, public and banking employees, the paramilitary police forces and the plainclothes police – have organized themselves, either independently or within the trade-union framework, and in some cases even 'illegally'. The official or semiofficial status of certain unionized public servants – the police, for example – has created ambiguous and difficult situations for the authorities. Yet, on the whole, they have preferred the use of the normal channels of the negotiating table rather than dismissals and arbitrary reprisals when confronted with delicate or embarrassing strikes or open challenges. Pragmatism rules now.

The spectacular increase in corporate and associational density in Spain has led to some awareness of the rise of an incipient 'neocorporatism' in the country.[1] Thus anticorporatist feelings were aired in influential, liberal and 'progressive' quarters when the socialist government gave notice that it intended to put forward a law for the regulation of professional colleges and corporations which, if implemented, would introduce a considerable measure of intervention in their lives and would probably lead to overregulation, overdiscipline and a tight state control over them (editorial comment in *El Pais*, June 14 1983). However, a widespread debate has not yet arisen on such issues. Observers have failed to relate corporate density in general to the persistence of multilateral pacts between the several 'social forces' in the production of economic, political and cultural reality. In the several analyses of the transition to democracy and its consolidation, the all-important issues of a budding, Western-style corporate society, are absent.[2]

---

[1] An early statement on the new corporatism in Spain can be found in the works of Martínez Alier. In an article in *El Pais* in December 1981 he asked the interesting question of why was it that Spain had imported neocorporatist terminology (and institutions) into its new political makeup but had not imported the debate (cf, also with Martinez Alier 1983). For another statement on the old and new corporatism in Spain see Giner (1982b).

[2] Martínez Alier (1983) chides Education Minister, J.M. Maravall, for ignoring corporatist theory and perspectives (even for not rejecting them explicitly) in his treatment of contemporary Spanish politics (cf, Maravall 1982).

References to de facto powers and haphazard reflections on the limits of the possible are not enough.

The stark contrast with the recent dictatorial past and the gravity of the current economic situation may be barriers for a lucid analysis of corporatist trends in democratic Spain. Corporatism itself – in its new 'pluralist' guise – may be seen as part and parcel of that efficiency, modernity and rationality to which the government so outspokenly aspires. By its own admission the goals of its socialist ideology must first wait for the updating and transformation of the antiquated arrangements and institutions inherited by it. Corporatism thus appears, if at all, as an abstract and remote entity, and certainly not a danger. If anything the party now in power has been practicing it for quite a while. And peaceful modernization as its leaders see it, include the bargaining processes and power structures of modern corporatism. The official goals of 'industrial reconversion' (which includes the dismantling of unproductive industries), educational reform, fiscal and financial improvements and administrative efficiency, are (according to government spokesmen) those that bourgeois and conservative governments in the past ought to have carried out long ago. They must now be achieved before thought can be given to other, more 'ideological' issues. Such goals are, no doubt, important. However, they tend to overshadow other no less important problems. Some are very visible and traditional, such as the ever pending agrarian reform.[1] Others, such as the growing corporatization of social life, seem less pressing, but are insidious and in the long run may become more serious than overconfident modernizers may think. With the highest unemployment figures in Western Europe, continued uncertainties about entry in the European Community, unrelenting inflation, economic stagnation, the unabated force of the nationalist cleavages – to mention only a few problems – the subtler questions of modern corporatism continue to elude serious analysis. There is no sense of urgency about them. This is perhaps surprising in a country whose culture contains a forceful and original strand of libertarian thought (that is libertarian thought writ large and not just restricted to the anarchist tradition).

Be that as it may, there is little in the new corporatist structuration of Spanish society that may look unfamiliar or surprising to an observer from

---

[1] Some have claimed that modernization of agriculture and the new methods of cultivation and exploitation have made the agrarian reform unnecessary. By 1983, however, labourers' occupations of large *latifundia* and peasant unrest were still endemic in Andalusia. Only the combined resources of the welfare state seem to have been able to contain the problem within more manageable and 'civilized' limits than in the past. By late 1983, however, the Andalusian regional government (Socialist controlled) managed to put forward a mild agrarian reform programme, emphasizing productivity and modernization rather than collectivization and land redistribution (cf Sevilla and Taberner 1983).

and advanced western democracy. Spain's *differential specifica* still lies else-where, in a number of cultural patterns, social institutions and ethnic characteristics, a combination of which is unique. For that reason the advantages of a newly achieved democracy leave open the possibility that Spaniards may still be able to confront successfully the more negative aspects of modern corporatism without sacrificing too much of their hard-won liberty.

References

Campo Vidal, M. (1983) La sentència pel 23–F ha desarmat els ultres, *El Món* May 6.

Carr, R. and Fusi, J.P. (1979) *Spain, Dictatorship to Democracy*, London, Allen and Unwin.

Cebrián, J.L. (1983) El latifundio del poder, *El Pais* April 17.

Díez Nicolás, J. (1971) La transición demográfica en España, *Revista de Estudios Sociales* pp13–72.

Gamar, L. (1980) *Política Económica de España*, Madrid, Alianza Universidad.

Giner, S. (1978) La Estructura Social de España, in A. López Pina (ed) *Poder y Clases Sociales*, Madrid, Tecnos.

Giner, S. (1982a) El porvenir de la religión es España, *La Vanguardia* April 29.

Giner, S. (1982b) España entre el viejo y el nuevo corporatismo, *La Vanguardia*, March 24, 5.

Giner, S. (1983) Clase, poder y privilegio en la sociedad corporativa, *Papers Revista de Sociología*, No. 20, pp13–60.

Giner, S. (1983b, forthcoming) Ethnic nationalism, centre and periphery in Spain, in C. Abel and N. Tarrents (eds) *Spain: Conditional Democracy?*, London, Croom Helm..

Giner, S. and Pérez Yruela, M. (1983) *La Sociedad Corporativa*, Madrid, CIS.

Giner, S. and Sevilla, E. (1980) From despotism to parliamentarianism: class domination and political order in the Spanish State, in R. Scase (ed) *The State in Western Europe*, London, Croom Helm.

González García, M. (1976) The armed forces, in P. Preston (ed) *Spain in Crisis*, London, Harvester. (Also, see *L'avenç*, special issue (December 1982) L'exèrcit dins l'Espanya contemporània, 1898–1977).

Jerez, M. (1982) *Elites Políticas y Centros de Extracción en España (1938–1957)*, Madrid, CIS.

Leguina, J. (1972) Análisis del envejecimiento de la población española, *Revista de Estudios Sociales*, Vol. 5.

Linz, J.J. (1981) A century of politics and interests in Spain, in S.D. Berger (ed) *Organizing Interests in Western Europe*, Cambridge, Cambridge University Press.

Maravall, J.M. (1982) *La Política de la Transición*, Madrid, Tecnos.

Martinez Alier, J. (1983) The old corporatist ideology and the new corporatist reality in Spain, Florence, *European University Institute, Summer School on Comparative European Politics, multicopied publication 203/83*.

Miguel, A. de (1975) *Sociología del Franquismo*, Barcelona, Euro.

Miguel, A. de (1977) *La Pirámide Social Española*, Barcelona, Ariel.

Miguel, J.M. de (1973) *El Ritomo de la Vida Social*, Madrid, Tecnos.

Morales, J.L. and Celada, J. (1981) *La Alternativa Militar: el Golpismo Después de Franco*, Madrid, Editorial Revolución.

Naredo, J.M. (1971) *La Evolución de la Agricultura Española*, Barcelona, Estela.

Naredo, J.M. et al (1974) *La Agricultura en el Desarrollo Capitalista Española*, Madrid, Siglo XXI.

Olson, M. (1982) *The Rise and Decline of Nations*, New Haven, Yale University Press.

Paricio, J.M. (1983) *Para Comprender a Nuestros Militares*, Madrid, Tecnos.

Perlmutter, A. (1977) *The Military and Politics in Modern Times*, New Haven, Yale University Press.

Pitarch, J.L. (1983a) La UMD, el derecho y la política, *El País*, March 7.

Pitarch, J.L. (1983b) Ante la sentencia del Tribunal Supremo, *El País*, April 28.

Ros Hombravella, J. (1979) *Política Económica Española, 1959–1973*, Barcelona, Blume.

Sepúlveda F.L.D. (1983) Ejércitos y poder fáctico, *La Vanguardia*, January 10, 5.

Sevilla, E. (1979) *La Evolución del Campersinada en España*, Barcelona, Peninsula.

Sevilla, E. and Taberner, J. (1983) Reforma agraria e regañadientes, *Diàid*, November 17.

Appendix

Political and economic development in post war Spain: a summary

The Francoist economy initially had been highly autarkic, both through choice (maintaining artificially high exchange rates) and constraint (between 1946 and 1950 it was isolated by UN sanctions). The economy was under strong central control; firms required licences for all investments exceeding 50 000 pesetas, and there were import quotas even for advanced technology. As part of the autarkic strategy the government also established a state holding institution, INI, responsible for creating new industrial companies and investing in existing firms in key sectors. These policies were reinforced by a narrow and regressive tax base and repressive labour laws.

This strategy allowed the economy to recover after the devastation of the Civil War and expand modestly. However, a relatively inefficient agricultural sector still dominated the economy (accounting for two-fifths of employment in 1960), the industrial sector was highly dualistic and, by the late 1950s, there were mounting deficits both in state budgets and trade balances. Eventually there was a turnabout in economic policy; Opus Dei technocrats were included in the sixth government in 1957 and in the next two years Spain moved towards fuller international integration, becoming a member of the OECD, the IMF and the World Bank. Above all, the 1959

Stabilization Plan symbolized the reorientation; public expenditure was reduced, the peseta was devalued (to encourage tourism and investment), and investment controls were relaxed, so that up to 50 percent of foreign holdings in Spanish companies were permitted (Baklanoff 1978; Wright 1977).

The results of these policies were spectacular, with GDP growing by seven percent per annum between 1960 and 1974, although there was a notable difference between agriculture (three percent) and manufacturing (nine percent). Foreign investment played a key role especially in the chemicals, metal goods, vehicles, nonferrous metals and food processing sectors, and Spain eventually became the world's ninth largest industrial producer (Lawlor 1975; Muñoz et al 1979). During the 1960s growth was maintained with low inflation rates and balance of payments surpluses, while real incomes approximately doubled. The proportions employed in agriculture fell (from 40 to 29 percent) while those in industry and the tertiary sector increased (to 37 and 34 percent respectively).

Both emigration and tourism contributed to growth. During the peak years of emigration (the 1960s) over 200 000 persons left Spain each year, and even in the mid 1970s there were over half a million Spaniards still resident abroad. Their remittances made an important contribution to the balance of payments whilst also reducing unemployment levels in some regions, and overall social and political tensions (Aceves and Douglas 1976). Tourism may have been even more important for, with the number of foreign visitors increasing from 6 million in 1960 to 34 million in 1973, tourist receipts came to cover about 70 percent of the trade deficit.

In contrast, the agricultural sector remained poorly developed. The reasons for this included the early emphasis on autarky (leading to excessive concentration on cereals production) and polarization of agriculture between *latifundia* in the south and west and *minifundia* in the north. Whilst two-thirds of farms in Extremadura and Andalusia were larger than 250ha, average farm size in Galicia was about 3ha, with excessive parcelization (Giner and Sevilla 1977; O'Flanagan 1980). State policies were limited to irrigation and colonization schemes (as in Badajoz – see Naylon 1966), and consolidation of plots in the *minifundia* zones, but there was no attempt tat land reform (Naylon 1967, 1973; O'Flanagan 1982). Such a measure would, of course, have undermined one of the major bastions of support for the Francoist regime, the rural aristocracy. However, there were changes in agriculture with significant advances in commercialization and mechanization, contrasting examples being the development of Nestlés creameries in

Santander and the introduction of capital intensive technology in Almeria to produce 'out-of-season' crops.

Generally, economic growth was regionally uneven being concentrated in Madrid, Catalonia and the Basque country and some of the larger cities such as Valencia and Zaragossa. The areas of Madrid, Barcelona and Bilbao experienced employment gains in excess of 1 percent per annum in the 1960s while in most of the South and West employment levels *decreased* by the same amount. This was associated with drift from the land as some 1.8 million left agriculture during these years. There were internal migration flows (especially from Andalusia to Catalonia) and waves of emigration (Bradshaw 1972), both of which contributed to some convergence of per capita incomes although differences remained substantial; extremes were Madrid, 38 percent above the national average, and Extremadura, 39 percent below this. There were attempts to reduce these inequalities, notably through a series of policies (initiated in the First Development Plan, 1964–1967) to promote growth centres in less developed regions. Experiences varied but these seem to have served national growth requirements better than regional development needs. Many of the policies were based on capital-intensive industries and lacked significant spread effects (Naylon 1981).

After the 1973–1974 oil crisis, the growth of the Spanish economy (which was dependent on imports for about 70 percent of energy requirements) slowed down appreciably. Between 1974 and 1980 growth only averaged 2 percent per annum, a far cry from the achievements of the 1970s and only half the OECD average. Declines both in tourist receipts and emigrant remittances contributed to this. For example, the growth in the number of tourists had been 14.5 percent in 1970 but fell to 4 to 5 percent per annum in the late 1970s and even declined in particular years. The number of emigrants also fell to 14 500 by 1977, only a quarter of the number of returned migrants in that year. Employment has continued to decline in agriculture (−6 percent per annum, 1974–1979) but there were also losses in industry so that only the tertiary sector exhibited growth (Lieberman 1982).

The broad economic changes described above had profound implications both for the political evolution of Francoism and for events since 1975. These are discussed in the main body of the chapter and only a chronology of the major political developments since 1975 are presented here. After Franco's death in November 1975, Arias Navarro remained Prime Minister hoping, with Juan Carlos' support, to achieve limited political reforms. These aroused considerable friction within the cabinet and, in July 1976, he resigned. Suárez became Prime Minister and, following a careful strategy (with the tacit support of many groups) he 'imposed democracy from above' on Spain. His most remarkable achievement was persuasion of the Cortes to dissolve itself, with new elections being held for a legislature to prepare a new constitution.

Elections were held in June 1977 and Suárez's Democratic Centre Union (UCD) party obtained approximately half the seats, the Socialist Workers Party (PSOE) led by González had a third of the seats and the Popular Alliance (AP) led by Fraga came a poor third. In due course, in 1978, the new constitution was approved: Article 1 stated that Spain was a parliamentary monarchy and Article 2 guaranteed the rights of the Spanish 'nationalities' to autonomy (see Maravall 1982; Serfaty 1981). This guarantee brought regionalist and nationalist questions to the forefront of Spanish parliamentary politics, although Catalan and Basque movements had become increasingly active since the 1960s (Medhurst 1977).

New elections were held in 1979 but these did not significantly affect the balance of power. Suárez continued in government and, by the end of the year, had completed the transfer of some powers to the Basque and Catalan regions. The local elections, however, saw important advances by the regional political parties at the expense of the national parties. Elements within and outside the UCD became alarmed at the prospect of further transfers of powers to the regions, especially as ETA terrorist activities continued in the Basque country. The government, therefore, contrived to block further rapid regional devolution (it obtained a technical 'no' vote in the referendum on autonomy in Andalusia).

The party, and Suárez in particular, are considered to have handled events badly and the Prime Minister was barely able to survive a vote of no-confidence in parliament in 1980. In a sense, this marked the end of concensus politics and in the general election of 1982 the centre-right UCD was decimated. The Socialists gained an absolute majority and the right-wing Popular Alliance became the major opposition party. Spanish politics were becoming increasingly polarized.

References

Aceves, J.B. and Douglas, W.A. (1976) *The Changing Faces of Rural Spain*, Cambridge, Mass., Schenkman.

Baklanoff, E.N. (1978) *The Economic Transformation of Spain and Portugal*, New York, Praeger.

Bradshaw, R.P. (1972) Internal migration in Spain, *Iberian Studies*, Vol. 1, pp68–74.

Giner, S. and Sevilla, E. (1977) The latifundio as a local mode of class domination: the Spanish case, *Iberian Studies*, Vol. 6, pp47–57.

Lawlor, T. (1975) Foreign investment in Franco Spain, *Iberian Studies*, Vol. 4, pp21–30.

Lieberman, S. (1982) *The Contemporary Spanish Economy*, London, Allen and Unwin.

Maravall, J. (1982) *Politics in Spain Since Franco*, London, Croom Helm.

Medhurst, K. (1977) The Basques and Catalans, *Minority Rights Group Report No. 9*, London.

Muñoz, J. Roldan, J. and Serrano, A. (1979) The growing dependence of Spanish industrialization on foreign investment, in D. Seers, B. Schaffer and M.L. Kiljunen (eds) *Underdeveloped Europe*, Sussex, Harvester Press.

Naylon, J. (1966) The Badajoz Plan; an example of land settlement and regional development in Spain, *Erdkunde*, Vol. 20, pp44–60.

Naylon, J. (1967) Irrigation and internal colonisation in Spain, *Geographical Journal*, Vol. 133, pp178–191.

Naylon, J. (1973) An appraisement of Spanish irrigation and land settlement policies since 1939, *Iberian Studies*, Vol. 2, pp12–17.

Naylon, J. (1981) Iberia, in H.D. Clout (ed) *Regional Development in Western Europe*, Chichester, Wiley.

O'Flanagan, T.P. (1980) Agrarian structures in North West Iberia: responses and their implications for development, *Geoforum*, Vol. 11, pp157–169.

O'Flanagan, T.P. (1982) Land reform and rural modernization in Spain, *Erdkunde*, Vol. 36, pp48–53.

Serfaty, M. (1981) Spanish democracy: the end of the transition, *Current History*, Vol. 466, pp213–7.

Wright, A. (1977) *The Spanish Economy, 1959–76*, London, Macmillan.

PART TWO

GENERAL THEMES

CHAPTER SIX

POPULATION MOBILITY: EMIGRATION, RETURN MIGRATION AND INTERNAL MIGRATION

Russell King

1. Introduction

'Up there in Switzerland it seemed like an earthly Paradise. It was a pleasure working with other people, exchanging talk: your mind was opened and your wits sharpened. But I missed my family terribly: so much I had to come back. And then I turned back into a block of wood: I felt I was in Hell'.

'When I came back to Sicily, I took heart again. We were back in our own land. I felt better, we all talked the same'.

Two Sicilian migrants returned from Switzerland express very different reactions to their migratory experience. Their words (from Dolci 1968) show how difficult it is to generalize about the personal experiences of southern Europe's migrant population. The illustration has more than anecdotal value for it is symptomatic too of the scholarly disagreements that exist within social science of how labour migration of the southern European type is to be interpreted and evaluated.

The debate can be illustrated by focussing upon the effects of emigration on the southern European sending countries. On the one side are those who see these largely in beneficial terms: 'Migration in western Europe represents . . . the equivalent of a large effort in development assistance rendered by the countries receiving labour to those sending it' (Hume 1973). 'Migratory workers acquire new skills whilst working abroad and thus are able to improve their economic and social status, either in foreign countries or after their return home . . . Those who migrate are usually superfluous to the economy at home' (Kosiński 1970). Both Kindleberger (1965) and Griffin (1976), after reviewing a number of economic theories on the emigration-economic growth dynamic, concluded that emigration was a positive force for growth in southern Europe. Lutz (1961) went even further and argued that emigration was a necessary precondition for the industrial expansion of southern European countries; only when a substantial proportion of the surplus population had left, she maintained, would incomes rise sufficiently to generate demand for industrial goods. In summing up the 'promigration' view, however, it should be pointed out that virtually all the arguments rest on economic theory largely unsupported by empirical data.

On the other side of the debate are writers, many of them of a Marxist or neo-Marxist persuasion, who see emigration in a much more critical light. The first authoritative critique came from the then governor of the Bank of Greece, Xenophon Zolotas (1966). More widely-known is the book by Castles and Kosack (1973) which attacks not only the economic arguments advanced above but also is widely heralded as the Marxist answer to the assimilationists who dominated studies of migration and race relations until the 1960s. In complete contrast to Hume, quoted above, Castles and Kosack (1973) conclude that '. . . labour migration is a form of development aid given by the poor countries to the rich countries'. Following Marxist orthodoxy they see migrants' class position in terms of the social relations of economic production, with the ruling classes of industrial Europe actively manipulating the concept of race to fragment the working class. They argue that the primary function of prejudice against immigrant workers is to conceal and legitimate the exploitation of their labour, by alleging that they are congenitally inferior. According to the Marxist analysis, southern Europeans' role as a reserve army of labour assured the receiving countries sustained industrial growth in the postwar period, and relieved northern European workers of the necessity of doing a whole range of unpalatable jobs (Ward 1975a). The internationalization of the European labour market sees the expansionist tendencies of western Europe capital recruiting labour from an ever-widening orbit: initially Italy, Greece, Spain and Portugal, later Turkey, North Africa and the Third World (Sasson-Koob 1978; 1980). As the migration mechanism annexes different countries, so these become graded and a basis is laid for a chain of sub-imperialism. This takes place either within the emigration countries themselves (the schism between northern and southern Italy is the clearest example of this), or by the 'first order' emigrant countries ultimately becoming immigration countries, importing labour from countries further down the chain (Nikolinakos 1975). This is precisely what is happening now in southern Europe, with new flows of North African and Third World migrants coming into the main urban and tourist centres of Italy, Greece, Spain and, less so, Portugal. We shall return to this point later.

Yet to see migrants merely as pawns in a game which they neither control nor understand, pushed and pulled by the interests of capital as represented by ruling elites, is an oversimplification. Class analysts who place migrant workers as part of the working class of the reception society are denying ethnicity and are ignoring the perspective of return, either as an ideology or as an actual act. Not only do migrants make choices, they utilise and manipulate various kinds of networks for their own ends; they are the creators and receivers of well-thought-out rationales for their own behaviour. Douglas (1970) shows how Basque migrants have open to them a wide range of 'mobility ploys': North and South America, France, Switzerland and various Spanish destinations. In that they can choose where to migrate, when, and for how long, they are the architects of their own destinies.

The remainder of this chapter is in three main parts. The first examines emigration from the southern European countries. This looks at the temporal and geographical patterns of the flows that have developed since about 1960, at the character of the migration and at the impact on the sending areas. The second part concerns return migration, of particular importance during the late 1960s and mid 1970s, and evaluates the role of returnees in promoting socioeconomic change in their home areas. In the final section attention switches to internal migration. Although less publicized than international migration, rural–urban and inter-regional flows are important adjuncts of social and economic change in the southern European countries.

2. Patterns of emigration

The researcher's task of finding reasonably reliable migration data for southern European countries was made much easier by the creation of SOPEMI (Continuous Reporting System on Migration) in 1973. The SOPEMI Annual Reports, issued in mimeographed form by OECD, are the main source for Table 6.1 which gives annual emigration total for the period 1960–1980. But it should be stressed straight away that SOPEMI tabulations rely on data supplied by individual countries, and these countries differ in their approaches to defining and recording their emigrants. The Spanish figures, for instance, are only for officially assisted emigration to Europe. The Portuguese data include an estimate for the huge quantity of clandestine movement based on post facto regularization in destination

Table 6.1   Emigration 1960–1980

	Spain	Portugal	Greece	Italy
1960	30,500	32,732	47,748	383,908
1961	43,000	34,796	58,837	387,123
1962	65,336	38,210	84,054	365,611
1963	83,728	53,970	100,072	277,611
1964	102,146	86,282	105,569	258,482
1965	74,539	116,974	117,167	282,643
1966	56,795	132,834	86,896	296,494
1967	25,911	106,280	42,730	229,264
1968	66,699	104,149	50,866	215,713
1969	100,840	153,536	91,552	182,199
1970	97,657	173,267	92,681	151,854
1971	113,702	151,197	61,745	167,721
1972	104,134	104,976	43,397	141,852
1973	96,088	120,019	27,525	123,302
1974	50,695	70,273	24,448	112,020
1975	20,618	44,918	20,330	92,666
1976	12,124	33,207	20,374	97,247
1977	11,300	28,758	18,350	87,655
1978	11,993	30,253	14,482	85,550
1979	13,019	20,622	11,050	88,950
1980	14,065	18,044		83,007

Notes: Spain: assisted emigrants to Europe (workers only).
Portugal: official emigration, plus 'regularizations' in emigration countries (except for 1979 and 1980).
Greece and Italy: all emigrants.

Sources: Cerase (1979).
Rocha Trinidade (1979a; 1979b).
Statistical Yearbook of Greece, 1972 and 1978, Athens, National Statistical Service.
SOPEMI (Continuous Reporting System on Migration) *Reports* for 1974, 1977, 1978, 1980 and 1981, Paris, OECD, Directorate for Social Affairs, Manpower and Education.

countries like France and Venezuela. The Italian and Greek data are probably more comprehensive, but the fact that they do not tally with the larger numbers of Italians and Greeks recorded as entering destination countries (by West Germany, for instance) indicates some underestimation here too. The four columns in Table 6.1 are therefore not comparable with each other. The figures do have greater validity in comparing trends through time, however.

The Italian flow was already well established by 1960. Throughout the period 1947–1959, annual emigration totals were within the range 200,000–350,000, and the postwar emigration peak was reached as early as 1961, with 387,000 migrants leaving in that year. Switzerland, France and Belgium took the bulk of the early postwar flow to Europe, West Germany only assuming importance after 1960. Throughout the perid 1960–1980 West Germany and Switzerland were the main destinations, with Switzerland in most years taking around 20–40 percent more Italian immigrants than Germany. Also important, especially in the early postwar years, were overseas or intercontinental flows; these were the modern continuations of much heavier outpourings of Italians to South America and the USA in the late nineteenth and early twentieth centuries. Interestingly, the EEC's Free Movement of Labour provisions, inserted in the Treaty of Rome largely at the insistence of Italy, have had little noticeable effect on the pattern of Italian emigration to EEC countries (King 1976). Indeed, during the 1960s (the period when the 'free movement' provisions progressively came into force), the quantity of Italian emigration to EEC countries declined more rapidly (180,700 in 1960, 66,900 in 1969) than it did to the main non-EEC destination of Switzerland (128,250 in 1960, 69,650 in 1969).

The migration profiles of the other three countries have similarities to, and differences from, the case of Italy just outlined. All have historical origins in mass emigrations in the last century – of Spaniards to South America, of Portuguese to Brazil and the African colonies, and of Greeks to the USA. The postwar trend of emigration, however, developed with a somewhat different temporal and spatial pattern. Whereas Italians emigrated to a wide spectrum of European countries, migrants from the other three countries have been rather more specialized in their European destinations. Iberian migrants have gone mainly to France, and Greeks to West Germany. The peaks of emigration have come later; during 1963–1965 and 1969–1970 for Greece, during 1964 and 1969–1973 for Spain, and during 1969–1971 for Portugal. Also very marked are the effects of the 1966/1967 recession which affected West Germany and (less so) France, and the reduction in emigration numbers since the oil crisis of 1973/1974 which caused most receiving countries to stop recruiting migrant workers. These cyclical effects are, however, hardly visible in the Italian figures, since Italians could not be kept out by the receiving countries. As a result the Italian annual totals decline steadily over the entire period 1966–1980.

The changing annual totals of emigrants portrayed in Table 6.1 are of course aggregates which reflect the balance of fluctuating movements to individual destination countries. The case of Portugal can be used to illustrate this point. As Table 6.2 shows, France absorbed more than two-fifths of legal emigrants from Portugal during 1960–1980, and the Portuguese are the largest foreign nationality group in that country. Significant numbers of Portuguese also migrated to West Germany, especially during the years 1965–1967 and 1969–1973. At the same time, certain longer-established destinations, such as Venezuela, the USA and Canada, continued to be important in the postwar years, whilst the Brazilian flow dwindled after the early 1960s. However, clandestine emigration, mainly to France, adds very considerably to these figures, in some years doubling the legal emigrants, as a comparison between the appropriate columns in Tables 6.1 and 6.2 shows. During 1973–1974 the principal European outlets, France and West Germany, were blocked off. Return flows, previously small, grew in size, stimulated not only by the northern European recession but also by the changed political climate of Portugal in the heady days following the 1974 revolution. A further very significant event was the repatriation of between 500,000 and one million (estimates vary) *retornados* from former Portuguese colonies during the mid-1970s. Clandestine movement out of Portugal is thought to have tailed off recently, but seasonal migration, mainly to France and Switzerland, developed strongly in the late 1970s (4,361 in 1977, 13,295 in 1980) – this consists of migrants on fixed-term contracts of less than 9 months recruited for specifically seasonal jobs mainly in agriculture and tourism. Seasonal migrants are not included in the figures of Tables 6.1 and 6.2. Also in the late 1970s and early 1980s emigration developed to new overseas destinations. In 1979, 9 percent of all overseas migrants went to countries in North Africa and the Arabian Gulf; this new movement consists almost entirely of males working on fixed contracts on projects connected directly or indirectly with the oil industry. By 1980 the estimate for Portuguese migrants living abroad was 2.757 million, of whom 1.1 million were living in Europe (90 percent of them in France), 1 million in the Americas and 500,000 in Africa. This total is equivalent to 29.3 percent of the Portuguese population living in Portugal.

Regional variations in the intensity of southern European emigration have been described by Livi Bacci (1972) and Salt and Clout (1976). Postwar emigration has been heaviest from rural upland areas where poverty and underemployment are widespread. Often these were the areas of fastest demographic increase, but this factor has slowed down of late, partly due to the effects of emigration itself. Whilst the majority of emigrants come from village (though not necessarily farming) origins, some either originate from the towns or are 'step-migrants' who move from the country to the town as a

Table 6.2   Portuguese emigration 1960–1980

Year	Brazil	Venezuela	USA	Canada	France	West Germany	All countries
			Destination countries:				
1960	12,451	4,026	5,679	4,895	3,593	54	32,318
1961	16.077	3,347	3,370	2,635	5,446	277	33,526
1962	13,555	3,522	2,425	2,739	8,245	483	33,539
1963	11,281	3,109	2,922	3,424	15,223	1,039	39,519
1964	4,929	3,784	1,601	4,770	32,641	3,868	55,646
1965	3,051	3,920	1,852	5,197	57,319	11,713	89,056
1966	2,607	4,697	13,357	6,795	73,419	9,686	120,239
1967	3,271	4,118	11,516	6,615	59,415	22,042	92,502
1968	3,512	3,751	10,841	6,833	46,515	4,886	80,452
1969	2,537	3,044	13,111	6,502	27,234	13,279	70,165
1970	1,669	2,927	9,726	6,529	21,962	19,775	66,360
1971	1,200	3,500	8,839	6,983	10,923	16,997	50,400
1972	1,158	3,641	7,574	6,845	17,800	14,377	54,084
1973	890	4,294	8,160	7,403	20,692	31,479	79,517
1974	729	2,550	9,540	11,650	10,568	3,049	43,397
1975	1,553	1,903	8,975	5,857	2,866	1,072	24,811
1976	837	1,812	7,499	3,585	1,787	346	17,458
1977	557	3,613	6,748	2,280	1,435	215	16,995
1978	323	3,580	8,171	1,871	1,604	112	18,044
1979	215	3,944	8,181	2,805	2,168	76	20,622
1980	229	2,744	4,981	3,269	1,862	67	18,044
Totals:	86,227	71,826	155,068	109,482	421,817	134,892	1,057,301

Notes: The above figures are for legal emigration only, and therefore do not tally with those of Table 1 which include corrections for clandestine emigration. Movement to the former 'Overseas Provinces' (chiefly Angola and Mozambique) is excluded (it averaged 34,000 per annum during 1960–1970).

Sources: Rocha Trinidade (1979b).
SOPEMI (Continuous Reporting System on Migration) *Reports* for 1978, 1979, 1980 and 1981, Paris, OECD, Directorate for Social Affairs, Manpower and Education.

prelude to emigrating abroad. The main areas of intense emigration are northern Portugal, western Spain (including Andalusia), southern and north-eastern Italy, and northern Greece.

These regional variations also indicate some of the causes of emigration; only a brief review of these is provided here, and this should be considered in conjunction with the later discussion of internal migration. Rural economies with relatively stagnant agricultural bases (as in Portugal, Greece and parts of Spain) or experiencing a decline in the demand for labour as a result of modernization (latterly in Italy) offer relatively poor job prospects

and little opportunity to accumulate wealth. In addition, at least until the
1970s, there were very inadequate levels of infrastructural and social provisions in the rural areas of southern Europe (see also Chapter 8). For many,
if not most, there was no way to break the vicious circle of poverty by
remaining within these rural areas (Clout and Salt 1976). Emigration
offered one strategy for escaping poverty, and, though it did not always
bring the hoped for training or social benefits, it provided the means for
many to accumulate savings. Emigration was not, of course, the only
strategy and development of tourism-related crafts or services, and internal
migration provided alternatives. However, it held the additional advantage
that it offered an escape from prevailing oppressive political conditions in
Greece, Spain and Portugal (and also from military conscription for the
African wars in the latter).

The character of postwar emigration

Böhning (1974) characterizes southern European labour migration as a
'polyannual' movement with the migrant moving typically for about 2–5
years, giving an annual turnover of around 30–40 percent. Many migrants,
however, have drifted beyond the polyannual period, a process which
contributes to the 'maturing' of the migration stream and to its 'self-feeding'
character (to use Böhning's terminology again). Initially most migrants
view their stay as temporary but, given continued employment, they tend to
postpone continually a definitive return and are gradually slipping into
quasi-permanent status. In this respect much depends on whether the
migrant gets married and is able to move his wife and family too, although
there are many variants. Some migrants, for instance, bring only their
wives, leaving their children in the care of grandparents, a device aimed at
maximizing earning power since then the wife can work full-time. Others
get married when abroad to someone of the host nation or of another
migrant nationality; these migrants are the least likely to return to their
home countries. Independent (though organized) female emigration is
another subtype, characteristic particularly of Spain, from which young
women emigrate to work in domestic service in France. In prerevolution
Portugal many young men emigrated clandestinely in order to escape
compulsory 4-year military service.

Southern Europe's migrant workers are employed in three main fields: as
industrial workers (mainly in industries where the jobs are arduous,
unpleasant or boring); in the construction industry (where the work is again
tough, as well as insecure); and in marginal service sector occupations

which are regarded as socially undesirable by the native populations (examples are street-sweepers, hospital porters and domestic servants). Whilst workers in the industrial sector are likely to be at the mercy of economic fluctuations, those in 'marginal' positions are in fact more secure in the sense that their jobs carry a very low social status in the eyes of north Europeans who would rather go on the dole than accept employment as, say, dustmen or hospital cleaners. This explains why, in spite of strong British legislation against excessive labour immigration, non-EEC workers from Spain and Portugal can easily find work in the catering, hotel and hospital trades in London and elsewhere in the UK.

Thus it is clear that it is the host countries' economic and cultural demands which determine the unskilled nature of the migrant population. The misconception that foreign workers are by definition unskilled, illiterate and unprepared for any skilled or complex job has its origins precisely in these demands and not in the true make-up of the migrant population (Giner and Salcedo 1978). Migrant workers are faced with capitalism's historic tendency to simplify the job to the assumed level of the worker, or even to 'deskill' the worker to the mundane level of certain job tasks, rather than raise the migrant workers' skill to the level of the job (Ward 1975b).

The enforcement of a system of temporarily employed labour – encapsulated in the German term *Gastarbeiter* or 'guest-worker' – has meant that the host economies have enjoyed the supply of a very flexible pool of labour-power without incurring all the additional social costs of upbringing or of retirement which would arise if migrants with their dependents became permanent settlers. Although, as we shall see shortly, policies of officially encouraging return are limited to the case of France, nonrenewal of short-term job contracts is a powerful ploy to rotate or decrease the stock of migrant labour at the whim of the host country. It is, therefore, not hard to view the large-scale returns of 1966–1968 and 1974–1976 as the export of unemployment, by which the industrial countries were able to cushion their own populations from the worst effects of slumps. The burden thus hit the southern European countries, poorer to start with, who had to contend with their own economic problems of recession as well as the return of hundreds of thousands of their own unemployed migrants.

Impact of emigration on southern European countries

What are the effects of emigration on those areas from which the migrants leave? This question can be answered at two different levels. At the micro level emigration's effect on local demographic structures, village social patterns and the local-scale rural economy can be examined. At this scale the effects of emigration abroad are much the same as the effects of rural–urban migration within the country (although there may be some differences as regards ties to the rural area, frequency of return visits etc.). Because of this overall similarity, discussion of the effects of rural out-migration at the local or regional scale is postponed to the section towards the end of this chapter on internal migration and its consequences. In the present section the effects of emigration at the macro or national scale are examined, concentrating particularly on the effects on the labour market. The question of remittances and savings is touched on in the second main section of this chapter on return migration.

One theory, based on the equilibrium rationale, argues that emigration removes unemployed and underemployed surplus labour, thereby making the remaining labour-force more productive and efficient. Reduction of unemployment results in higher wages which in turn forces the rationalization of agriculture by enlargement of holdings and mechanization. Where emigration removes mostly unskilled labour, the quality of the remaining labour force is improved. There is also the additional benefit of reduced welfare pay-outs wherever unemployed workers emigrate.

So much for the theory. The reality is, in fact, somewhat different. Rather than review all the evidence and opinions on this vexed question, perhaps the best way to appreciate what the two sides of the debate have to say to each other is to refer to the interesting exchange of views between Böhning (1975; 1976) and Griffin (1976).

Böhning started his 1975 paper by noting that emigration provokes a 'potentially serious conflict between private gains and social costs'. He concedes that emigration generally improves the financial status of the emigrant and his family and that it may relieve unemployment, but he questions whether the effect on the sending country as a whole is very positive. He points out that emigration also takes out of the sending country many skilled workers while those who remain behind become so dependent on money from abroad that farming is neglected. Mechanization and consolidation of holdings may provoke further unemployment, he argues. A consumer mentality, fuelled by the behaviour of returned migrants, may induce inflation and stimulate further outmigration. The results are a spiral of outmigration and neglect, and a deepening dependency on the part of the sending country on the countries receiving their migrants.

Griffin (1976) claimed that Böhning's pessimism was entirely misplaced. He saw the emigration of 'ordinary working people' to higher paid jobs abroad as '. . . a major avenue of escape from poverty and oppression'. In contrast to Böhning's view of private gains and social costs, for Griffin it is a case of social gains contributed to by the private costs of emigrants' sacrifice, hard saving and frugal living whilst abroad. Emigration is good, he argues, because it increases the wealth of the migrant's family, it increases the man-land ratio and therefore agricultural productivity, it reduces unemployment and increases wages, and it will increase the amount of investment capital for development. Griffin then concludes these mostly well-worn economic arguments by saying that '. . . if low income, low productivity peasants from underdeveloped countries migrate to high income, high productivity employment in the urban centres of western Europe . . . overall output and efficiency will rise, not fall'.

In his reply Böhning (1976) responds to this assertion by questioning '. . . efficiency for whom, for which countries, and for what goals?' According to Böhning the primary beneficiaries of migration are the receiving countries. 'Immigration greatly contributes to raising welfare in developed countries. Through it, the poor developing countries become ever more closely tied to the system of hierarchical dependency; they are left with precious little more than the crumbs from the table of the rich in the form of remittances'.

From the point of view of the economy and society of the sending countries, then, emigration can be debilitating. It deprives the nation of skills and initiative; investment in upbringing and education is lost. Some Greek studies are very revealing here. Not long after the growth of emigration in the 1950s, labour shortages started to appear in several sectors of the Greek economy. They appeared first in agriculture, after about 1955. Pepelasis and Yotopoulos (1962) judged that they had affected the evolution of the farming pattern, holding back the expansion of new labour-intensive crops like cotton and citrus fruit. Extensive wheat cultivation was extending over land previously under crops yielding higher returns but necessitating larger amounts of labour. Nor has emigration had the anticipated 'freeing' effect on the rural land market. Except in a few areas where land can be sold speculatively for building and tourist development, emigrants hold on to their land, preventing land consolidation. If anything, emigration *reduces* the mobility of the land market since so many owners are abroad (Filias 1972). During the 1960s, labour shortages started to appear in Greek industry too. Scarcities of skilled workers and technicians were affecting several branches of manufacturing and construction, holding back planned investment projects which would have expanded production. By 1972

Greek industry was reported to be suffering a deficit of 50,000 workers, mainly in important export sectors like textiles, machinery, metals and chemicals. Progress in important public works was also being hampered by lack of skilled and semiskilled workers (Nokolinakos 1973).

From emigration to immigration

A final trend worthy of comment is for southern Europe to become a region of immigration. It is difficult to date the beginnings of this movement since Spain and Portugal have always had significant numbers of foreign nationals from Latin America and the former Portuguese colonies living within their borders for educational and other reasons. In Italy, where the foreign worker presence is most developed, the trend may be dated to the late 1960s, when labour shortages in northern industry stimulated an influx of Yugoslav labour and when North Africans started to move into western Sicily to replace local labour which had fled the Belice valley earthquake of 1968.

The coexistence of emigration and immigration in the countries of southern Europe may seem contradictory, but it can be easily explained. Just as wage levels in southern Europe are significantly below those of northern Europe, so too are they significantly above those of North Africa and the Third World. Italian average wages are four times those of Tunisia and seven times those of Morocco, for instance. Hence North Africans, and other foreign workers from poor countries, are prepared to work in Italy for wages far below those acceptable to Italians. This explains the anomaly of migration into a country which already has more than 2 million unemployed (60 percent of them under 24 years of age), and substantial numbers of recently returned migrants. We are, therefore, witnessing the development of a tiered system in which African and Third World labour migrates to southern Europe to replace those local workers who have moved north. The Malians who froze to death in the winter of 1973/1974 trying to enter Italy illegally across the Alps may have been the first victims of this new subimperialist migration chain (Ward 1975b).

Southern European immigration is a largely undocumented phenomenon in which workers arrive clandestinely to take up a certain rangs of jobs. Although there are some who have relatively stable jobs in industry (in northern Italy for example), most work in marginal employment in the tertiary sector and in jobs where the work is heavy, seasonal or insecure (agricultural harvesting, dockyard labour, construction etc.).

In Italy, where SOPEMI estimated a presence of 500,000 foreign workers in 1980, 63 percent live in six major cities (Rome, Milan, Turin, Genoa, Naples, Bari), drawn there by the availability of employment in domestic services, restaurants and hotels. There is also a substantial involvement of North Africans in seasonal agricultural labour and in fishing in Sicily. Apart from North Africans (Moroccans, Algerians, Tunisians, Egyptians), the main nationalities are Ethiopians (especially Italian-speaking Eritreans), Yugoslavs and Filipinos. The Maghreb and Yugoslav flows are partly related to the closure of traditional north European outlets in 1973/1974. The illegal status of Italy's immigrants enables them to be ruthlessly exploited. Del Rio (1979) has described the working conditions of Rome's estimated 7,000–8,000 Filipina domestic workers. Almost all are clandestine. Not speaking Italian, they are kept ignorant of labour laws and of their rights regarding minimum pay, insurance and job security. Many work 10–12 hours per day for a pittance. The nature of their work keeps them isolated and prevents collective action.

Similar situations are found in Greece, Spain and, to a lesser extent, Portugal. In 1979 Spain recorded 50,000 foreigners with work permits, of whom the largest group were Portuguese (14 percent). But there were thought to be a much larger number of clandestine workers with no permits, especially from Portugal, Morocco, the Philippines and Latin America. They tend to work in the same sectors as those noted above. Nikolinakos (1973) has written of the import of Africans into Greece where they work in the building sector, as agricultural labourers and in the dockyards of Piraeus. They constitute a device to relieve local labour shortages but also to retain competitiveness and maximize profits. Athens has its own Harlem, where live thousands of Africans from Sudan, Ethiopia, Nigeria and Egypt. Portugal also has its immigrants, although they are rather less numerous; in 1981 52,000 foreign nationals were enumerated, including 25,000 from Cape Verde. Again, there is a concentration in the construction, tertiary and domestic sectors.

3. Return migration

It is impossible to gain accurate figures on the quantity of return migrants who have gone back to their home countries in southern Europe in recent years. The statistical shortcomings have if anything grown more serious of late and SOPEMI acknowledges that its sources on return flows are fragmentary. Böhning (1979), whose estimates are probably amongst the most well-informed, calculates that at least 1.5 million Mediterranean migrants retreated from the European industrial countries during 1974–1978, indicating that the real figure could be as high as 2 million. Around a third of this number returned to countries that are not of direct concern in this chapter (Turkey, Yugoslavia, Algeria, Tunisia, Morocco). The bulk of the return, especially of those with a weak legal status – the non-Italians – seems to have taken place in the years immediately following the oil crisis, i.e. 1974–1976.

Table 6.3 gives the available SOPEMI data on annual returns for the period 1970–1980. No figures are available for Portugal; those from Spain are merely estimates. Although the figures are not strictly comparable, being collected on different criteria, there is an overall similarity in the temporal pattern. Returns to both Spain and Greece peaked in 1975, since when there has been a steady decline to levels below those of 1970. Italy also follows this trend, except that the 1975 peak is not well-pronounced. Italian figures are steadier because of the free movement of labour and job security provisions that Italians enjoy as EEC members.

Table 6.3   Return migration 1970–1980

	Spain	Greece	Italy
1970	66,000	22,665	112,933
1971	88,000	24,709	105,927
1972	80,000	27,552	113,657
1973	74,000	22,285	101,771
1974	88,000	24,476	96,359
1975	110,000	34,214	101,948
1976	74,000	32,067	96,150
1977	62,500	29,950	81,042
1978	52,000	23,359	68,086
1979	39,000	17,279	67,537
1980	30,000		62,240

Notes: Spain: workers and their families returning from European countries (estimates).
Greece: workers only, from Europe and overseas.
Italy: workers and their families returning from European countries.
No data available for Greece 1980 or for Portugal at any date.

Source: SOPEMI (Continuous Reporting System on Migration) *Reports* for 1973, 1976 and 1981, Paris, OECD, Directorate for Social Affairs, Manpower and Education.

Circumstances surrounding return

Return migration from northern to southern Europe is often interpreted as the result of the 1973/1974 oil-induced recession (for example, Lebon and

Falchi 1980). This, however, is only part of the story. The 'recruitment stop' of West Germany, France and other countries had a more dramatic effect on emigration flows than on returns, the former falling much more sharply than the latter rose. Moreover the incidence of redundancy and return has not been at all straightforward. The experience of West Germany contradicts the assumption that those migrants who return are the ones who are most easily sent home, for during the years 1973–1975 the number of Turks in West Germany only decreased by 4 percent whereas Italians and Spaniards both dropped by 30 percent. Slater (1979) suggests that German employers have tended to keep on the more 'docile' Turks (Spaniards and Italians are more active in political and union affairs). He also points out that Turks are unlikely to want to return because of the poor state of the Turkish economy, whereas the Spanish, Italian and Greek economies have been more buoyant in the 1970s and have, at least theoretically, offered some job prospects for returnees.

Secondly, the pattern of returns, at least for the three countries for which there are figures, was well established before 1973. Polyannual migrants who had left during the 1950s and early 1960s were already reaching the end of their migratory cycles and were already returning in large numbers from countries like France and Belgium which had started their recruitment of foreign labour soon after the end of the war. The West German recession of 1966/1967 also sent large numbers of southern European migrants home. Employment of foreigners in Germany fell from 1.313 million in September 1966 to 991,000 a year later, a drop of 24.5 percent. However, Kayser (1972), who studied these cyclically-determined homeward flows, found that on the whole the return was temporary: by 1968 or 1969 many migrants were back in Germany, either in their old jobs or in new ones. Of course, as long as an open-door policy was maintained, migrants were relatively free to come and go. But this situation changed in November 1973, so that a non-Italian migrant leaving West Germany during the last 10 years has little chance of reentry.

In the case of another receiving country, France, a policy of deliberately encouraging repatriation operated from 1977 to 1982, initially for unemployed migrant workers, later for all migrants. Up to the end of 1980, when Spaniards and Portuguese were excluded from the scheme, 88,542 individuals received the 'aid to return' of 10,000 francs (5,000 francs for nonworking spouses and children). Portuguese (35.9 percent) and Spaniards (17.7 percent) were the main nationalities benefiting. The scheme did not apply to Italians who have free movement rights, nor did it apply to Greeks. The fact that three-quarters of the beneficiaries of the scheme were in employment (four-fifths for the Spaniards and Portuguese) indicates that the return-bonus merely functioned as an additional factor in expediting returns that probably would have happened anyway (Poinard 1979; Rogers 1981).

Finally, southern European migrants suffered immense social problems. Chief among these were appalling housing and racial conflict. Italians and Spaniards were not numerous in the notorious French *bidonvilles*, but Portuguese were. Algerians bore the brunt of the violent xenophobia of the early 1970s in France, but racist attitudes spilled over to other migrant groups as well. Racial tension also increased sharply at this time in West Germany, Switzerland and the Netherlands, although it should be pointed out this tension has not always been aimed at the same nationalities. In Switzerland, for instance, there is strong hostility towards Italians and Spaniards, while these nationalities are relatively favourably received in Germany in comparison to the more recently arrived Turks and Maghrebins. Whatever the national variations, however, it is clear that growing racial tension was a factor of some importance in the political decisions taken after late 1973 to suspend immigration and encourage return.

Return migration and socio-economic change

Twenty years ago it was generally thought, at least by southern European governments, that return migration would emerge as a dynamic force for development. Such thoughts were given weight by the analyses of economists such as Kindleberger (1965) who, arguing theoretically but largely in the Greek context, stressed the positive role of returning migrants trained in the northern industrial countries and the value of remittances in boosting foreign exchange earnings and in promoting productive investment in domestic industry and other capital projects. Kindleberger acknowledged that remittance-derived capital formation may have low productivity in cases such as a farm with strongly diminishing returns or a shop in a dying village, but the rapid rates of growth in remittance-supported economies like Greece and Portugal (both of whose remittance income was equivalent to over half the total value of merchandise exports in 1970) seemed to vindicate his basic argument (see Chapters 2, 4 and 7).

However, subsequent findings, particularly those of the 1970s, seem not to bear out this argument. Indeed the similarity of the return migration experience across all southern European countries is quite striking (King 1979). In most cases returnee businesses are traditional enterprises whose existence is linked to the prestige of independence rather than to economic rationality. Many are likely to fail eventually, or to be sustained only by the subsidies from other migrant investments such as land, property or bonds. The proposition that return migration has a positive impact on the long-term development of the sending rural areas must be rejected. Instead, return migration involves a kind of 'cosmetic' development in which villages are given a face-lift but little of a long-term productive nature is actually created. Indeed, to the extent that returnees, with their (by local standards) luxurious houses full of consumer goods, encourage further emigration, return migration may actually hasten a village's economic decline, particularly in terms of prising people out of farming, which is increasingly seen as a socially undesirable and economically unrewarding occupation.

This dual process of superficial modernization and continued under-development is portrayed very well in two papers on Andalusia by Rhoades (1978; 1979). Here the accent is on emigration to, and return from, West Germany. The returnees are known simply as *los alemanes*. The visual connection is reinforced by new cars bearing German number plates. Inside the splendid new returnee villas the atmosphere is again distinctly nonlocal. The furnishings are copied from those of German lower middle class houses — chandeliers, wall plaques, Black Forest cuckoo clocks, German stereo equipment and lavish bathroom fittings. Reyneri (1980), in a study of emigration and return in central Sicily, concludes that the region continues to exist only as a 'subsidized system'. Remittances do not support the capitalization of development initiatives but are spent on the purchase of houses, goods and services which do not promote increased productivity locally. The region experiences waste of capital and fragmentation of labour, both of which are obstacles to economic progress.

But is this at all surprising? What alternatives are there? Migrants left because they perceived that their villages held no future for them. If the home that the migrant left was a remote village in Andalusia, or in Sicily, or in a dozen other exhausted upland regions of southern Europe, the likelihood is that it offers him less today than it did then, except a root in an otherwise rootless life, a place to which to return to enjoy some temporary prestige. Who can blame him for wanting to spend his hard-won savings on a new home and on improving the material standard of living of his family? Is it not the most natural thing to expect, given the near-universality of the house as a prestige symbol? And in upland areas where agriculture holds little promise of intensification, what else is there to invest in?

Of course the situation might be very different for migrants returning to economically more progressive areas — to regions of rich agriculture, to industrial towns or to tourist zones— but empirical material on these forms of return is very fragmentary. Returness to such developing areas may either be of local origin or they may have originally emigrated from more depressed parts of the country. In the Spanish case a fairly clear pattern is observable for returnees who originated from country areas: those who are younger and single tend to be drawn back to the urban areas, whereas families tend to return to their villages. 'Retirees' are overwhelmingly village-oriented.

Surveys carried out in the 1960s in a series of Montecatini-Edison (now Montedison) chemical plants in different parts of Italy showed minimal presence of returned migrants in the workforces (Vigorelli 1969). The situation may well have changed since then, however, for many of the younger generation of labour migrants who departed in the late 1960s and 1970s have a far higher industrial orientation than their more peasant-minded predecessors. The problem, at least for the past 10 years, has been the stagnation of industrial employment in much of southern Europe so that returnees aspiring to industrial jobs have great difficulty finding them.

The social dynamics of return migration have been much studied, particularly in the context of changing village society. Returnees see themselves, and are seen by others, as a nouveau riche class characterized by new-found wealth and material possessions, chief amongst which is a new and often ostentatious house. Migrants are no longer peasants, and have no wish to return to working the land. Depending on the point of view, this social change is seen either as a modernizing influence or a regrettable loss of 'Greekness', 'Italianness' or whatever. Culturally, the return migrants' most striking characteristic is their ambivalence. Return migration often brings a kind of reverse culture shock equal to that experienced when moving abroad. At least for a time, returnees feel like strangers in their own land, which they perceive as backward. Old habits annoy — the litter, the gossip, the corruption. The ambivalence is reciprocally balanced: when abroad migrants identify with the home country; when at home they tend to exhalt the virtues of Germany or Switzerland. Ambivalence is frequently noted in anthropological studies of migrant workers; some would say that it is an inevitable fact of migratory life (Bernard and Ashton-Vouyoucalos 1976). Cultural — and linguistic — problems are particularly acute for second-generation children, born and perhaps partly educated abroad, who are brought back to southern Europe when their parents return. Some migrants fail to resolve their ambivalence and become 'shuttle migrants', going back and forth, perpetually dissatisfied with where they are, restless spirits with no real home.

A question of policy

To stand any chance of making a successful contribution to southern European development, return migration must be organized and migrants must be kept fully informed as to possibilities in their home countries. A comprehensive system of selection, communication and incentives must be set up in order to effect the necessary fine tuning; at the moment most governments are still groping. Some of the new regional administrations in Italy have passed statutes to help returning migrants, with loans made available for housing and the establishment or improvement of enterprises like commercial farms, small industries and touristic developments. So far, few migrants have availed themselves of these aids, largely because the measures are not widely known and because of the mistrust ordinary people feel towards the Italian bureaucracy. Some of the Italian incentives are for the establishment of cooperative enterprises, yet migrants by nature tend to seek change through individualistic action — mainly by accumulating savings through extreme self-denial when abroad— and are not disposed to collective enterprise, either in collaborating with the authorities or working with each other in cooperatives and trade-unions (Signorelli 1980).

The responsibility for reintegrating returning migrants and extracting full economic benefit from them does not rest entirely with the migrants' countries of origin, however. There was much debate in the 1970s on the role that the country of immigration can play in migrants' vocational training (Abete 1976; Wagner 1977). Although it has to be acknowledged that the jobs many migrant workers do (refuse collectors, construction labourers, hospital porters etc.) require little or no training, some schemes have been put into operation and there is enormous potential for further effort in this field.

Most recently the question of compensation has arisen, since it is now widely acknowledged that the engagement of migrants, skilled or otherwise, creates value added which is largely, if not exclusively, internalized in the country of employment and thus further increases its economic power relative to the country of origin (Böhning 1979). The suggestion has been made that part of the direct taxes paid in the host country by a migrant worker should be transferred to his country of origin to compensate for the costs of raising and educating that migrant. Since income is more or less related to education, such an income-based tax would take into account varying levels of human capital investments. If it appears doubtful that receiving countries would part with tax receipts, such payments might be deducted as a proportion of migrants' wages and paid into a trust fund which would either be given to the migrant upon his return or, if he does not return, handed over to his mother country as proper compensation for its original expenditure on education and training. These, however, are only some suggestions and countries like France, Germany and Switzerland still have a long way to go before they can be said to be doing anything more than paying lip-service to the issues of compensation and vocational training for their southern European migrant workers.

4. Internal migration

So far we have considered only external migration. It needs, therefore, to be stressed that emigration and return migration from abroad are overlain by important internal migratory movements, some of which are of considerable age and remarkably stable. It is also worth pointing out that regions of net loss to internal migration do not necessarily coincide with regions of net loss abroad. In Spain, for instance, Galicia has been a region traditionally of emigration overseas; compared to rural areas of Castile and the south, it participates relatively little in the currents of internal migration. The Italian Mezzogiorno, on the other hand, has been deeply affected by outmovement both abroad and to northern Italy.

Internal migration is a rather more complex phenomenon than international migration for it encompasses a wide range of types and scales of movement. Rural–urban migration, much of which is also interregional, has been the dominant type historically, but we should also mention rural–rural, interurban, intraurban and urban–rural movements. Examples of all these kinds of internal migration can be found although they are not always easy to document, given the limitations of the data available. In Portugal and Greece there are almost no statistics on internal migration. Use can be made of the intercensal residual method but this also reflects international movements. Spain and Italy have an annual registration procedure whereby residential moves must be notified to local authorities. In theory these annual data on registrations and cancellations of residence should provide an up-to-date source of local and regional migration trends. Unfortunately, the quality of these data is not good, especially in Spain, and there is a very limited range of accompanying information on demographic, social and occupational characteristics.

Main patterns of rural–urban migration

Turning now to a description of the main patterns, it seems that, at least until the 1970s, the four countries were all characterized by strong rural–urban currents, leading to rapid urbanization, especially of the main industrial and administrative cities, coupled with rapid depopulation of upland, marginal regions (see Chapter 8). Internal migration has also been marked to burgeoning tourist areas such as the Mediterranean coasts of Spain. Some interesting maps constructed by Fielding (1975) showed that rates of both urbanization (in Barcelona and Madrid) and depopulation (over most of western and central Spain) were greater in Spain during the 1960s than in any other West European country. Almost equally rapid depopulation occurred in north-eastern Portugal.

It is very difficult to generalize about the factors controlling temporal rates and spatial patterns of rural outmigration. Clearly factors like poverty, population pressure, demographic growth and the intensity and stability of local agriculture can all play a part, but much can also depend on migratory traditions established in the past. Thus Barcelona's continued ability to attract southern migrants dates from the 1920s when Andalusians worked on the construction of the Barcelona Fair and the Metro (Bradshaw 1972). Some local studies have shown that young people living in rural areas close to towns depart more readily than their counterparts in remote areas. At the same time there is a clear indication that the smaller the settlement the greater its chance of rapid loss through migration; larger villages, with their wider range of job opportunities and social facilities, have a better basis for maintaining their populations.

Little is known of the modal distances moved by rural–urban migrants, except that they embrace a range from long distance interregional movement (Calabrians to Milan, Andalusians to Barcelona) to moves to local market towns or tourist centres. With their higher incomes and wider range of industrial and service sector jobs, large cities and capitals naturally tend to draw migrants from wider areas than the more localized urban fields of regional nodes and market towns. Whilst it is true to an extent that interregional and rural–urban migrations reflect spatial differences in job opportunities and wage levels, there is a danger of oversimplification. Rural workers from rich Po Valley farms moved to urban areas even though factory jobs paid lower wages than agriculture: the attraction was the urban way of life (Romanos 1979).

Land tenure may also play a crucial role in local and individual migration propensities. Other things being equal, one might expect migration to be stronger from villages and regions having many landless peasants than from areas where land ownership is widely distributed. There is evidence to support this contention from Spain where since the 1950s the areas of highest outmigration have been the *latifundio* provinces of the south and south-west, especially Badajoz, Cáceres, Córboda, Jaén and Granada (Bradshaw 1972).

At the individual level, who stays and who leaves may be closely related to inheritance practices. Primogeniture deprives younger offspring of land, encouraging them to leave. Partible inheritance, on the other hand, gives all siblings a stake in the land, thereby ensuring at least some economic foothold in the rural economy. This relationship is upheld by village studies of migration in Spain, especially in the north where the custom of *mayorazgo* — passing the land to the eldest son — prevails (Douglass 1971). Disinherited siblings have been leaving Basque farms for generations; indeed this rural exodus is '. . . the fundamental precondition of the survival of Basque agriculture' (Greenwood 1976). Most depart soon after leaving school; their destination is overwhelmingly in factory jobs in the urban industries of the Basque region.

The Basque case is also interesting in that it shows that when industrial employment is available within the region, rural–urban migration is predominantly intraregional. Much of the same happened in Catalonia and in northern Italy. Likewise in southern Italy recent industrialization has undoubtedly 'captured' many rural southerners who in earlier decades would have gone north or abroad. Rodgers' (1970) analysis of net migration patterns for the provinces of the Italian Mezzogiorno for the period 1950–1965 revealed a clear tendency for government-sponsored industrial development in nodes such as Brindisi, Taranto and Siracusa to dampen down the rates of migratory loss from their respective provinces and to eventually lead to net inmigration. More spatially refined analyses, using 1961–1971 intercensal commune data for the islands of Sicily and Sardinia, showed strong relationships between migration and the service sector; expansion in tertiary sector employment was the key variable in 'explaining' inmigration or low outmigration (King and Strachan 1980a; 1980b).

Effects of rural outmigration

In the countryside the effects of internal and external migration cannot easily be separated. Both contribute to the gradual process of abandonment

— of land, of dwellings, sometimes of whole villages. In severely marginal areas such as the high Pyrenees, the Mani peninsula in Greece, the Calabrian uplands and some of the minor Italian islands, settlement abandonment has been almost complete (Wagstaff 1968; Majoral 1977; King and Young 1979). Hillside terraces, the work of generations, slip away. Once fastidiously cultivated, they are gradually obliterated by scrub and maquis. This creeping paralysis of the rural landscape is characteristic of upland areas in all four countries.

If departing migrants were willing to sell their land, some farm rationalization might result with holdings becoming bigger and more efficient. Rarely does this happen. Generally migrants prefer to retain their land as a kind of insurance policy. Sometimes such land will be worked by a relative, or rented to another farmer, or simply used as common grazing. Absentee land ownership by migrants has the result of fossilizing the landholding pattern, making many forms of land planning or agricultural improvement virtually impossible. Although mechanization is sometimes invoked as a cause of rural outmigration, in most cases it has taken place in response to loss of labour, developing only after the flight from the land was established (Bradshaw 1972). In fact, much land cannot be mechanized because of slope, small plot size and the nature of the crops grown.

The selectivity of outmigration from rural areas inevitably causes imbalances in the residual populations. This has been demonstrated many times over by a wealth of studies by anthropologists, rural sociologists and human geographers. In Italy Barberis (1968) has documented the feminization and senescence of the agricultural labour force consequent upon the exodus of most of the young males. In the southern region of Basilicata he found that 79 percent of agricultural workers were female— a new role for these 'women of the shadows' who traditionally were kept subservient and within the confines of the village (Cornelisen 1976). O'Flanagan (1976) has described the increasing dominance of old people in Galician demography. In this region of Spain 94 percent of *municipios* have net population losses due to migration. Most of the loss has taken place over the last 25–30 years, in some cases halving the population left behind. Majoral (1977) finds similar results in the western Pyrenees, except that here outmigration of young females has been heaviest.

Abandonment and decay are not the whole story, however. Studies on rural–urban migrants in southern European cities show that they retain close ties with their natal villages to which they return for holidays and, if the distance is not too great, for weekends. 'He has gone back to his village' is a remark frequently heard in Athens, for a large proportion of the city's residents are of rural origin. Greek rural society is more egalitarian than in the other three countries, and channels for upward mobility are generally more fluid. Educated people from humble rural backgrounds often get white-collar or trade-type jobs in cities. On their regular return visits to see parents and relatives, they act as channels for the diffusion of modernization and national 'urban' culture (Friedl 1959).

Perhaps the most forceful exemplar of the 'migration-prosperity' thesis is Brandes's (1975) monograph on Becedas, a Castilian village 200 km west of Madrid. In contrast to other regions of southern Europe, where outmigration has led to increasing marginalization, social atomization and cultural disintegration, Brandes sees in Becedas a community with an ongoing integrity, the new economic adaptations and cultural patterns brought on by migration being phased into familiar structural frameworks. Far from leading to a downward spiral of impoverishment and marginalization, emigration and prosperity are closely linked in Becedas. Money is channelled back to renovate village houses for summer residences. It enters the village in many other ways too: supporting local agriculture, local festivals and local shops. In contrast to the past when there was much poverty and landlessless in the village, now most farmers have sufficient land and are switching to commercial agriculture. The key to this process of 'positive backwash' is the nearness of the village to Madrid, where most of the migrants have settled. Close kinship ties and frequent visits enable the rural and metropolitan worlds to interpenetrate in a symbiotic, mutually supporting way. Another relevant consideration is the way in which migrant land has been readily released at cheap prices and rents to enable non-migrant farmers to enlarge their operations, contrary to the general pattern in southern Europe. Becedas clearly contains points of relevance for other rural settlements in southern Europe, particularly those affected by internal outmigration. It is a pity that Brandes nowhere tries to evaluate the representativeness or uniqueness of his village study— a common failing of social anthropologists working in the Mediterranean (Davis 1977). It should also be pointed out that in his conclusion Brandes virtually stands his own argument on its head by predicting that in the long run the community may well disintegrate. The present phase of survival and prosperity is only interim. As the old villagers die off and are not replaced; as agriculture, although modernizing, struggles to survive in the face of competition from more physically favoured regions; as villagers, under the influence of their urban cousins, become more individualistic and private in their behaviour;

as the binding power of the church declines: so the socio-economic cohesion of the community is threatened — not to mention its very demographic existence. Only tourism, thinks Brandes, can prevent the village's ultimate demise.

The implications of internal migration go well beyond the simple redistribution of population. Rural–urban migration involves restructuring the whole fabric of society. Certainly in Italy and Spain, the rural classes have been replaced by the new urban proletariat as the largest national social group. The political implications of this should not be overlooked. In the past the strength of traditionalism in the social and political structure depended largely on the passive support of the peasantry, many of whom in reality were outside the formal or active political life of the countries. The voice of the new urban working class has a more active role and a more direct message: greater social mobility, better education and welfare and a say in trade-union matters are a few of them (see Chapters 3 and 8).

The problems of rural–urban migration are not limited to the rural areas of migratory loss. Internal migrations have created enormous problems for southern European cities, especially in the fields of housing and public services. Some migrants can be found in innercity tenements but most end up in postwar suburbs on the urban periphery, in public or private apartment blocks. Many of these are built at very high densities with little or no provision for open space or other communal facilities. Other areas can best be described as shanty-towns. Bradshaw (1972), writing of Spain, sums up the problem equally well for other countries: 'Although for some, arrival in the city has meant the start of a new and better life, for others it has been merely the exchange of the poverty of the countryside for the poverty of the town; and in the town poverty is more acutely felt'.

Regional flows

Few flow maps have ever been published to indicate visually the directional pattern of internal migration streams in southern Europe. Nevertheless, the general outlines are fairly clear. They depend very much on the simple geography of the countries concerned. Portugal and Greece are very similar in this respect. In both countries the major metropolis is the country's principal port, industrial centre and capital, and acts as far and away the most powerful magnet for internal movement. Depopulation in both countries has been most severe from the northern mountainous regions. And just as Lisbon–Setúbal can be compared to Athens–Piraeus, so too can Oporto to Thessaloniki: both are northern coastal towns which act as secondary nodes for more localized migratory flows. A set of equally striking parallels exists between Spain and Italy. In both countries migration has been strong to northern industrial regions (Catalonia and the Basque provinces in Spain; the North Italian Plain, Genoa and Florence in Italy) and to the centrally located capitals of Madrid and Rome, whilst outmigration has been heavy from virtually all rural areas, especially if they are highland or southern.

The Italian case, which has been copiously researched, including some excellent studies in English, will now be considered in more detail. Since Italy tends to pioneer internal migration trends in southern Europe, and Italian migration data are the best of the four countries, the choice is appropriate. Interregional net flow data for 1955–1970 are mapped in Figure 6.1. This covers the period of greatest internal mobility; after 1971 rates of migration slowed down. As Table 6.4 shows, northern and central regions which in the 1950s and 1960s had lost population by outmigration (Trentino-Alto Adige, Umbria and Marche) became net gainers of migrants in the 1970s, as did some southern regions (Abruzzi-Molise, Apulia and Sardinia). Traditional regions of very heavy outmovement, such as Basilicata and Calabria, saw their rates of loss lessen in the 1970s.

Returning to Figure 6.1 the pattern portrayed can be largely explained by reference to regional differences in demography (particularly rates of natural increase) and in economic structure and growth. The beginning in the decline of the birth-rate started in the North long before it affected the South. Many northern regions have for a long time had a lower fertility-rate than that required to replenish the population. They now have negative natural increases and an old population. In southern Italy, on the other hand, the fertility-rate remained high until just a few years ago and is still ensuring a steady natural increase of just under 1 percent per year. The contrast in demography can be appreciated by comparing north-western Italy and mainland southern Italy. Both have similar populations (13 and 12.4 million respectively), and yet the former added, by natural increase, just 63,000 persons to the labour force during 1961–1971, whereas the latter added 1.3 million (Golini and Geseno 1981).

Regions of demographic increase correlate inversely with regions of economic growth in Italy. Until the 1950s patterns of internal movement were mainly localized rural–urban flows, the major exceptions being the draining of population out of the Alps and north-eastern Italy towards the growing industrial centres of the Po Plain. During 1921–1931 Veneto (−11.4 per thousand) and Friuli-Venezia Giulia (−13.1 per thousand) had annual rates of net migration loss comparable with those of southern Italian

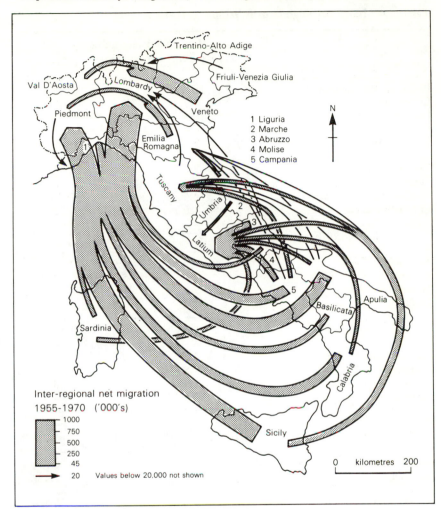

Figure 6.1   Italy: interregional net migration, 1955–1970 (after
Migliorini 1976).

regions during the 1950s and 1960s (see Table 6.4). After the war Italy's
famous economic miracle drew workers largely from the South towards the
industrial north-west, especially to the cities of Milan and Turin. At the
same time, the bureaucratic and commercial expansion of Rome stimulated
currents from central and southern regions (Figure 6.1). Finally, Tuscany

Table 6.4 Italy: net migration by region 1951–1977

| | Net annual migration rate (%) | | |
	1951–1961	1961–1971	1971–1977
Piedmont-Val d'Aosta	10.9	9.3	3.2
Lombardy	7.7	7.3	2.7
Liguria	10.9	4.6	2.8
Sub-total North-West	9.1	7.6	2.9
Trentino-Alto Adige	−2.2	−1.0	1.0
Veneto	−9.9	0.7	2.7
Friuli-Venezia Giulia	−4.5	4.9	5.1
Emilia-Romagna	−1.0	2.1	3.8
Sub-total North-East	−5.2	1.6	3.6
Tuscany	1.2	2.9	4.3
Umbria	−8.7	−5.3	3.4
Marche	−9.6	−2.9	2.0
Latium	6.6	6.8	3.2
Sub-total Centre	1.0	3.2	3.4
Abruzzi-Molise	−19.5	−9.5	3.5
Campania	−7.5	−8.8	−1.7
Apulia	−11.9	−9.4	0.3
Basilicata	−18.4	−20.4	−4.9
Calabria	−20.0	−18.2	−4.1
Sub-total South	−12.9	−11.1	−1.0
Sicily	−9.2	−13.0	0.2
Sardinia	−8.6	−8.9	1.1
Sub-total Islands	−9.1	−12.1	0.1
Total Italy	−2.7	−1.0	1.8

Source: After Golini and Gesano (1981).

and Emilia-Romagna were also regions of some in-movement, whilst the north-eastern region of Veneto continued to lose migrants to north-western regions.

Less amenable to quantification, but no less important, are the social and planning stresses caused by the flooding of northern Italian cities by southern immigrants. These have been well described in studies of Milan and Turin (Fofi 1970; Bielli 1973). The southern rural migrant arriving at the Milan or Turin central railway station in the heyday of the 'move to the North' faced a situation not unlike the international emigrant arriving in a totally alien, foreign city. The lucky ones were met by friends or relatives and looked after for the first few days until some kind of job and accommodation were found. Most internal migrants group themselves into nuclei based on the village or region of origin: thus there are Sicilian districts, Calabrian quarters etc. Yet their range of acquaintances is narrow, and they are exploited in many ways, especially by unscrupulous landlords and by the *padroni* and 'labour cooperatives' through which they find jobs in building yards and factories. Most southerners have little or no job security, insurance cover or other rights; '. . . they are exploited and isolated, they have bitter experiences behind them, and there is no one to give them the perspectives, the social, cultural and political education that they need' (Fofi 1970). Many work in small 'black market' concerns, taking in work subcontracted from the bigger industries. This 'outwork' system is a conspiracy to defraud the state of tax and other payments, and to keep Italian industry competitive; no social benefits are paid, working conditions are poor and wages often below the minimum legal rates. More than anybody else, it is the southern migrant who is the victim of the crisis of Italian capitalism.

5. Conclusion: migration – the future

The brief survey of internal migration can be concluded by identifying three likely future trends; these are based partly on the work of Clout (1976) and Fielding (1982):

1. Rates of natural increase in rural areas are being threatened by local distortions in the population structure which are the product of outmigration. Chief among these is the removal by outmigration of the most fertile cohorts of the population.
2. Flows of migration from the countryside may be stemmed by the

establishment of holding points or 'key settlements' equipped with services and employment opportunities. To be effective, these rural nodes must be linked to their hinterlands of smaller villages by adequate systems of public and private transport.

3. Urban–rural countercurrents, the result of taking suburbanization beyond the urban fringe, are increasing in intensity. This 'counter-urbanization', noted in North America and north-west Europe from about the beginning of the 1970s (Vining and Kontuly 1978), is starting now to affect certain regions of southern Europe too. Once again, Italy provides the best exemplification of this for its data sources are far superior to those of the other three countries. During the 1950s and 1960s, as we have just seen, rural depopulation was the dominant trend everywhere, especially from the South and upland areas; net migration gains were mainly concentrated in the northern 'industrial triangle' of Turin–Milan–Genoa and in Rome. Further regional differentiation of internal migratory trends then occurred in the 1970s. By about 1978 gains to the big industrial cities of the North had disappeared and a tendency towards counter-urbanization in this region had set in. On the other hand, the net migration gains of Rome remain high. Rural depopulation continues in some central and southern districts, but at a much slower pace than in the 1950s and 1960s. Some medium-size cities, in all regions of the country, continue to gain from inmigration. Return migration, both of internal movers and of emigrants coming back from abroad, has revitalized many rural areas, even in quite remote districts. Many villages which had been losing population for decades started to gain in the 1970s. The exact nature of the economic forces framing the turnabout in internal migration trends is difficult to pin down: the growth of pension and other state welfare benefits, the diffusion of small and medium scale industry into rural areas and the expansion of certain artisan trades are certainly some of the relevant influences. So too is the repulsive effect of increasingly noisy, overcrowded, polluted and badly planned cities (see Chapter 8). It will be interesting to see whether this 'rural revival' continues throughout and beyond the 1980s, and to what extent the Italian evidence is paralleled by similar trends in Iberia and Greece.

The course of future internal migration patterns will, in part, be dependent on the future course of emigration. The changing scales and geographical features of emigration have largely been influenced by economic conditions in the destination countries. However, it is true that the policies adopted by the French and West German governments against emigrants from non-EEC countries have also been influential. This is illustrated by the example of Portugal which, in 1982, sent more emigrants to the UK (although only measured in hundreds) than to either France or West Germany. In general terms, there has been a shift of southern European emigration from Western Europe to the USA and more traditional destination countries in South America, as well as to new ones in the Middle East. Nevertheless, access to West European labour markets will be an important issue; the Treaty of Rome already guarantees this for Italy and, by the late 1980s, after a transitional period, the same conditions will be extended to Greece. The major question, therefore, is whether Spain and Portugal (assuming their eventual membership) will be granted the same terms. At best, lengthy negotiations and transitional periods are likely to delay completely free access until the end of this century. In the meantime, changes in labour demand elsewhere could lead to a further sharp decline in the level of emigration and there could be no revival in the West European economies. This raises the question of whether considerable increases experienced in standards of living during the 1960s and 1970s can be repeated or, perhaps, even maintained in the 1980s and 1990s.

References

Abete, G. (1976) Vocational training courses for returning migrants before their departure from the country of immigration and after their arrival in the country of origin, *International Migration*, Vol. 14, pp120–133.

Barberis, C. (1968) The agricultural exodus in Italy, *Sociologia Ruralis*, Vol. 8, pp179–188.

Bernard, H.R. and Ashton-Vouyoucalos, S. (1976) Return migration in Greece, *Journal of the Steward Anthropological Society*, Vol. 8, pp31–51.

Bielli, C. (1973) Aspects of the social integration of immigrants in Milan, *Genus*, Vol. 29, pp183–192.

Böhning, W.R. (1974) The economic effects of the employment of foreign workers, with special reference to the labour markets of Western Europe's post-industrial countries, in W.R. Böhning and D. Maillat (eds) *The Effects of the Employment of Foreign Workers*, Paris, OECD.

Böhning, W.R. (1975) Some thoughts on emigration from the Mediterranean Basin, *International Labour Review*, Vol. 111, pp251–277.

Böhning, W.R. (1976) Migration and policy: a rejoinder to Keith Griffin, in W.R. Böhning, Basic Aspects of Migration from Poor to Rich Countries: Facts, Problems, Policies, *Migration for Employment Project, Working Paper 6*, Geneva: ILO, World Employment Programme.

Böhning, W.R. (1979) International migration in Western Europe: reflections on the last five years, *International Labour Review*, Vol. 118, pp401–414.

Bradshaw, R.P. (1972) Internal migration in Spain, *Iberian Studies*, Vol. 1, pp68–75.

Brandes, S.H. (1975) *Migration, Kinship and Community: Tradition and Transition in a Spanish Village*, New York, Academic Press.

Castles, S. and Kosack, G. (1973) *Immigrant Workers and Class Structure in Western Europe*, London, Oxford University Press.

Cerase, F.P. (1979) Italy, in D. Kubat (ed) *The Politics of Migration Policies*, New York, Centre for Migration Studies.

Clout, H.D. (1976) Rural–urban migration in Western Europe, in J. Salt and H.D. Clout (eds) *Migration in Post-War Europe: Geographical Essays*, London, Oxford University Press.

Cornelisen, A. (1976) *Women of the Shadows*, London, Macmillan.

Davis, J. (1977) *People of the Mediterranean: An Essay in Comparative Social Anthropology*, London, Routledge and Kegan Paul.

Del Rio, A. (1979) Filipina domestic workers in Italy, *Migration Today*, Vol, 24, pp20–22.

Dolci, D. (1968) *The Man Who Plays Alone*, London, MacGibbon and Kee.

Douglass, W.A. (1970) Peasant emigrants: actors or reactors?, in R.F. Spencer (ed) *Migration and Anthropology*, Washington, University of Seattle Press.

Douglass, W.A. (1971) Rural exodus in two Spanish villages, *American Anthropologist*, Vol. 73, pp1100–1114.

Fielding, A.J. (1975) Internal migration in Western Europe, in L.A. Kosiński and R.M. Prothero (eds) *People on the Move: Studies on Internal Migration*, London, Methuen.

Fielding. A.J. (1982) Counterurbanisation in Western Europe, *Progress in Planning*, Vol. 17, pp1–52.

Filias, V. (1972) Restructuring of agricultural enterprises affected by emigration: Greece, in C.A.O. van Nieuwenhuijze (ed) *Emigration and Agriculture in the Mediterranean Basin*, The Hague, Mouton.

Fofi, G. (1970) Immigrants to Turin, in C.J. Jansen (ed) *Readings in the Sociology of Migration*, Oxford, Pergamon.

Friedl, E. (1959) The role of kinship in the transmission of national culture to rural villages in mainland Greece, *American Anthropologist*, Vol. 61, pp30–38.

Giner, S. and Salcedo, J. (1978) Migrant workers in European social structures, in S. Giner and M.S. Archer (eds) *Contemporary Europe: Social Structures and Cultural Patterns*, London, Routledge and Kegan Paul.

Golini, A. and Geseno, G. (1981) Regional migration in the process of Italian economic development from 1881 to the present, in J. Balán (ed) *Why People Move: Comparative Perspectives on the Dynamics of Internal Migration*, Paris, The Unesco Press.

Greenwood, D. (1976) The demise of agriculture in Fuenterrabia, in J.B. Aceves and W.A. Douglass (eds) *The Changing Faces of Rural Spain*, New York, Schenkman.

Griffin, K. (1976) On the emigration of the peasantry, *World Development*, Vol. 4, pp353–361.

Hume, I. (1973) Migrant workers in Europe, *Finance and Development*, Vol. 10, pp2–6.

Kayser, B. (1972) *Cyclically-Determined Homeward Flows of Migrants*, Paris, OECD.

Kindleberger, C.P. (1965) Emigration and economic growth, *Banca Nazionale del Lavoro Quarterly Review*, Vol. 74, pp235–254.

King, R.L. (1976) Long range migration patterns within the EEC: an Italian case study, in R. Lee and P.E. Ogden (eds) *Economy and Society in the EEC*, Westmead, Saxon House.

King, R.L. (1979) Return migration: a review of some case studies from southern Europe. *Mediterranean Studies*, Vol. 1, pp3–30.

King, R.L. and Strachan, A.J. (1980a) Spatial variations in Sicilian migration: a stepwise multiple regression analysis, *Mediterranean Studies*, Vol. 2, pp60–87.

King, R.L. and Strachan, A.J. (1980b) Patterns of Sardinian migration, *Tijdschrift voor Economische en Sociale Geografie*, Vol. 71, pp209–222.

King, R.L. and Young, S.E. (1979) The Aeolian Islands: birth and death of a human landscape. *Erdkunde*, Vol. 33, pp193–204.

Kosiński, L.A. (1970) *The Population of Europe*, London, Longman.

Lebon, A. and Falchi, G. (1980) New developments in intra-European migration since 1974, *International Migration Review*, Vol. 14, pp539–579.

Livi Bacci, M. (1972) The countries of emigration, in M. Livi Bacci (ed) *The Demographic and Social Pattern of Emigration from the Southern European Countries*, Florence, Dipartimento Statistico-Matematico dell'Università di Firenze, Serie Ricerche Empiriche 7.

Lutz, V. (1961) Some structural aspects of the southern problem: the complementarity of emigration and industrialisation, *Banca Nazionale del Lavoro Quarterly Review*, Vol. 59, pp367–402.

Majoral, R. (1977) The consequences of depopulation in the western Pyrenees of Catalonia, *Iberian Studies*, Vol. 6, pp24–33.

Migliorini, E. (1976) Spostamenti di popolazione in Italia nell'ultimo quarto di secolo, in A. Pecora and R. Pracchi (eds) *Italian Contributions to the 23rd International Geographical Congress 1976*, Rome, Consiglio Nazionale delle Ricerche.

Nikolinakos, M. (1973) The contradictions of capitalist development in Greece: labour shortages and emigration, *Studi Emigrazione*, Vol. 30, pp222–235.

Nikolinakos, M. (1975) Notes towards a general theory of migration in late capitalism, *Race and Class*, Vol, 17, pp5–17.

O'Flanagan, P. (1976) The changing population structure of Galicia 1900–1970, *Iberian Studies*, Vol. 5, pp61–80.

Pepelasis, A. and Yotopoulos, P.A. (1962) *Surplus Labour in Greek Agriculture 1953–1960*. Athens: Centre of Planning and Economic Research, Monograph Series 2.

Poinard, M. (1979) Le million des immigrés: analyse de l'utilisation de l'aide au retour par les travailleurs portugais en France, *Revue Géographique des Pyrénées et du Sud-Ouest*, Vol. 50, pp511–539.

Reyneri, E. (1980) Emigration and sending area as a subsidised system in Sicily. *Mediterranean Studies*, Vol. 2, pp88–113.

Rhoades, R.E. (1978) Intra-European return migration and rural development: lessons from the Spanish case, *Human Organization*, Vol. 37, pp136–147.

Rhoades, R.E. (1979) From caves to main street: return migration and the transformation of a Spanish village, *Papers in Anthropology*, Vol. 20, pp57–74.

Rocha Trinidade, M.B. (1979a) The Iberian peninsula, in D. Kubat (ed) *The Politics of Migration Policies*, New York, Center for Migration Studies.

Rocha Trinidade, M.B. (1979b) Portugal, in R.E. Krane (ed) *International Labor Migration in Europe*, New York, Praeger.

Rodgers, A.L. (1970) Migration and industrial development: the southern Italian experience, *Economic Geography*, Vol. 46, pp110–133.

Rogers, R. (1981) Incentives to return: patterns of policies and migrants' responses, in M.M. Kritz, C.B. Keely and S.M. Tomasi (eds) *Global Trends in Migration*, New York, Center for Migration Studies.

Romanos, M.C. (1979) Forsaken farms: the village to city movement in Western Europe, in M.C. Romanos (ed) *Western European Cities in Crisis*, Lexington, D.C. Heath/Lexington Books.

Salt, J. and Clout, H.D. (eds) (1976) *Migration in Post-War Europe: Geographical Essays*, London, Oxford University Press.

Sasson-Koob, S. (1978) The international circulation of resources and development: the case of migrant labour, *Development and Change*, Vol. 9, pp509–545.

Sasson-Koob, S. (1980) The internationalization of the labour force, *Studies in Comparative International Development*, Vol. 15, pp3–25.

Signorelli, A. (1980) Regional policies in Italy for migrant workers returning home, in R.D. Grillo (ed) *'Nation' and 'State' in Europe: Anthropological Perspectives*, London, Academic Press.

Slater, M. (1979) Migrant employment, recessions and return migration: some consequences for migration policy and development, *Studies in Comparative International Development*, Vol. 14, pp3–22.

Vigorelli, P. (1969) Returning migrants re-employed in Italian industry, *Migration News*, Vol. 18, pp3–13.

Vining, D.R. and Kontuly, T. (1978) Population dispersal from major metropolitan regions: an international comparison, *International Regional Science Review*, Vol. 3, pp49–73.

Wagner, M. (1977) Vocational training for returning migrants, *Migration Today*, Vol. 21, pp117–124.

Wagstaff, J.M. (1968) Rural migration in Greece, *Geography*, Vol. 53, pp175–179.

Ward, A. (1975a) European capitalism's reserve army, *Monthly Review*, Vol. 27, No. 6, pp17–32.

Ward, A. (1975b) European migratory labour: a myth of development, *Monthly Review*, Vol. 27, No. 7, pp24–38.

Zolotas, X. (1966) International labour migration and economic development, with special reference to Greece, *Papers and Lectures 21*, Athens, Bank of Greece.

CHAPTER SEVEN

CAPITAL ACCUMULATION: THE INDUSTRIALIZATION OF SOUTHERN EUROPE?

R. Hudson and
J.R. Lewis

1. Introduction

There is no more popular image with those seeking to demonstrate the economic transformation of southern Europe than that of heavy industrial complexes; photographs of the red-and-white hooped chimneys of petrochemical plants or diagrams of the production cycle of steel works dominate the pages of brochures proclaiming the industrial advantages of the Tagus, Taranto, Tarragona or Thessaloniki. In these same brochures, tables of manufacturing output statistics and graphs of exports are presented as further proof that Greece or Italy or Portugal or Spain is an industrial economy with a record of rapid growth and prospects of further expansion. The evidence is indeed impressive, for Italy and Spain have the world's ninth and eleventh largest economies respectively, all four countries have between 30 percent and 50 percent of their GDP from industry and had industrial growth rates exceeding 6 percent per annum during the 1960s. Furthermore, the country studies in this book (chapters 2–5) show the economic, political and social consequences of industrialization to have been profound. In this chapter we shall examine the reasons for these changes by considering the changing position of southern Europe in the world economy and the different types of flows of capital that have been involved in industrial investment. It will become clear that both the types of industrial development and the relative importance of different forms of organization of capital are qualitatively different from those of the classic models of European industrialization of either the past — for example, nineteenth century Britain— or the present— for example, FR Germany.

This means that the industrialization that has taken place so far raises a new set of issues when future trends are considered.

Before this highly compressed and oversimplified argument can be presented, however, it is necessary to draw attention to the limitations of the data on which any analysis is based. The data problems encountered in studying the movements of people (summarized in chapter 6) seem almost trivial when compared with those encountered in analysing the movements of capital. At the international level not only are there variations in practice between nations in recording flows but there are also unrecorded items (for example, part of workers' remittances) and misclassified ones (most notably due to 'transfer pricing' by multinational companies). Intranational movements remain shrouded by the secrecy of banking systems and the labyrinthine complexities of State taxation and payment systems, while the presence of a significant 'black' or 'subterranean' economy in the small firm sector reduces the reliability of estimates for industrial production or employment. This has a further consequence for, when official statistics are incomplete (and out of date), it even becomes difficult to be sure of the representativeness of sample survey results so that Sokrates' maxim — 'I know that I know nothing' — applies in this field of study with some force.

2. Southern Europe in the world economy

Even if it were possible to examine the economies of southern Europe in isolation prior to 1960,[1] the spectacular growth of world trade during the 'postwar boom', the rise of the multinational company, the increasing importance of supranational bodies such as the European Communities (EC) and internationalization of labour 'markets' have all meant that an awareness of the world economic context is an essential prelude today. The fact that each of the economies — and, in particular, their industrial sectors — is now closely involved in the capitalist world economy is not only a result of the general tendencies summarized above but also reflects the series of political choices taken by the States concerned. In the case of Italy, it was the choice of membership of the EC with its policies for free international movement of capital and labour in 1957 but for Greece it was the 1961 Association agreement with the EC which gave a major boost to inward investment under the 1953 law on foreign capital. Portugal, in contrast, joined the European Free Trade Association (EFTA) in 1959, reduced controls on foreign capital in 1965 and became formally associated with the EC in 1972. Spain first 'liberalized' with the 1959–1961 Stabilization Plan and then sought to join the EC in 1962, but was considered politically unacceptable so association was only agreed in 1970 (see also Chapter 1).

However, the world economy itself was changing as southern Europe became more involved, affecting the sorts of industrial development that would be possible during the decades after the 'opening' of its economy. Three changes were of special significance. The first was the replacement of the UK as the leading industrial power in Europe by FR Germany for both German companies' search for European markets for their capital goods and their increasing involvement in investment abroad had a greater impact in southern Europe than UK firms' earlier colonial strategies. By 1975, FR Germany was the major source of all imports for Italy and Greece and second (to the world's largest industrial economy, the USA) in both Portugal and Spain. Considering supplies of machinery alone, FR Germany was the largest supplier to all the countries with from 21 percent (Portugal) to 42 percent (Italy) of imports (Schlupp 1980). The second shift of importance was the international resurgence of Japan, initially on the basis of exports of consumer goods. Although not significantly affecting southern European internal markets, this increased competition in parts of northern European markets has limited the growth of southern European exports of these products. The exception is when more recent Japanese investments in, say, Portugal are aimed at the EC market. Thirdly, the most recent important trend has been the growth of the Newly Industrializing Countries (NIC's) in South East Asia, partly as a result of Japanese investments. Most commentators on the NIC's (for example, Balassa 1981) include at least Greece and Portugal in their lists based on industrial growth rates or increases in industrial exports, and it is clear that there is now some direct competition between the southern European NIC's and those elsewhere. However, it will be argued later in this paper that the similarities between those groups of economies are often overstated.

Just as there is considerable heterogeneity in a group such as the NIC's, so too it is important to be aware of the differences between the countries of southern Europe in order that generalizations about their industrial development are treated with appropriate caution. The most important aggregate indicators of their internal economic structure are presented in Table 7.1 which focuses on Gross Domestic Product (GDP) in 1980. These show clearly the different sizes of the four economies, ranging from $394 b. (Italy) to $24.1 b. (Portugal). This is not a function of population size alone, for once GDP is expressed per caput the range is reduced considerably but still suggests the same 'ranking'. Italy is the largest and wealthiest economy,

Table 7.1   Gross domestic product, 1960–1980

	Greece	Italy	Portugal	Spain
GDP, 1980 ($US, billions)	40.4	394.0	24.1	211.1
GDP, per caput, 1980 ($US)	4,210	6,910	2,430	5,650
Growth of GDP, 1960–1970 (annual average percentage)	6.4	5.3	6.2	7.1
Growth of GDP, 1970–1980 (annual average percentage)	4.9*	3.0	4.6	4.0
Percentage GDP from agriculture, 1980	16	6	13	8
Percentage GDP from industry, 1980	32	43	46	37
Percentage GDP from services, 1980	52	51	41	55

* 1970–1979
Source: World Bank (1982)

followed by Spain, while the two countries with the smallest populations are some $1500 (Greece) and $3000 (Portugal) per caput poorer than Spain. Turning briefly to Table 7.2, which presents part of a joint ranking by Linge and Hamilton (1981) of countries according to their annual national production and of companies according to their annual turnover (using 1976 data), these disparities are underlined in a more unusual way. This ranking of 'economic units' confirms the importance of both Italy and Spain in world terms with at least double the value of production of Exxon, the largest corporation (rank 22, turnover $49 b.). However, Greece is only ranked at 43, smaller than 6 corporations and Portugal, at 52, is smaller than 10 corporations.

In terms of GDP growth rates (Table 7.1), there is considerable uniformity between the countries in each of the decades considered, with rates of 5–7 percent in the 1960s falling to 3–5 percent in the recessionary 1970s. There has also been a tendency throughout the period for Italy's annual growth rate to be 1 percent lower than the others, which has meant some convergence in GDP size within the group. The composition of GDP in 1980 shows significant variation in the importance of agriculture between, on the one hand, Greece and Portugal (with 16 and 13 percent respectively) and, on the other, Italy and Spain (6 and 8 percent). However, the relative share of industry is highest in Portugal (43 percent) and lowest in Greece (32

Table 7.2 Major companies and countries, ranked by annual turnover/national production, 1976

Rank	Name	Turnover/production ($ billion)
1	U.S.A.	1697
2	U.S.S.R.	709
3	Japan	554
4	F.R. Germany	458
5	France	347
6	China	343
7	U.K.	226
8	Canada	174
9	ITALY	171
10	Brazil	125
11	SPAIN	104
12	Poland	98
.		.
.		.
.		.
40	Mobil	26
41	Hungary	24
42	South Korea	24
43	GREECE	24
44	Bulgaria	20
.		.
.		.
.		.
50	Kuwait	17
51	Gulf Oil	17
52	PORTUGAL	16
53	Thailand	16
54	IBM	16

Source: Hamilton and Linge (1981)

percent) and Spain (37 percent), both of which have large service sectors in employment (Table 1.4) and output terms.

What these contemporary comparative data cannot do is indicate the important differences in the evolution of the economies, particularly of their industrial structures. Yet the long history of manufacturing production (including exports to northern Europe) in areas like Lombardy in Italy or the Basque country in Spain does mean that they have a more highly interdependent industrial economy and a more clearly identifiable urban proletariat than in all but the odd textile town of Greece or Portugal. Furthermore, the development of functional specialization between firms in the traditional industrial areas of Italy and Spain went beyond the sphere of production and included a good basic network of business services and banks that facilitated the growth of indigenous industrial capital. The influence of these different initial conditions on patterns of industrialization in the rapidly changing world economy of the last two decades will become clear once we have reviewed the types of capital movements that have acted as stimuli.

International and intranational Capital movements

The simplest distinction amongst the various flows of capital that have given rise to the contemporary sectoral and spatial patterns of industrial activity is between those that cross national boundaries and those that do not. In both cases, the movement may actually take place within the same company, as when Exxon disinvested in Greece or Fiat initiated plants in southern Italy, but such transfers are hard to trace properly, as are those from one branch of production to another. Therefore, most attention has to be given to the least badly recorded movements — those between areas.

International movements

If Lipietz (1983) is roughly correct in arguing that in Spain international private investment was worth under 5 percent of domestic investment between 1967 and 1980 (and it is likely to have been even less important in the other three countries), it is unfortunate that it should be international movements that are easiest to identity, both in balance of payments records and in the more concrete form of multinational company plants. With this reservation about their relative weight in mind, it is possible to distinguish and examine in turn three major forms of international capital movement— workers' remittances, private capital and official capital. The absolute values of these flows are given in Table 7.3 which summarizes the main elements of the balance of payments for the two most recent years currently available, usually 1980 and 1981, and for 1972, the last year before the first great increase in oil prices. Apart from the striking evidence of a considerable increase in trade deficits for all the countries over the ten years, this table shows just how important the three types of capital flows are in offsetting these deficits.

Transfers— which largely consist of workers' remittances— now run at

Table 7.3 Balance of payments, 1972, 1980 and 1981 ($m)

	Greece 1972	Greece 1980	Greece 1981	Italy 1972	Italy 1980	Italy 1981	Portugal 1972	Portugal 1980	Portugal 1981	Spain 1971	Spain 1979	Spain 1980
Imports	860	4094	4750	18480	76857	74825	1296	4616	4089	3201	24022	32389
Exports	−2197	−9813	−10281	−18425	−93193	−85385	−2023	−8667	−9251	1419	18352	20928
Trade balance	−1337	−5719	−5531	55	−16336	−10560	−727	−4051	−5162	−1782	−5671	−11461
Services	388	1929	2099	1540	5442	1750	205	−12	−441	875	5015	4425
Transfers	575	1083	1036	448	1213	693	872	3015	2893	451	1782	2048
Private long term capital	478	1275	na	−956	−32	4237	62	293	765	502	2835	4020
Official long term capital	478	1275	na	−169	3597	4480	−191	425	517	33	382	174
Short term capital and errors	69	240	363	−2243	−1192	949	56	1236	1268	−215	−830	246
Nonmonetary balance	173	−1192	na	−1327	−7308	1549	277	906	−160	−136	3513	548

Sources: OECD Country Economic Surveys 1980, 1981–1982 and 1982–1983

about \$1000 million each year in Greece and Italy,[2] nearer to \$2000 million in Spain and an astonishing \$3000 million in Portugal. These levels of inflow are relatively most important in Greece and Portugal, where they represented 3.9 percent and 8.3 percent respectively of GDP over the period 1970–1977 (Fua 1980) and, by 1980, had risen to 7.5 percent and 12.5 percent. In contrast, in Italy and Spain they are seldom worth more than 1.5 percent of GDP. However, it is somewhat misleading to view workers' remittances as a similar flow to that of private or official capital since numerous studies have shown that most of the money is either spent on consumer goods (often imported) or invested in items such as improved housing or better education for children— see Chapter 6 for examples. In such circumstances, the actual impact of this influx on the country's production structure is much less than the absolute figures might suggest. Moreover, given the clear preference for the service sector amongst those returned emigrants who do invest their savings in businesses, the effect on industrial development is smaller still.[3]

Private capital flows into Greece, Portugal and Spain have been seen by commentators like Baklanoff (1978) and Murolo (1982), as a major reason for the 'economic miracles' that followed the increasing openness of these economies. Certainly, Table 7.3 shows that their value has increased during the past decade. Spain has always been the major recipient with over \$4,000 million in 1980, representing about 2 percent of the country's GDP throughout the 1970s. However, such flows may be relatively more important in Greece as the 1980 receipt of \$1,275 million of *both* official and private capital was equivalent to 3.1 percent of GDP— and had averaged 4.7 percent in 1970–1977 (Fua 1980).[4] In contrast, Italy usually appears as a net exporter of capital but the amount of surplus has gradually declined in recent years as inward investment increasingly matches the export of capital by such firms as Fiat and Agip.

The uses of these direct and portfolio capital flows are seldom given in detail but the few studies that are available show the importance of industrial investments. Thus when the *Banco de Portugal* compared the flow of foreign investments in 1974 and 1978, the proportions in manufacturing were 50 percent and 48 percent, respectively, while services took 25 percent and 29 percent, finance, 11 percent and 9 percent, and mining 9 percent in both years. Official statistics for Spain show that 69 percent of foreign investment during 1979 was in the manufacturing sector, followed in importance by 20 percent in trade and tourism. Turning from flows to stocks, Schlupp (1980) indicates that 43 percent of the identifiable 2,880 million DM stock of FR German investment in Spain in mid-1977 was in manufacturing, although this was less than the 48 percent accumulated in hotels during the tourism boom. A similar calculation for Italy showed that 88 percent of German investment was then in manufacturing. Figures for stocks of all foreign direct investment in Greece for the much earlier date of 1969 reveal that 83 percent was industrial (Hadjimichalis 1981) and there is little reason to expect that this proportion has declined dramatically in the 1970s.

Clearly there is a wide range of reasons for the considerable size and persistence of these flows but, if activities such as tourism and banking are ignored and attention confined to industrial investments, four factors appear to explain most inward investments. First, the availability of natural resources in southern Europe has attracted several multinational companies, although the fragmented nature of many mineral deposits has usually meant small-scale investments like those in the wolframite mines of northern Portugal. The best example of large-scale investment is Pechiney-Ugine-Kuhlman processing bauxite at Itea in Greece (Mouzelis 1978; Nikolinakos 1984) which is also famous because of the concern expressed about the environmental damage caused by this type of industrialization. Indeed, the willingness of governments to allow activities that pollute can be seen as a second attraction for foreign investors. At a time when FR German chemical firms are having to spend about one third of their research and development budgets on meeting anti-pollution standards, it is not surprising that relocation in countries which are less likely to enforce their environmental protection laws appears prudent. When, as in the wood pulp industry, the savings on antipollution measures can be combined with easy access to natural resources (such as timber) investments such as those in paper making along the Portuguese coast are the result.

The third, and most important single reason— according to Paine (1979, 1982) and Vaitsos (1982)— is market access. This can be an influence at two levels, starting with access to those domestic markets which have generally been highly protected. For Greece, Vaitsos (1982) reports that 90 percent of the production of foreign-owned manufacturing plants in 1977 was for the local market and the Spanish market took the same proportion of all sales by the major foreign firms there in 1974. For Spain, in particular, by far the largest of the more 'closed' markets, 'the local market provided the main incentive for most of the foreign direct investment' (Tsoukalis 1981). It is this motive that explains the significant presence of foreign investors in producing consumer goods — such as paints, detergents, perfumes, soft

drinks and photographic equipment in Spain and it is also partly responsible for investments by companies like Gulf Oil, ICI and Bayer AG in
chemical and petroleum production. However, EC membership or association means that industrial investment in any of the four southern European
countries is now a means of gaining better access to the EC market for
multinational firms based in countries like Japan and the USA. Thus
further Spanish evidence shows that the proportion of exports in foreign
manufacturing firms varies not only sectorally but also by country of origin,
with US firms producing automobiles and chemicals having a higher level of
exports than other, EC based, firms (Vaitsos 1982). It is this level of market
access that helps account for the large share of all foreign investment coming
from the USA— 36 percent of that into Greece in 1953–1977 (Murolo 1982)
and 58 percent of the cumulated total from 1960 to 1975 in Spain, although
only 19 percent of the stock in Portugal in 1978 (Tsoukalis 1981).

The fourth factor to consider is the availability of relatively low-cost,
'flexible' labour. In Greece, Portugal and Spain this reflected not only
demographic increase and the agricultural exodus but also the political
restrictions on trades unions for much of the period before the mid-1970s.
In each of these countries, wages — and other labour costs such as social
security payments— are lower than in the USA and most West European
countries. Consequently, with improvements to the transport system and
the development of production on Taylorist lines, it has become profitable
to locate the more labour intensive parts of production there (Fröbel et al
1980; Froöbel 1982; Lipietz 1983). The textile industry is the best known
example, having great variation in wages: hourly rates for a seamstress in
1975 within Europe varied between 10DM inn FR Germany, 5.7 DM in
Italy, 3.3 DM in Greece and 3.2 DM in Portugal. This has encouraged firms
to relocate or subcontract production in southern Europe (or areas such as
North Africa and South East Asia where costs are lower still). While the six
main West European textile producing countries lost 858,000 jobs (−30
percent) in this sector between 1965 and 1977, the four South European
countries gained 255,000, an increase of 28 percent (Hudson and Lewis,
1982).

There has also been significant relocation of production in the assembly
of consumer electronics and automobile components through the investments of firms like Phillips, Siemens, Grundig, Texas Instruments, Ford
and Renault. It can also be argued that low wages have attracted some more
capital intensive types of production to southern Europe, the most obvious
illustrations being the automobile plants of Spain and Portugal in which

production is as much for export to the EC as for the domestic market. However, it is not only the relatively low wages that companies consider attractive but also the absence of strong trade unionism amongst the sort of workers that are often recruited — people with little industrial experience. There is little quantitative evidence on this but a mass of incidental observations suggest that employers can introduce changes in production methods more readily and that the labour force can be redeployed with less delay than is usual in countries with a strongly unionized, urban-industrial proletariat. This is an advantage of rural areas that is discussed further in relation to Italy below.

The third important type of capital flow recorded in Table 7.3 is that of official capital and consists primarily of loans or financial transfers to governments. In absolute terms, the flow to Italy has been the most significant in recent years, with some $4,500 m in 1981 alone, while Portugal's receipts are notable as the flow has changed from being a net repayment of loans in 1972 to an inward movement of $400–500 m per annum. This reversal is indicative of Portugal's increasingly serious foreign debt problem as the amount owed has shot up from $485 m in 1970 to $6,313 m in 1981, or from 7 to 27 percent of GDP, and was costing $641 m in interest payments in this latter year (World Bank 1983). Details on the use made of this official capital flow are scarce but its relevance for industry can be seen from the use made of one such flow, that of 'pre-accession aid' from the EC to Portugal. This has already reached 625M ECU's, largely through European Investment Bank loans either for productive infrastructural projects such as improvements to the port of Leixões (near Oporto) or schemes to assist the small-medium scale industrial sector. Such aid is reinforced by separate loans from countries like FR Germany ($60 m loan for the Cova de Beira project) and the Netherlands (21m Fl. to modernize the fishing industry).

In sum, the composition of international capital flows varies between the four countries but the different types of long-term capital flows have clearly been important in the recent industrialization of Greece, Portugal and Spain. In general Italy has been less affected by international capital movements,[5] although considerable flows of official capital to the Mezzogiorno continue to influence the speed and character of development there.

Intranational movements

It is difficult to present even tentative conclusions about the movement of capital *within* these countries as intersectoral and interregional flows are almost entirely unrecorded. The sorts of movements discussed above —

from remittances to private and public capital flows— must exist but their magnitude and direction can only be assumed from their effects. Remittances seem largely to act as a counter-flow to the migration of workers so that an urban–rural direction seems likely to have contributed to the start of the 'rural revival' (noted in Chapter 6), but, as with international remittances, they have more impact on private consumption than on productive structures.

Movements of private capital are hard to trace but there appears to be two opposing tendencies. On the one hand, Cuadrado Roura (1981) has shown that during the 1970s the private banking system in Spain has persistently lent more money in the Basque Country, Madrid and Catalonia than the value of deposits there (to the tune of 19,000 m Ptas, 12,000 m Ptas and 2,750 m Ptas respectively in 1973). However, on the other hand, there is a limited spatial decentralization of industries from metropolitan area (for example, see Barquero Vazquez 1983; Ferrão 1983; Garofoli 1983; Stathakis 1983). Such evidence is not contradictory for the capital flows through the banks include investments in housing, services and those industries which have remained predominantly urban. Productive decentralization has— with the exception of Italy— not usually involved great industrial investment outside the metropolitan regions but rather in the sort of metropolitan peripheries like Attica-Beotia around Athens (Leontidou-Emmanuel, 1981), which Ferrão (1984) has shown to be the most profitable locations. How far these movements of private capital initially stimulated industrial growth at the expense of agricultural investment remains open to speculation, as does the question of the effects of the current wave of investment in property— from workers' apartments to tourist villas— on further industrial growth.

Finally, intranational official capital movements deserve a brief mention. Yet again, there is little doubting the importance of financial transfers through the state of influencing patterns of regional development but detailed studies of this are rare. Much of the transfer is in the form of collective social service investments in schools, drains, clinics and the like or direct payments of pensions or welfare benefits to individuals. The sociopolitical implications of this phenomenon in areas like the Mezzogiorno are considerable (see Pinnaro and Pugliese 1979 or Pugliese 1984) but its impact on industrial development is more limited, especially when compared with the public funds directed to productive infrastructure. This latter category is best exemplified by the operations of the *Cassa per il Mezzogiorno* (summarized in King 1981 or Ronzani 1980) which has spent some £250 m per annum on investments in irrigation works, transport improvements and urban renewal. However, similar sorts of expenditure were associated with the Spanish 'growth pole' programme of the 1960s (Hebbert and Alonso Teixedor 1982), the Sines project in Portugal (Lewis 1983; Lewis and Williams 1982) and were proposed for the abortive Pylos project in southern Greece. Taking all interregional flows through the public sector together, Cuadrado Roura (1981) shows that, in 1973, Spanish regions like Andalusia, Castilla-Leon and Galicia received more than they contributed in taxes while Catalonia, the Basque Country and the Balearic Islands recorded net deficits — a pattern roughly the reverse of that for private flows.[6]

4. Forms of industrialization

The net effect of these capital movements can be judged from Tables 7.4 and 7.5 which show the relative importance of the four countries in the capitalist world's industrial production and changes in the value of output during the 1970s. It is clear from Table 7.4 that Spain has substantially increased its share of production (from 0.9 to 1.6 percent) between 1963 and 1977 but that industrialization in Greece and Portugal has had more modest effects as neither accounted for more than 0.3 percent of production in 1977. Italy's share has slightly declined, like that of the other leading industrial countries. In terms of manufactured exports, Italy remains the

Table 7.4   Share of selected countries in the capitalist countries' industrial production, 1963 and 1977, and world manufacturing exports, 1963 and 1976

	Industrial production		Manufactured exports	
	1963	1977	1963	1976
U.S.A.	40.3	36.9	17.2	13.6
F.R. Germany	9.7	8.9	15.5	15.8
U.K.	6.5	4.2	11.1	6.6
France	6.3	6.2	7.0	7.4
Japan	5.6	9.1	6.0	11.4
Italy	3.4	3.3	4.7	5.5
Spain	0.9	1.6	0.3	1.1
Portugal	0.2	0.3	0.3	0.2
Greece	0.2	0.3	0.0	0.2
S. Korea	0.1	0.7	0.1	1.2

Source: Linge and Hamilton (1981)

most important and the shares of both Spain and Greece have risen between 1963 and 1976. However, none of these industrial growth rates matches those of Japan or South Korea. Evidence of more recent relative performances in industrial production is provided in Table 7.5 which shows the 1977 gap between manufactured output per caput in Italy and Spain, on the one hand, and Portugal and Greece on the other. It also underlines Spain's rapid growth which appears from the index figures to have been concentrated in the period before 1975. What appears to be impressive growth in Portugal is partly due to a low level of industrial production in the base year, 1975, due to postrevolutionary changes. Increasing industrial production has also meant a growing share of employment over the period 1960–1980, as shown in Table 1.4. In 1980 Greece had 28 percent, Portugal 36 percent and Spain 40 percent of the labour force in industry— a shift that was most rapid in the case of Greece. In Italy, however, despite a substantial increase in industrial employment, there has been a relatively small increase in the industrial share of all employment.

In addition to the size of the industrial sector, it is necessary to consider its internal structure using the information of Table 7.6. With its unfortunately large category of 'other industries' some distinctions between countries are lost but the contrast between Greece and the remaining countries is still obvious. With 20 percent of value added coming from food and agricultural product processing and another 26 percent from textiles in 1979, Greece most closely resembles the 'traditional' industrial structure of southern Europe. Even Portugal, with its substantial machinery sector due largely to car production, appears to have become more like the diversified and sophisticated industrial countries of Western Europe. A similar pattern is evident in terms of trading relationships (Table 7.7) for, while Greek imports of machinery and transport equipment were worth 38 percent of

Table 7.5   Value of industrial output, 1970, 1978 and 1979

	Date	Greece	Italy	Portugal	Spain
Manufacturing output	1970	770	2204	n.a.	1704
p.c. (1975 $)	1978	1346*	2892	1623	2690*
Index of industrial	1970	66.4	92.2	77.7	71.0
production (1975 = 100)	1979	128.7	122.8	134.0	115.0

* 1977 not 1978
Sources: World Bank (1982); Eurostat (1980).

Table 7.6 Distribution of value-added in manufacturing, 1979

	Greece	Italy	Portugal	Spain
Food and agriculture	20	10	13	12
Textiles and clothing	26	15	20	19
Machinery and transport equipment	8	26	20	17
Chemicals	8	9	10	10
Other	38	40	37	42

Source: World Bank (1982)

Table 7.7 Structure of merchandise trade, 1979

	Greece	Italy	Portugal	Spain
Percentage share of imports:				
Food	10	16	17	15
Fuels	21	24	20	30
Other primary commodities	7	15	11	13
Machinery & transport equipment	38	19	25	19
Other manufactures	24	26	27	23
Percentage share of exports:				
Fuel, minerals and metals	21	8	2	5
Other primary commodities	33	9	22	22
Textiles and clothing	17	12	31	5
Machinery & transport equipment	4	30	12	26
Other manufactures	25	41	33	42

Source: World Bank (1982).

the total in 1979, the other countries tended to import more food and raw materials — including a substantial amount of fuel in all cases. In exports too, Greece still relies heavily on primary products (54 percent of 1979 exports) and products like textiles, whereas Portuguese trade has a sizeable proportion of machinery and other manufactures to set alongside its long-standing agricultural and textile exports. Both Italy and Spain show a predominance of such 'advanced' industrial products.

These aggregate figures do help in establishing broad trends over the past two decades but give little idea of how industrial production is currently organized — and thus its likely development in the future. To obtain such a picture it is useful to subdivide the industrialization process in two ways:

First, according to its markets, and secondly, by the type of organization of capital. These two aspects are treated in turn below.

Market relationships

Within the industrialization process a distinction can be made between import reproducing,[6] export processing and export platform activities. From the point of view of governments in southern Europe, there is considerable merit in encouraging the growth of import-reproducing industries for, by moving towards self-sufficiency, this can cut import bills and so ease balance-of-payments problems. Consequently such developments have been encouraged over a wide range of industries but especially those that provide inputs into other nationally-based forms of production. Examples are cement for the construction industry and, above all, iron and steel which is linked to the growth of import-reproducing car or other consumer durable industries and machinery production. Thus Italian steel production rose from 8.5m tonnes in 1960 to 24.8m tonnes in 1981 (overtaking the French total of 21.3m tonnes in the latter year) while, despite reductions in investment plans after 1974, complexes such as Seixal (Portugal), Eleusis and Thessaloniki (Greece) have given relatively important steel-making capacity to the smaller countries (Judet 1980). Hence, crude steel output continued to rise in southern Europe throughout the 1970s, even with the overall crisis of overproduction in the world steel industry (Mandel 1978). In other industrial sectors, setting up import-reproducing plants has often been part of an agreement with the state whereby quotas for other imports have been increased, so that this is one channel through which private capital is able to get access to the national markets of southern Europe.

The second and third forms of industrialization are both export-oriented developments which national Governments have encouraged to boost exports and tackle balance of payments difficulties. The first of these is export-processing production. This can take a variety of forms but mainly falls into one of two categories: either the processing of minerals and other raw materials or the processing in various ways of agricultural raw materials — canning fruit and vegetables in Greece or Spain for example. Clearly not all such production is export-oriented, but the high shares of 'food and agriculture' in total value added in manufacturing (Table 7.6) is indicative of the way in which 'traditional' food processing industries, producing for regional or national markets, may come to co-exist alongside, or be converted to, export production for international markets.

Table 7.8 Destination and value of manufactured exports, 1962 and 1979

| | Percentage share of manufactured exports to: | | | | | | | | Value ($m) | |
| | Industrial market economies | | Nonmarket industrial economies | | High income Oil exports | | Developing economies | | | |
	1962	1979	1962	1979	1962	1979	1962	1979	1962	1979
Greece	52	66	4	4	3	14	41	16	27	1,773
Italy	64	68	5	4	2	6	29	22	3,490	60,125
Portugal	53	82	0	3	1	0	46	15	205	2,529
Spain	57	59	1	3	1	4	41	34	205	13,347

Source: World Bank (1982).

Table 7.9 Principal OECD economies' imports of selected manufactured goods*, 1976 ($m)

	USA	Japan	EC	(France	FR Germany	UK)	Total
Greece	33	6	482	44	292	17	520
Portugal	35	5	449	46	103	187	703
Spain	522	27	2,049	825	504	218	2,932
Hong Kong	2,015	140	1,917	980	823	694	4,991
ALL N.I.C.'s and developing countries	11,626	2,079	10,928	1,915	4,035	2,261	28,283

* Goods manufactured from Plastic, Glass, Leather and Wood; Vehicle Tyres, Cotton Fabrics, Cutlery, Engines, Office Machinery, Machine Tools, Radio Receivers, Motor Vehicles, Clothing, Footwear, Toys, Watches, Gramophones, Furniture.

Source: Edwards (1979).

The final form of production is that of export-platform, the establishment of factories or even production complexes in southern Europe to serve not national but international markets. These are not attracted by the domestic market or by the availability of raw materials but rather by the profitable conditions for production described earlier. In addition to these conditions, the generous grants and financial concessions made by national Governments keen to attract capital to promote industrial development as part of an intensifying global competition for mobile investment is always a useful bonus. Nevertheless, while part of the recent industrial growth of southern Europe has been of this export-platform type, it is important not to overexaggerate its importance. While it is true that the shares of manufactured exports from southern Europe to the advanced capitalist world have increased (Table 7.8), it is equally clear (Table 7.9) that their exports form a relatively small share of even those of the 'Newly Industrializing Countries' to the OECD bloc (the comparison with Hong Kong being especially revealing). Moreover, as with their agricultural exports, the dependence of southern Europe's export-oriented manufacturing industries on access to the EC market via various treaty agreements is again starkly emphasized. In particular, the dependence of Greece upon access to FR Germany's markets, of Portugal on access to the UK's, and of Spain on access to France's is marked.

5. The organization of capital in south European industry

The second major feature of industrialization is that of the organization of capital, in which international firms, state corporations and indigenous small or medium capital can be distinguished. The role of one major form of organization, multinational corporations, has already been hinted at in relation to all three forms of industrialization. The nations of southern Europe fit into their global production and marketing strategies in a variety of ways. It is worth bearing in mind that several of these corporations are 'larger' than some of the national economies (Table 7.2), not least as it effects the balance between corporate power and the political authority of southern European governments. This balance has implications for the latter being able meaningfully to influence, if not control, the investment and disinvestment decisions of the former in relation to national and regional development objectives (see Amin 1984; Nikolinakos 1984). Such potential problems have not prevented southern European Governments actively encouraging multinational capital to locate within their national territories and they have come to dominate in similar sectors in the three

Table 7.10   Share of foreign capital in industrial production in Greece (1979), Spain (1975) and Portugal (1975)

	Greece		Spain[3]	Portugal[4]	
	% Employment[4]	% Assets[2]	% Value Added	% Employment	% Production
Food	12.7	7.5	⎫	6.1	14.5
Beverages	31.0	36.9	⎬ 36.2	10.9	10.4
Tobacco	—	—	⎭	20.1	4.0
Textiles	3.7	15.4	⎫ 39.7 ⎫		
Clothing	16.7	16.8	⎬ ⎬	5.2	5.6
Leather	13.7	5.7	⎭ 7.3 ⎭	4.0	4.1
Wood	2.9	37.1	—	4.4	6.3
Furniture	—	—	—	1.2	2.8
Paper	12.0	15.6	11.7	10.1	19.2
Printing	—	0.5		1.8	3.7
Rubber	14.9	30.3	—	24.2	43.8
Chemicals	25.7	43.4	40.7	26.1	24.3
Petroleum products	9.1	72.7	—	—	—
Nonmetallic mineral products	9.4	27.6	22.0	8.5	11.7
Iron and steel	⎫		2.7 ⎫		
Base metals	⎬ 30.1	47.5	22.6 ⎭	12.2	27.4
Metal products	8.4	9.0	20.1	5.4	12.1
Nonelectrical equipment	10.2	12.4	18.3	18.9	23.2
Electrical equipment	42.1	50.8	57.9	65.2	68.0
Transport equipment	12.1	42.5	18.8	26.1	31.4
Miscellaneous	24.0	55.5	56.2	16.8	25.3
Total	13.3	29.2	19.9[5]	12.2	16.6

[1] Foreign capital defined as those firms with a foreign shareholding of over 35 percent in the top 5,000 companies.

[2] Foreign capital defined as those firms with a foreign shareholding of over 49 percent (including joint ventures and overseas Greek investment) in the top 5,000 companies.

[3] Foreign capital defined as those firms with a foreign shareholding of over 49 percent in the top 700 companies.

[4] Foreign capital defined as those firms with a foreign shareholding of over 49 percent.

[5] The total includes mining and utilities.

Sources: Dokopoulou (1983); ILO (1979); Tsoukalis (1981); Gianntsis (1983).

countries covered in Table 7.10[7]. These include electrical equipment and to a lesser extent nonelectrical equipment, chemicals and beverages, although it should be noted that there are important national differences in some other sectors such as base metals and textiles.

In contrast to the decisions of foreign, multinational capital, those of the second major type of agent of industrialization in southern Europe— State holding companies, public and nationalized industries — are in principle much more amenable to domestic political control. Such forms of direct Government intervention are prevalent in all southern European nations not least because of the perception of their Governments of the need for public control or direction of 'key' industries so as to promote a more general industrialization. The selectivity of public control or ownership of 'key' industries thus offers, in principle, a mechanism of considerable power through which national Governments can influence not only the overall sectoral pattern of development but also the spatial allocation of such activities within their national territories. Perhaps the best-known example of this is the activities of the Italian State holding companies of which IRI (Instituto per la Ricostruzione Industriale) and ENI (Ente Nazionale Idrocarburi) are the most important and have important shares of national steel, petrochemical, shipbuilding and mechanical good production. From 1957 onwards these were required to locate at least 40 percent of total investment in the South and to allocate at least 60 percent of new investment there (these proportions were raised to 60 percent and 80 percent respectively, in 1971). Despite the capital-intensive character of the production association with such investment, notably in their iron and steel and petrochemical companies, the result of such investment requirements has been that the share of employment in the Mezzogiorno in the state holding companies has risen from 13 percent in 1958 to 18 percent in 1965 and 27 percent (or about 700,000 jobs in all) in 1978 (Ronzani 1980).

The third major form of organization of capital in the industrialization of southern Europe is that of the indigenous small and medium-sized firms. Such small capitals are of much greater importance in the southern than the north western European economy (Table 7.11). Thus in all four countries over three quarters of manufacturing plants had under 10 employees during the 1970s and none had more than 3 percent with over 100 employees while the proportions for the UK at this time were 39 percent and 15 percent respectively. This proliferation of small manufacturing firms is closely related to the specialization of the southern European economies within the international division of labour. It is precisely in the export-oriented 'tradi-

Table 7.11   Distribution of manufacturing plants by size

		Number of employees			
	Date	1–9	10–49	50–99	>100
Greece	1978	93.3	5.5	0.6	0.6
Italy	1971	86.1	10.9	1.6	1.4
Portugal	1971	78.9	15.9	2.6	2.7
Spain	1978	76.6	18.5	2.5	2.4

Source: Garofoli (1982); INE (1977); Stathakis (1983).

tional' industrial branches, such as clothing and textiles, leather, shoes, furniture and woodworking, and ceramics, that these small firms are particularly concentrated. Nevertheless, one response to the crises of the 1970s was for related forms of decentralized production to spread over a wider range of industries — for example in engineering — not simply into small factories but also into home-working. This was an attempt to contain labour costs and maintain the labour-market flexibility that is vital to their international competitiveness. While formally independent from the point of view of production, such small capitals are dependent upon the wider international market. Choice of product, of methods and techniques of production, are very heavily constrained by this international context and the need, for example, to compete with similar industries in the Mediterranean and south east Asia (for example see Balassa 1981; Edwards 1979).

The link between the necessity for flexible labour-market conditions and the growth of small manufacturing firms has become a focus of considerable recent research in Italy (see, for example, Arcangeli et al 1980; Bagnasco 1977, 1982; Fua 1983; Garofoli 1981, 1983a, 1983b) but the phenomenon is by no means restricted to the Italian case (for other examples, see Lewis and Williams 1980; Andrikopolilou-Kafkala et al 1982; Garofoli 1982; Barquero Vazquez 1983). Much of the postwar industrial growth of the Italian economy, prior to 1963, was associated with export-oriented small firms in traditional industries, many located in the established economic core region of the north west. In 1962/3 (and again at the end of the 1960s), however, real wages were pushed up sharply as a result of a series of major strikes and industrial disputes (see Chapter 3). This posed a threat to those traditional industries where wage costs formed a large part of total production cost and which, because they were operating with mature technologies (which offered little scope for development to reduce the amount of living labour required in production), needed to seek out new locations with low wage costs and more flexible labour markets.

The required conditions were found in the adjacent central and north eastern regions, especially Emilia-Romagna, Veneto and, to a lesser extent, Tuscany, not least because of the persistence of a significant number of small farms, based on family labour. Within these there were considerable reserves of labour, a reflection of agricultural under-employment, which could be cyclically drawn from the agricultural sector and returned to it by these small manufacturing firms as demand for their products rose and fell. This system of double-labour was extremely important to the small firms in two senses: it helped to hold down wages and also preserved the necessary flexibility to recruit and fire wage-labour. This stemmed from the general tendency among those drawn from agriculture into industry on this irregular basis to regard industrial wages as a supplement to their livelihood from agriculture and to remain nonunionized (see Chapter 9). In any case, the spatial diffusion of these small firms and production units itself militated against unionization while dispersion into the existing built environment helped cut the firms' fixed capital investment costs. The result of these processes of diffuse industrialization and the decentralization of production was that particular locations within central and north eastern Italy came to specialize in these forms of production.

This represents but one example of a much more widespread aspect of industrialization within southern Europe: that is, the distinctive locational patterns associated with particular forms and agencies of industrialization. In the broadest sense, these locational differences reflect the importance of market access and the different connotations of market access for different agents and forms of industrialization. Import reproducing industries tend to be located with respect to internal domestic markets, existing centres of economic activity and concentrations of population; to this extent, they often reinforce spatial imbalances associated with previous phases of economic growth and exacerbate problems of uneven, internal spatial development. Export processing industries tend to be more tied by the location of raw materials but export-platform industries tend to locate in ports which themselves are often major urban and industrial centres. Within southern Europe, Athens is the most extreme case of urban-industrial concentration (see Leontidou-Emmanuel 1981 and see also Chapter 2) but the trend is a general one (Courtot, 1978). Small firms, on the other hand, particularly those in 'traditional' branches of manufacturing which are dependent upon flexible labour market conditions, have tended to relocate away from major existing urban-industrial concentrations. Nevertheless, this spontaneous (in the sense of a simple response to market forces) decentralized development is itself a selective process, not only in terms of branches of industry but also in terms of the regions in which it takes place: it has not, for example, spread into southern Italy.

More generally, there are large areas within the national territories of the southern European states which, for a variety of reasons, remain excluded from or marginal to the national growth process. Governments have attempted to pursue regional policies designed to draw such regions into the accumulation process as locations for production (as opposed to sources of internal and international migrant labour). These regional policy measures have taken a variety of forms but essentially can be classified either in terms of major, publicly-funded infrastructure projects (to provide industrial sites, ports, roads, etc.) which have often required substantial Government borrowing to fund them, or financial incentives (grants, soft loans, tax holidays, tax-free profits, etc.). Such regional planning and policy packages can be found in all the southern European states (for example, see Hebbert and Alonso Teixedor 1982; Ronzani 1980; Ramos 1980; Stathakis 1983) and have often proved a compelling attraction to multinational capital. This is particularly the case when they are additional to any general measures to attract such capital, especially in those branches such as petrochemicals which require heavy fixed capital investment. Such industrial developments were not always appropriate to the needs of the regions in which they were implanted according to Nikolinakos (1984), although they may have been central to national development plans. Furthermore, the response from private capital, in terms of type of industry and length of commitment to the location, was not always necessarily that anticipated by Government regional development plans.

6. Conclusions: issues for the future

As this last example demonstrates, managing the industrialization process often poses severe problems for southern European governments. Yet, in a sense, they have no choice but to try to do so given the growth in the importance of the industrial sector within their economies and their commitment to transform their territories into modern industrialized nation states. Such problems exist not simply at the level of the spatial distribution of industry within the country but also at that of managing the national economy. The increasing, but selective, integration of industry in southern

Europe into the sphere of the industrialized economies of the advanced capitalist world create new dilemmas for the states of southern Europe. These centre on the implications for national economic management of such features as profit repatriation, technological dependence (for example, see Cuadrado Roura et al 1984), dependency upon access to foreign exports markets in an era of unstable currencies, and international trade flows being intra-company ones.

In the longer term such problems may intensify and new ones appear. For example, the implications of European Community enlargement on industries in the Community itself, in southern Europe, and in those states which have industrial trade agreements with the Community are likely to be considerable (see Chapter 10). As with agriculture, it is Spanish entry that will pose the greatest threat: in sectors such as steel, shipbuilding and motor cars, Spanish entry will only add to capacity in sectors already severely in crisis within the Community (see Hudson and Lewis 1981). There are significant implications for these industries in Spain and in the rest of the Community when Spain joins. Furthermore, the implications for southern Europe of further industrial development in the Newly Industrializing Countries of the Middle and Far East must be taken into account. For example, a question mark hangs over the future of the export-platform petrochemicals complexes around the coasts of southern Europe when the new complexes currently under construction in Saudi Arabia and other Gulf States come on stream in the next year or so. In addition, small firms producing in traditional sectors are likely to experience greater competition as Far East producers, such as Hong Kong and Singapore, now deliberately begin to restructure into higher value-added products, following the lead of many southern European producers as one, generally successful, response to the 1970s crisis. Alternatively, developments in micro-electronics, in new control and production technologies, may allow a further decentralization and fragmentation of production processes and the survival of the southern European model of decentralized production in the face of this intensifying international competition. Without such a shift in the type of industrialization in southern Europe, the apparently profound transformation of these countries into industrial states could turn out to be shallow and short lived.

Footnotes

1. In practice, it is difficult to comprehend the earlier economic development of any of the countries without reference to their colonial empires (in the cases of Italy, Portugal and

Spain), their trading relationships with northern European countries and their substantial intercontinental migration flows.

2. This is a net figure and other methods of estimation suggest a greater inflow. The World Bank (1981), for example, suggests $3000 million in 1979, some seven times larger than the OECD figure, and much closer to expectations based on the number of Italian migrant workers.

3. In addition to the evidence summarized in Chapter 6 there is support for this generalization in the results of a recent survey of returned emigrants in central Portugal (Boura et al 1984). They found that even when rapidly growing urban areas were included in the survey only 28 percent of emigrants had invested in business and that of these 54 percent had chosen commercial activities, 23 percent agricultural ones and 15 percent invested in industrial firms. Since the average employment in these new establishments was 2.3 persons, the spread effects would also appear limited.

4. OECD surveys of Greece do not subdivide these two types of capital movements but data presented by Bienefeld (1982) for 1971–1976 and Evangelinides (1979) for 1975 show that at least 87 percent of net receipts in these years was due to private capital. If this ratio has remained typical then the relative importance of private capital to Greece remains higher than in Spain.

5. It may well be the case that the investment abroad by Italian firms like Montedison, Pirelli and — of course — Fiat has had a greater impact than inward investment during the 1960s and 1970s. Whether this continues (and starts to apply to Spain with its companies' growing investment in Latin America) in the 1980s will largely depend on location trends in the chemical and automobile industries.

6. 'Import reproducing' seems more apt than the more widely used 'import substituting' as the new products are usually similar to those previously imported in terms of materials and even advertising, as they are often made by the same firm.

7. Note the different definitions of foreign capital used for the Greek figures. Since Dokopoulou ignores joint ventures and 'overseas Greek' her employment figure refers to firms which owned only 15.3 percent of all assets. Even though Iannitsis has shown that foreign capital in all its forms is relatively less important now than in the 1960s, it has yet to reach this low level.

References

Amin, A. (1984) Restructuring in Fiat and the decentralization and production into southern Italy, in R. Hudson and J.R. Lewis (eds) *Accumulation, Class and the State in Southern Europe*, London, Methuen.

Andrikopoulou-Kafkala, E., Hermanns, H., Kafkala, G., Napoli, O. (1982) *Industrialisation, Regional Labour Markets and Productive Investment by Remigrants in a Peripheral Regional: The Case of Thraki in Northern Greece*, Project Report 3, Thessaloniki, University of Thessaloniki.

Arcangeli, F., Borzaga, C. and Goglio, S. (1980) Patterns of Peripheral development in Italian regions, 1964–1977, Papers of the Regional Science Association 44.

Bagnasco, A. (1977) *Tre Italia*, Bologna, Il Mulino.

Bagnasco, A. (1982) Economia e societa della piccolo impresa, in S. Goglio (ed) *Italia: Centri e Periferie*, Milan, Franco Angeli Editore.

Baklanoff, E.N. (1978) *The Economic Transformation of Spain and Portugal*, New York, Praeger.

Balassa, B.A. (1982) *The Newly Industrializing Countries in the World Economy*, Oxford, Pergammon.

Barquero Vazquez, A. (1983) Industrialization in Rural Areas: The Spanish Case, Paper presented to the Conference on Rural Entrepreneurial Capacities, Senigallia, Italy.

Bienefeld, M.A. (1982) Impact on Industry, in D. Seers and C. Vaitsos (eds), *The Second Enlargement of the EEC*, London, Macmillan.

Boura, I.M., Jacinto, R.M.M., Lewis, J.R. and Williams, A.M. (1984) Economic impact of returned emigrants: Evidence from Leiria, Mangualde and Sabugal, in M. Porto (ed) *Emigração e Retorno na Região Centro*, Coimbra, CCRC.

Carr, R. and Fusi, P. (1979) *Spain: Dictatorship to Democracy*, London, Allen and Unwin.

Courtot, R. (1978) Geographie des investissements industriels recents en Espagne, *Méditerranée*, 4.

Cuadrado Roura, J.R. (1981) Los flujos financieros interregionales, in R. Acosta España et al (ed) *La España de Las Autonomías*, Madrid, Espasa-Calpe.

Cuadrado Roura, J.R., Granados, V. and Aurioles, J. (1984) Technological dependency in a Mediterranean economy: The case of Spain, in A. Gillespe (ed), *Papers in Regional Science 12*, London, Pion, pp118–131.

Dokopoulou, E. (1983) Technology Transfer from Multinational Enterprises to Small Developing Countries, Paper presented to the Conference on Multinational Companies and the Third World, Birmingham, UK.

Edwards, A. (1979) *The New Industrial Countries and Their Impact on Western Manufacturing*, Economist Intelligence Unit, Special Report 73.

Evangelinides, M. (1979) Core-periphery problems in the Greek case, in D. Seers, B. Schaeffer and M.L. Kiljunen (eds), *Underdeveloped Europe*, Sussex, Harvester.

Ferrão, J. (1983) Alguns aspectos regionais da evolução recente da indústria transformada em Portugal, Paper presented to the III Coloquio Iberico de Geografia, Barcelona.

Ferrão, J. (1984) Regional variations in the rate of profit in manufacturing industry in Portugal, in R. Hudson and J.R. Lewis (eds) *Accumulation, Class and the State in Southern Europe*, London, Methuen.

Fröbel, F. (1982) The current development of the world economy, *Review*, 5, pp507–555.

Fröbel, F., Heinrichs, J. and Kreye, O. (1980) *The New International Division of Labour*, Cambridge University Press.

Fuà, G. (1980) *Problemi Dello Svilippo Tardivo in Europa*, Bologna, Il Mulino.

Fuà, G. (1983) Main Features of the NEC (North-East and Centre) Model, Paper presented to the Conference on Rural Entrepreneurial Capacities, Senigallia, Italy.

Garofoli, G. (1981) Lo sviluppo delle 'aree periferiche' nell' economia italiania degli ani settante, *L'industria*, Vol. 2, pp391–404.

Garofoli, G. (1982) Areas of Specialised Production and Small Firms in Europe, Paper presented to the Conference on National and Regional Development in the Mediterranean Basin, Durham, UK.

Garofoli, G. (1983a) Uneven Regional Development and Industrial Restructuring:

The Italian Pattern in the 1970s, Paper presented to the Conference on European Integration, Naxos, Greece.

Garofoli, G. (ed) (1983b) *Industrializzazione diffusa in Lombardia*, Franco Angeli Editore.

Gianntsis, T. (1983) *I Ellenkiti Viomihansa*, Athens, Gutenberg.

Hadjimichalis, C. (1981) *The Geographical Transfer of Value*, PhD Thesis, UCLA.

Hebbert, M. and Alonso Teixedor, L.F. (1982) Regional planning in Spain and the transition to democracy, in R. Hudson, and J.R. Lewis (eds) *Regional Planning in Europe*, Pion.

Hudson, R. and Lewis, J.R. (1982) The Regional Problem in the Enlarged European Community, Paper presented to the Conference of the Institute of British Geographers, Southampton, UK.

International Labour Office (1979) *Employment and Basic needs in Portugal*, Geneva, ILO.

Judet, P. (1980) O desenvolvimento da indústria siderurgica no Mediterrâneo, *Economia e Socialismo*, Vols. 46/47, pp59–74.

King, R. (1981) Italy, in H. Clout (ed) *Regional Development in Western Europe*, 2nd edition, Chichester, Wiley.

Leontidou-Emmanuel, L. (1981) *Working Class and Land Allocation: The Urban History of Athens, 1880–1980*, PhD thesis, London School of Economics.

Lewis, J.R. (1983) Regional policy and planning, in S. Bornstein, D. Held and J. Krieger (eds) *The State in Capitalist Europe*, London, Allen and Unwin.

Lewis, J.R. and Williams, A.M. (1981) Regional uneven development on the European periphery: the case of Portugal, *Tijdschrift voor Economische en Sociale Geografie* Vol. 72, pp86–88.

Lewis, J.R. and Williams, A.M. (1982) Desenvolvimento regional desequilibrado em Portugal: Situação actual e impacto provável da adessão à CEE, *Desenvolvimento Regional*, No. 14/15, pp71–139.

Linge, G.J.R. and Hamilton, F.E.I. (1981) International industrial systems, in F.E.I. Hamilton and G.J.R. Linge (eds) *Spatial Analysis, Industry and the Industrial Environment*, Vol. II, Wiley.

Lipietz, A. (1983) Sur les Fordismes peripheriques de l'Europe du Sud, Paper presented to the Conference on European Integration, Naxos, Greece.

Mandel, E. (1978) *The Second Slump*, London, New Left Books.

Mouzelis, N. (1978) *Modern Greece: Facets of Underdevelopment*, London, Macmillan.

Murolo, A. (1982) The Greek economy: The role of the transnationals and the EEC, *Mezzogiorno d'Europa*, Vol. 2, pp197–220.

Nikolinakos, M. (1984) Transnationalisation of production, location of industry and the deformation of regional development: The case of Greece, in R. Hudson and J.B. Lewis (eds) *Accumulation, Class and the State in Southern Europe*, London, Methuen.

Paine, S.H. (1979) Replacement of the West European migrant labour system by investment in the European Periphery, in D. Seers, B. Schaeffer and M.L. Kiljunen (eds) *Underdeveloped Europe*, Sussex, Harvester.

Paine, S.H. (1981) International investment, migration and finance: Issues and policies, in J.A. Girão (ed) *Southern Europe and the Enlargement of the EEC*, Lisbon, Economia.

Pinnaro, G. and Pugliese, E. (1979) Changes in the social structure of southern Italy, *International Journal of Urban and Regional Research*, Vol. 3, pp492–515.

Pugliese, E. (1984) Farm workers in Italy: Agricultural working class, landless peasants or clients of the welfare state?, in R. Hudson and J.R. Lewis (eds), *Accumulation, Class and the State in Southern Europe*, London, Methuen.

Ramos, M.H. (1980) Sistema integrada de incentivos ao investimento, *Desenvolvimento Regional*, Vol. 10, pp103–131.

Ronzani, S. (1980) Regional incentives in Italy, in D. Yuill, K. Allen and C. Hull (eds) *Regional Policy in the European Community*, London, Croom Helm.

Schlupp, F. (1980) Modell Deutschland and the international division of labour, in E. Krippendorff and V. Rittberger (eds), *The Foreign Policy of West Germany*, New York, Sage.

Stathakis, G. (1983) *Industrial Development and the Regional Problem: The Case of Greece*, PhD Thesis, University of Newcastle-upon-Tyne.

Tsoukalis, L. (1981) *The European Community and its Mediterranean Enlargement*, London, Allen and Unwin.

Vaitsos, C. (1982) Transnational corporate behaviour and the enlargement, in D. Seers and C. Vaitsos (eds) *The Second Enlargement of the EEC*, Macmillan.

World Bank (1981) *International migrant workers remittances: Issues and prospects*, World Bank.

World Bank (1982) *World Development Report 1982*, Oxford University Press.

World Bank (1983) *World Development Report 1983*, Oxford University Press on behalf of the World Bank.

Yannopoulos, G. (1979) The effects of full membership on the manufacturing industries, in L. Tsoukalis (ed) *Greece and the European Community*, Saxon House.

CHAPTER EIGHT

URBANIZATION: GROWTH, PROBLEMS AND POLICIES

J. Gaspar

1. Introduction[1]

Southern Europe has its own specific urban characteristics which are, on the one hand, part of its historical past and, on the other, the result of the recent urbanization process. This process is a fundamental component of the social and economic transformations experienced by these countries during the last 30 years. Preindustrial settlement in southern European countries had a large number of centres with urban or quasi-urban characteristics, which later evolved rapidly with the onset of industrialization, and which play an important role in determining the nature of contemporary urban networks. Late industrialization, which was not simultaneous in the different southern European countries, led to an urban explosion in the twentieth century, particularly after World War II (see Table 1.4). This recent urban development shows distinctive features, both in relation to the more developed countries, which industrialized earlier, and to other recently industrialized countries (NIC's), as well as developing countries. Distinctiveness also stems from the fact that dictatorial regimes prevailed in Portugal, Spain and partly Greece, during their years of most rapid economic and urban expansion. The present urban system represents the combination, sometimes conflicting and sometimes harmonious, of the forces generated by these two sources: this historical heritage and recent industrialization.

The wave of urbanization which occurred during the last 30 years in southern Europe is not just to be observed in urban expansion in these countries. For many people urbanization was linked with emigration to the

more developed European countries (reflected in total population changes
— see Table 8.1): first were the Italians immediately after World War II,
followed by the Spaniards and later the Greeks, Portuguese, Yugoslavs and
Turks. This particular form of urbanization sometimes had contradictory
results: on the one hand, immigrants added to the urban populations of the
recipient countries, sometimes even contributing to revitalization of the
degraded central areas of large cities but, on the other hand, when the
emigrants returned to their homeland, 'ruralization' could often be
observed. There may be a revitalization of rural areas as a result of the
inflow of funds (both occasional investments and regular transfers). This
process does not usually change the productive base of the rural settlements
but it has significant consequences for social behaviour and may influence
the future pattern of development (see Chapter 6).

Another implication of emigration is that returnees may settle in towns or
cities instead of their villages of origin. This phenomenon is most important
in Greece and is also significant in Spain and Italy, but is less marked in
Portugal where the majority of emigrants return to their area of origin.
There are exceptions to this pattern in Portugal and recent evidence shows
that some returnees settle in urban centres (Boura et al 1984), perhaps
because they are perceived as being more suitable for investment or because
they have children of school age. However, ruralization probably remains the
dominant trend and in this Portugal is exceptional. The trend may be
accounted for by the considerable efforts made to provide sanitation, electrifi-
cation, access roads, schools and health facilities in small villages (which,
only 15 years ago could have been expected to become totally depopulated).

Urbanization also has to be interpreted as part of the process of development which, in southern Europe, particularly after World War II, has been
associated with strong territorial and social imbalances in these countries.
These spatial imbalances, which are both interregional and intraregional,
frequently correspond to deep distortions in the urban systems, often
characterized by urban primacy (see Table 8.2) — in some cases at the
national level (Greece and Portugal) and in others at the subnational level
(Italy and Spain) (Lagopoulos 1971; Evangelinides 1979; Gaspar 1980a,
1980b; Burgel 1981; Ceccarelli 1981; Lewis and Williams 1981; Gaspar
1981a; Papayannis 1981; Ponsetti-Bosch 1981).

Although there is a certain common identity of process and form which
may be observed in Southern Europe there are characteristics specific to
each country, strongly correlated with their different stages of economic,
social and political development and different historical experiences.

Table 8.1 Population growth

Country	Crude birth rate per '000 population		Crude death rate per '000 population		Total fertility rate	Average annual growth of population (%)		Projected population (Millions)	
	1960	1978	1960	1978	1978	1960–70	1970–80	1990	2000
Greece	19	15	8	9	2.3	0.5	0.9	10	11
Italy	18	13	10	9	1.9	0.6	0.6	59	61
Portugal	24	18	8	10	2.5	-0.2	1.3	11	11
Spain	21	18	9	8	2.6	1.1	1.0	41	43

Source: World Bank (1982).

Table 8.2   Growth of major metropolitan areas (MAs)

Country	Average annual growth rate of largest MA (%)			Population of largest MA as a percentage of urban population[1]
	1950–1960	1960–1970	1970–1975	
Greece	3.0	3.2	2.1	54
Italy	2.2	2.1	1.7	16
Portugal	1.9	1.9	2.1	51
Spain	3.4	3.4	2.8	15

Note: [1] Latest available year.
Source: Gaspar (1981a).

2. Postwar urbanization

In 1980, official estimates of the levels of urbanization in southern Europe varied between 31 percent (Portugal) and 74 percent (Spain) of total population, with Italy and Greece at 60 percent and 62 percent respectively (Table 8.3). However, these estimates are only of relative interest because the national calculations are based on different criteria. For example, if the criteria applied to Portugal was adapted to take into account the country's settlement structure (and set at 2,000 instead of 10,000 population), then urbanization would be calculated at about 50 percent, which is probably a more realistic assessment. In Portugal most of the centres with less than 10,000 inhabitants and more than 2,000 inhabitants have industrial commercial and service functions which mark them as 'urban'.

The first major trend to note is that, in the 1970s, the three less urbanized countries registered high annual average population growth rates, with a maximum of 2.9 percent in Portugal and 2.6 percent and 2.2 percent in Greece and Spain. Italy had the lowest annual growth, 1.3 percent, which was less than the rates registered during the 1950s and 1960s. In fact, there was a tendency for urbanization rates to be lower in the 1970s compared to the two previous decades in all these countries, except Portugal (Table 8.3).

Another component of the urbanization process was an increase in regional imbalances and, in Portugal and Greece, the accentuation of urban primacy. In both countries it would actually be more accurate to speak of bipolar development around two metropolitan areas: Lisbon and Oporto in Portugal, Athens and Thessaloniki in Greece. The general tendency towards regional imbalance began to slow down in the mid 1970s, especially in Italy (Balbo et al 1980) and Spain, as was demonstrated by a decrease in

Table 8.3   Urban population characteristics

Country	Urban population as a percentage of total population		Average annual growth rate (%)		Percentage of urban population				Number of cities with over 500,000 persons	
					In largest city		In cities of over 500,000 persons			
	1960	1980	1960–70	1970–80	1960	1980	1960	1980	1960	1980
Greece	43	62	2.6	2.6	51	57	51	70	1	2
Italy	59	69	1.5	1.3	13	17	46	52	7	9
Portugal	23	31	1.3	2.9	47	44	47	44	1	1
Spain	57	74	2.6	2.2	13	17	37	44	5	6

Source: World Bank (1982).

the power of attraction of large cities and the emergence of new types of urban patterns based on smaller centres. Similar processes can also be observed in Portugal (Gaspar 1981b) and, to a lesser extent, in Greece (Papayannis 1981), although the growth of smaller centres did not surpass that of larger centres in these cases.

This new process is mainly related to the convergence of two interrelated phenomena: the reduction of migratory flows, both abroad and internally, and development of more spatially diffuse industrialization based on small and medium sized enterprises, frequently located in rural areas (see Chapter 7). This trend, which has parallels in more advanced economies, has been accompanied by a similar process in tertiary activities. Other explanatory factors include the rate of financial transfers to less developed regions, both internally (pensions, unemployment pay) and externally (emigrant remittances— see Chapter 6), the widespread growth of tourist facilities and the desire to escape some of the negative externalities of life in the larger cities.

The process of diffuse industrialization has been subject to many studies, especially in Italy (Bini 1976; Bagnasco 1977, 1981; Garofoli 1978, 1983; Fuá 1980) and more recently in Spain (Vasquez Barquero 1983). No attempt has yet been made to evaluate its overall influence on the urban system or to devise adequate planning policies to manage this kind of counterurbanization. If the trends continue during the remainder of this decade, which is likely given economic prospects, then serious problems may develop in the expanded smaller settlements with respect to infrastructure and social equipment. Scarcities may arise in the recently 'urbanized' areas alongside obsolescence in the larger urban agglomerations. However, if only the metropolitan areas, rather than the urban system in total is considered, dynamic growth was still evident in each of the four countries until at least 1975. Despite having annual rates of growth which were lower than those of the 1960s (excepting Lisbon), the largest metropolitan areas in each country still experienced notable growth between 1970 and 1975 (Table 8.2).

Although there are these common features of urbanization in southern Europe, there are also individual characteristics. In Italy, there was intense migration to the north during the period of most rapid industrialization, the 1950s and 1960s, but in the 1970s there was a tendency for greater stability in interregional movements. Recently, the larger cities have ceased to be poles of attraction while their surrounding regions have absorbed more population. Currently this process is more marked in the north, where small and medium sized cities and towns have expanded, producing spatially and functionally coherent urban networks. In the south, as a result of the development of specialized and isolated centres, such as the growth poles created by State policy in the *Mezzogiorno* or coastal tourist areas, loose-knit and poorly integrated urban networks have been established (Balbo et al 1980).

In Spain urban development since the 1950s has been closely linked with industrial development and modernization processes in the country. Modernization is important because it has affected agriculture, government administration and the service sectors as well as industry. Consequently in addition to urban growth in industrial areas, there has also been expansion in provincial capitals and in areas where commercial and service activities are concentrated. At the interregional level, a major factor has been population changes in the South (Andalusia and Extremadura), in the Centre (Castille and Leon) and in Galicia. Generally speaking, these rural areas (excepting some pockets along the Mediterranean coast or small areas of industrial development) lost population to Catalonia (especially Barcelona), Madrid and the Basque region. Growth was also registered, although less intensively, in the main cities in Levante (Valencia, Alicante and Castellon), Navarre and the Balearics, Seville and Zaragossa, tourist zones such as the Canary Islands, and Mediterranean and Atlantic Andalusia (Cadiz and Huelva in the latter case). During the 1970s an important change occurred: growth in the major cities started to slow down whereas the populations of medium sized cities began to stabilize and even to grow. Some traditional regional migration flows continued, especially to Catalonia, the Basque

Country, Madrid and Seville but, generally, only the interior areas (Castille, Leon, Extremadura and some interior provinces in Andalusia) stagnated or lost population. Demographic increases were registered in the other regions and the islands which, in turn, corresponded to a growth in provincial capitals and other cities (Ocaña 1979; Ponsetti-Bosch 1981).

Urbanization in Greece has centred on Athens and Thessaloniki where, in 1980, 70 percent (57 and 13 percent respectively) of the urban population was located. Some other cities have experienced significant growth, particularly those based on industry, transportation (Volos, Patras, Cavala), tourism (Heraklion) or agriculture (Larissa). However, of the southern European countries, Greece displays the greatest regional imbalance. In the 1950s Athens had 18 percent of total population but in 1980 it accounted for 57 percent, and this is expected to increase even further (Burgel 1981; Papayannis 1981).

In Portugal there was a substantial and widespread decrease in rural population between 1950 and 1970, surpassing 50 percent in several municipalities. In contrast, there were population increases in the main urban areas, especially in the Lisbon and Oporto areas, whilst there were lesser increases in small and medium sized towns. In 1980 the metropolitan areas of Lisbon and Oporto were estimated to account for nearly 40 percent of the country's population. However, during the 1970s, and particularly after 1975, all urban centres increased in population, even in the most remote areas; to some extent, this was due to the arrival of *retornados* from the African colonies. Nevertheless, the most significant trend was the increasing imbalance between the western coastal strip (extending from Braga in the North to Setúbal in the South) and the remainder of the country. This region, which covers only 32.5 percent of the area of the country, contained 72.8 percent of the population in 1980. The autonomous regions of Madeira and the Azores have their own distinct urbanization processes. In Madeira, there is only one city — Funchal — which has close to half the region's population and practically all of its urban functions, while in the Azores there is more balanced development amongst the three main urban centres, located on different islands (Gaspar 1980a, 1980b, 1981b; Lewis and Williams 1981).

3. Urban social movements

Since the late 1960s the urban process in most industrialized capitalist countries has been significantly influenced by urban social movements, somewhat disconnected from the main social movements related to the class struggle against capital. This new type of urban struggle was often interclass and polarized around issues of reproduction, usually housing and service provision by local government agencies. The specificity of these movements is synthesized by Castells (1975b, p7) as '. . . systèmes de pratiques sociales contradictoires qui remettent en cause l'ordre établi à partir des contradictions spécifiques de la problématique urbaine'.

Some commentators consider that urban social movements cannot be understood outside the broader context of the labour struggle. Della Seta (1978) points out that, in Italy, urban struggles have always been at the centre of the postwar workers' movement. Certainly urban social movements represent a new postwar development and are obviously the result of the overall economic, social and political processes in the capitalist city. As Santos (1983) stresses, the simple Marxist distinction between primary and secondary contradictions is no longer acceptable, at least in the advanced capitalist countries. The experience of the last decade shows that sometimes the secondary contradictions can generate more active mass movements: in most advanced capitalist countries, and also in the more developed Mediterranean countries (Italy and Spain), the contradictions which developed in housing and the supply of social services have been more acute than the direct contradiction between capital and labour. It is possible to argue that urban political movements have been one of the main features of urban social dynamics from the end of the 1960s up to the middle of the 1970s and that the events of May 1968 in France were the starting point for these. In Spain and, to a lesser extent, Portugal, these movements were also an important focus of opposition to nonrepresentative government.

For reasons associated with internal economic, social and political processes, Italy has been the Mediterranean country where urban struggles have been most advanced. In the other three southern European countries the same type of movement did emerge, but later, and only after the fall of their dictatorial regimes. During the dictatorships there had been several struggles against the political system and these were mainly based in the cities. Their immediate roots can be linked to the overall political movements which developed from the late 1960s, both in terms of external relations and of the social classes which supported them: the industrial proletariat and the new urban petite bourgeoisie. However, the immediate targets of these early movements were different, being orientated directly against the ruling powers and often focussing on specific national issues, such as the colonial wars of Portugal, the regional question of Spain and, to a certain extent, the Cyprus question in Greece.

In Spain the urban social movements began to be structured by the end of the 1960s with the emergence of neighbourhood associations (*asociaciones de vecinos*), the formation of which had been legally recognized in 1964. Sometimes the origins of the neighbourhood associations lay in local cultural or religious organizations which had mainly social preoccupations (Bier 1979). These associations, which nowadays represent one of the more important type of social movements, involving hundreds of thousands of dwellers, have appeared in many Spanish cities, though they are most active in Barcelona. Their role increased after the death of Franco and especially after the shift to democratic conditions (Castells 1978). Since 1969 the targets for these movements have been broadly similar (better housing, lower rents or prices, adequate or simple provision of infrastructure and equipment), but their strategies have changed. In many instances the neighbourhood associations managed to intervene in the preparation of urban plans and programmes, often making significant alterations and improvements and becoming a leading element in the planning process itself (Puig 1974; Borja 1977; Bier 1979).

Spanish urban social movements are often interclass but the *asociaciones de vecinos* exhibit many differences in their social composition, goals and political involvement. In the early stages some associations were created by the municipal authorities, sometimes in opposition to 'popular' associations created by residents who opposed the dictatorial regime (Bier 1979). Castells (1978) shows that there were seven types of neighbourhood associations in Madrid, with different social compositions and different demands: shanty town associations which were more involved in the solution of housing problems and local scarcities of basic equipment; provisional housing associations with similar aims; public housing movements, interested in housing improvements and rent levels; privately promoted associations, in the city or suburbs, demanding adequate sanitation and schools, and better transport both public and private; exclusive middle and upper middle class residential neighbourhood associations, struggling for promotion of social and cultural activities; and 'downtown' associations which, since 1975, opposed the transformation of city centres.

In Italy since 1969 and in the other countries since the fall of the dictatorships, the urban movements have mostly developed around the question of housing scarcities, the need for better social infrastructure or lower prices for social services (see Chapter 3). In Italy, the different targets of these social and political movements can be seen in a temporal sequence

(Marcelloni 1979). The first period, 1969–1970, was characterized by occupation of dwellings in older buildings, often subject to speculation. These movements, which were most clearly observable in Rome, were directed mainly by traditional political forces, namely the PCI, the PSIUP, and some left-wing catholics. The second period, 1971–1972, saw a division between the 'old' and the 'new' left, and an important role was played by forces like *Potere Operario*, *Lotta Continua* and *Il Manifesto*, who developed new squatting operations and defended earlier occupations; they sometimes caused confrontations and the PCI was the main target of their political attacks. In the third period, 1972–1973, the *comitati di quartieri* appeared, corresponding to a greater degree of implantation and organization of urban movements. Their efforts were more orientated to improvement of services and the creation of more social equipment, thereby enlarging the content of the housing struggles. After the rise in oil prices, most struggles focussed upon the rising prices of public services, transport, electricity and telephones, but, as early as 1974, housing occupations again increased, spreading to all major cities: there were 5,000 occupations in Rome alone and significant occupations in Milan, Turin, Naples, Florence, and other cities (Bagnasco et al 1979; Marcelloni 1979; Lagana et al 1982).

In Spain, urban political and social movements were less orientated towards conflict than in Italy, and corresponded more to a general increase in social demands for public services and to development of local political organizations.

In Portugal the revolutionary period, 1974–1975, witnessed a climax of urban struggles, accompanied by the appearance of revolutionary agrarian movements; together these accomplished large numbers of popular occupations, both of dwellings and of large estates. In both cases there was clear and sometimes active support from elements in the Armed Forces Movement (see Chapter 4) but the involvement of political forces was different in the housing and land occupations: the Communist Party (PCP) was deeply involved in the agrarian struggles, especially in the South, but it was cautious and even suspicious in the case of the urban struggles (Dows et al 1978; Leitão et al 1978).

Urban political movements in Portugal, in the period 1974–1975, can be divided into two main types. One, controlled and organized by the Communist Party, was orientated both towards the general demands of the working class and to the overall political trajectory of the revolution whilst another involved, in different proportions in different situations, all the forces to be found on the extreme left (from the Stalinists and the Maoists to the left-wing Catholics) and, in some cases, the Communist Party and some elements of the Socialist Party. The urban social movements mainly originated in the struggle for decent housing immediately after April 25 1974. By May 1974 there were already some state housing schemes which had been occupied by inhabitants from the shanties, and the peak of the urban movement — as measured by housing occupations — occurred in February 1975.

There were many cases of opportunism in the occupations: a well-known case occurred in Setúbal (a city in the Lisbon Metropolitan Area) where much of the squatting was undertaken by those who were not in need (Dows et al 1978). Several occupations were undertaken by the middle class who frequently succeeded in obtaining better houses with smaller rents. The inhabitants of the shanties generally were not involved in squatting; they preferred to cooperate with the SAAL process (which provided technical support for self-help schemes) and with the municipalities in order to obtain houses. By the end of 1976 the urban movements were in decline and a large part of the neighbourhood associations formed during the revolutionary period folded or went into decline, although their role was legally recognized by the 1976 Constitution. After this the organization of local power through local elections increased so that the major political parties played the dominant role (see Chapter 4). Most of the housing occupations occurred in the Lisbon Metropolitan Area, but a significant number occurred in the Oporto Metropolitan Area, and a few in other towns and cities. The occupations were concentrated in three types of building:

1. Old buildings, unoccupied and awaiting demolition for speculative reasons, mostly in central Lisbon.
2. New buildings in public housing schemes, not yet distributed and frequently not even completed; there were extreme cases of the base shells of houses being occupied.
3. Occupations of a number of recently-built private houses, although these were less numerous than the other types.

Whilst squatting has been the most evident and perhaps most political action among the 'nonpolitical' urban movements, others were also significant, especially the struggle for improvements in social equipment and infrastructure (such as transport, leisure space, children's nurseries, homes for the elderly) and, in the shanty areas or in the illegally built areas, for basic infrastructural provision, such as metalled roads, water supply, and garbage collection. However, housing demand has always been the major issue.

The experience of SAAL (*Serviço Ambulatório de Apoio Local* — Ambulatory Service for Local Support) in Portugal has been both interesting and controversial (Ferreira 1975; Leitão et al 1978; Dows 1980). SAAL was created during the early stages of the revolution to act as a link between government structures and the organized local movements in poor residential areas — either the shanties or old degraded urban neighbourhoods. A technical team was assigned to each problem area to work with the active involvement of the local populace on the solution of local residential difficulties. The most important initiatives were the construction of welfare housing through local housing cooperatives. However, at the end of the revolutionary period SAAL lapsed and very few of its initiatives have been even partially completed: the most important were in Lisbon (new welfare housing) and in Oporto (renewal of a small part of the most degraded zone in the old city). Curiously, in the different political context of the 1980s some of the SAAL projects have eventually been implemented in order to rehouse shanty populations.

In the second half of the 1970s there has been a decline in, if not the death of, urban social movements in all four countries, particularly in Italy and Portugal. This coincides with the increasing role of left-wing groups, namely the Communist and Socialist parties, in local politics, and their ability to control and direct social demands in the urban environment, particularly in the larger centres where the urban movements had been more active. Gradually, the most important cities in the four countries, with the exception of the two largest Portuguese urban areas, have become controlled by the left, either by individual parties or by coalitions. The exceptions of Lisbon and Oporto are relative for the suburban municipalities are, to a large extent, controlled by the left, usually the Communist Party in the Lisbon Metropolitan Areas and the Socialist Party in some of the Oporto suburbs.

There are different views concerning interpretation of the achievements of the urban social movements of the 1970s and late 1960s. There is one point of agreement: these movements, besides initiating improvements in living conditions among the most disfavoured classes, contributed in many cases to a reshaping of the process of urban development. Even if many problems still need to be solved, there was improvement of housing conditions and of access to basic infrastructure and social equipment. In all four countries it also became common practice in several urban centres for the population to participate in the decision-making process and in exercising some control over urban planning.

A more controversial issue relates to the overall political consequences of these movements (the Italian case must be analysed separately). In the countries where democracy has only recently been restored, the urban movements represented an important experience and contributed to consolidation of the political process. Moreover, in the Spanish case, as Castells (1978) indicates, neighbourhood association movements contributed to the crisis of Francoism. Borja (1977, p203) has also argued that urban movements became an important crisis factor in the political structures of Spain, '. . . through them the population exercises rights, creates organizations, expresses forcible demands and finds the institutional system unable to provide adequate responses or even a framework for their reception. Since such movements are not easily suppressed (because of their broad social base, the legitimacy of demands, etc.) the consequence is an accentuation of the crisis of local government structures. Furthermore, urban social movements often influence internal contradictions within dominant social groups and even within political institutions themselves. The fight against general planning schemes, deficiencies of housing and services, corruption and speculation, etc., not only accentuates these internal contradictions but highlights the incapacity of the rigid and unrepresentative political system to allow them free expression and resolution. In short, we can say that urban movements have a markedly democratic nature and represent the democratic option in Spanish society. . . .' Urban movements had a similar if weaker role in Portugal and de Costa (1975) has indicated the broader political significance of the tenants' movements organized in public housing areas in the early 1970s to oppose increased rents and repressive housing management methods.

There are two different views of the Italian case, represented by Della Seta (1978) and by Marcelloni (1979). The first view emphasizes the important historical dimension which the workers' movements (parties and unions) gave to the urban struggles, transforming these into a vehicle for reform. The latter view highlights the importance of gains by left-wing parties in local government elections, although this can also be interpreted in two different ways. On the one hand, the Communist Party (PCI) experiences difficulties in the urban local authorities it controls, as a result of central government continuing to be dominated by the Christian Democrats. On the other hand, there tend to be fewer struggles when unemployment is rising, even though the scarcity of housing is increasing and the level of services offered at local level is decreasing; residents' demands are less militant and '. . . often strangled by the bureaucracy of the local committees . . .' Marcelloni (1979, p266).

Nevertheless, election of left-wing majorities on local councils in many cities represents a driving force in national, political and social processes, and may be more significant in the three countries which recently relinquished dictatorial regimes. The urban social movements which developed from the late 1960s to the mid-1970s may represent not the beginning of a new era, but the end of an old era (Ceccarelli 1982). In all four countries, forces opposed to the main left-wing parties joined the urban movements, whilst the electorate increasingly supported these parties because experience has shown this to be the most likely means to realize social demands at the local level.

In order to understand changing trends in social movements at the urban level one must keep in mind the changing economic context in which 'the demand for jobs becomes more flexible' and 'attitudes and expectations toward work have changed' '. . . this process of change and adjustment does not mean that the causes of conflict have disappeared. But the entire present situation is less rigid than a decade ago, and there is little chance that urban social conflicts may explode again in the near future with the support of large social groups' (Ceccarelli 1982, p274).

The increase in competence obtained by local authorities — the major demand of some movements — has also had important implications for urban social movements in general. According to Ceccarelli (1982), decentralization represents adaptation by the State to the new context in order to reduce potential conflict. As Santos (1983) stresses '. . . Besides ideological resources, other means can be activated in order to neutralize the consequences of the politicization of the urban crisis. One of these is regionalization and decentralization whereby political conflict with the central State is fragmented or atomized into several conflicts with the local authorities. . . .' However, there is a need to distinguish between decentralization to the regional level, which is usually a result of the development of a regional bourgeoisie, and decentralization to the local level (Gaspar 1982). The increase in local decision-making capacity may represent a dilution of conflict with the central State but it may also lead to increasing confrontation between the dominant class interests represented at each level.

4. Urban policies

Spain and Portugal (and to a lesser extent Greece) experienced their most rapid growth during periods of dictatorial government. This is important because although the fundamental causes of the crises in urban areas arose from the process of uneven urban and regional development, the prevalent political systems conditioned the response of the State to these crises. This is most clearly illustrated by Spain and Portugal which had dictatorial governments throughout the years of most rapid economic and urban change. In the case of Spain, Naylon (1981) has argued that the problems of Barcelona were particularly acute for massive immigration led to rapid expansion beyond the city's territorial limits. There were several attempts to provide a coherent plan or planning framework for the larger metropolitan areas, but these were thwarted by a central government fearful of any moves which might encourage Catalan nationalism. Instead new urban developments mushroomed on the periphery of Barcelona and these were poorly serviced and badly integrated into the larger urban system. This disregard of popular needs is partly accounted for by the high degree of centralization in the Spanish state, which allowed municipalities few resources and little freedom for initiative. It was also due to the insensitivity of Francoist institutions to the needs of urban residents (Borja 1977).

A similar insensitivity to basic needs can be seen in Portugal where migration brought about rapid expansion in Lisbon and Oporto, creating a housing 'crisis'. The private sector was totally incapable of providing adequate levels of housing for the low-income urban working classes, and the State made no real attempt to bridge this gap. The consequences were obvious — overcrowded inner city areas and shanty towns. It has been suggested by Lewis and Williams (1984) that the State response can be accounted for by a number of factors including: the lack of autonomy granted to the municipalities; the particular use of state housing for legitimation purposes; the calls on state resources for economic investments and, latterly, war expenditure. It was also due to the fact that the Salazarist State was able to ignore the effects of rising housing costs on wage levels, because the latter could be restrained through the use of other, repressive means. In short, the existence of dictatorial governments in both Spain and Portugal gave additional twists to their already serious urban problems.

With the end of dictatorial regimes in Portugal, Spain and Greece and ensuing legislative reforms, municipal authorities (the local State) gained more power and responsibility, and acquired stronger financial bases. The reforms had different historical courses and differed in their extent, developing further in Portugal than in Greece. However, the powers of local authorities in these countries to control urban development is limited, whether through passive controls (territorial planning, for example) or active means (improvement of urban land and control of production).

The major reasons for the weakness of many local administrations in the Mediterranean countries are limited finances and, in most cases, a scarcity of qualified technicians. To a certain extent these handicaps can be explained by the small sizes of the municipalities which are below the thresholds necessary for the development of basic planning and management structures. To try and overcome these problems an experiment was attempted in Portugal after 1976, whereby central government directly created teams to provide technical support for coherent groups of municipalities. Most of these teams, composed mainly of engineers, architects and other technical staff, eventually were to be transferred to local authority control. These teams have been useful in assisting small authorities with their programmes for infrastructure and equipment and, sometimes, with planning and housing. This measure has been complemented by special means for financing intermunicipal projects, which has encouraged the foundation of municipal associations.

There are both differences and similarities in the urban policies followed by southern European countries since World War II and in the results of these. Generally, all governments have tried to reduce spatial imbalances in development whereby some areas become virtually abandoned while large urban centres continue to grow, apparently uncontrollably. Idealistic policies to promote harmonious development were proposed but these were usually contradicted by actual State policies which intensified economic growth and favoured the large urban concentrations. In order to cope with rapid urban growth that sometimes reached chaotic proportions, all four countries tried to establish a series of planning measures (which were also idealistic) and the Master Plan emerged as a common approach. In a few cases, physical planning achieved some successes but it usually failed and problems continued to mount. In many cases urban plans actually made a negative contribution to urban development because they acted as the driving force in speculation. In addition, physical planning relied on slow and hierarchical administrative processes, the inefficiency of which induced investors to ignore the plans, thereby increasing confusion in urban areas. The more precise and complex the planning system aimed to be, the worse were the consequences. For example, the Spanish system, despite having recognized defects, is more flexible and simplified than the Portuguese, and has been better adapted to controlling the urban 'explosion'. In contrast excessive red-tape in the urban planning system in Portugal has been a critical factor in the growth of numerous, extensive illegal developments.

Given the negative experiences of the Master Plans, there have recently been attempts to develop alternative 'planning solutions', including different ways of financing urban development and, at the same time, establishing general rules for urban land production. This qualitative change is found in the so-called Land Laws: these were instituted in Spain in 1975 reformulated in 1976; adopted in Portugal in 1976 and in Italy in 1977.

5. Some urban issues

Since the 1970s many Mediterranean cities, especially the larger ones, have experienced grave management difficulties, mainly resulting from financial pressures. National adaptations to the economic crisis often resulted in increased difficulties for the largest cities. On one hand, the shift of private investments to rural areas and to small towns (the pattern of diffuse industrialization already noted) and, on the other hand, the decline of some basic industries located in the metropolitan areas (for example, the automobile industry in Torino, and shipbuilding and repair in Lisbon) both led to severe problems for the major urban centres. Besides increasing unemployment levels, the local authorities have also had to face high levels of social demand at a time when local financial resources have declined because of falling tax revenues both from labour and capital. The increasing role of the 'black' economy may have helped to reduce the real level of unemployment but it has not helped to solve the problems of local authorities in meeting rising social demands.

In the present situation it will be difficult for the major cities to ameliorate the decline in their economic bases, especially the industrial sector; even with a decrease in wage levels it would be difficult to attract new industries (outside the 'black' economy). This is because of the higher costs of the reproduction of labour power stemming from increased wages, the costs of land and infrastructure, and demands for greater environmental controls in view of the new catastrophic level of pollution in some southern European cities. Neither the State nor the local authorities are able to subsidize, via service provision, these higher costs. Therefore, substantial transformations of the economic bases of the larger cities will be necessary if they are to adjust their roles in the new emerging spatial system. This may mean greater emphasis on higher order tertiary activities and a decline in the traditional industrial bases.

Services and commerce have been and continue to be the fundamental bases of the economies of the Mediterranean countries' urban agglomerations. However, the industrial sector has constituted the main factor in urban growth and the most intensive periods of urbanization correspond to the periods of greatest industrial expansion. Industrialization has assumed a different character in each of the southern European countries. In some cases a single sector (for example the building industry), had had an extremely important role in the urban economy and become the driving force behind urban growth. In contrast, modernization of agriculture has had a two-fold effect on urban growth because, on the one hand, it frees labour for the urban sector and, on the other hand, rural areas support the urban centre through increasing demand for products and services. National and international tourism has also contributed to urban growth, not only in the tourist zones but indirectly in the main commercial and administrative centres, as well. The development characteristics of the southern European States shape their urban economies but, in turn, these are particularly sensitive to international conditions as a result of their dependence on imported energy, raw materials, emigrants' remittances, tourism, capital and technological transfers (see Chapter 1). More specifically, it can be stressed that many of the problems which southern European cities face are a result of the fragility of their economic bases, either because they are specialized in economic sectors depending on demand from the wealthier countries or because they are experiencing strong competition from the NIC's.

Housing needs

The intensive rural–urban migration witnessed after World War II is the main factor behind the housing problems faced by all southern European countries, though these problems are on different scales and have qualitative variations. The problems are most severe in Portugal, followed by Greece, whilst Spain and Italy are in relatively stronger positions (Gaspar 1980a; Santillana 1980; Ceccarelli 1981; Papayannis 1981).

Housing needs result not only from the absolute lack of housing but also from obsolescence and the uneven regional distribution of the existing stock. Considerable efforts have been made by the public sector in Italy and, to a lesser extent, in Spain and in Portugal, to increase the supply of new houses since the 1950s. This has partly been accomplished through a decline in building standards and, consequently, large proportions of recently-built housing in each of these three countries are already in need of repair or, in many cases, replacement. Another reason for obsolescence in recently-built housing is the large proportion of postwar dwellings constructed illegally, with little regard for basic requirements; this occurs in all four cases but is most extensive in Greece, the only country where, in practice, public housing hardly exists. Increasing obsolescence also stems from the system of rent control, amounting sometimes (for example, Portugal) to a total freeze which obviously discourages owners from financing improvements. Attempts have been made to change rent controls in order to attract more private investment to the rental market but potential investors are discouraged by other considerations: high interest rates, the costs of construction and of land, and the existence of more attractive investment alternatives, namely in speculative property.

Housing shortages tend to be greatest in the major cities, despite the concentration of the construction industry and of public housing in these areas. In Portugal, the present housing shortage is estimated to be about half a million dwellings of which 40,000 correspond to the need to replace shanties, which have increased in number recently, particularly around Lisbon. Greece, with a similar population to Portugal, has a larger housing stock and a much higher average annual construction rate so there is not the same chronic absolute shortage of housing. In both countries, the available supply of dwellings would have been even lower had it not been for the illegal housing sector; this provides relatively cheap housing, often constructed to reasonable standards, but lacking infrastructure which eventually will have to be provided at increased costs (Williams 1981). In Portugal illegal building in the last decade represents nearly 20 percent of the total housing stock and, since the freezing of private sector rents in 1974, represents the only significant addition to the rental market. A marked decrease in the housing deficit has been experienced in Spain, where estimates of the present shortage vary between 300,000 and 600,000 dwellings, compared with 1 million in 1961. This is mainly due to extensive building activity in the 1961–1967 period (Santillana 1980). Housing shortages in Italy are relatively smaller but are increasing due to obsolescence and to regional and social inequalities (with the South having the largest deficit).

Meanwhile, public participation in the supply of housing has decreased sharply. In Italy the share of housing directly built by the public sector fell from an annual average of 18 percent in the early 1950s to less than 3 percent in the 1970s (Ceccarelli 1981). In Portugal the 1980s average is much lower than the already insufficient level of 10 percent of new stock built by the public sector during the 1970s. In Spain there is also a tendency towards a sharp decrease in public sector participation, which fell from 8.1 to 4.9 percent , 1973–1976. In Greece the level of public housing has always been low, representing only 1.6 percent during the period 1970–1975.

The public sector can also contribute to housing programmes through the provision of low-interest loans. This policy is utilized in all four countries but is of least importance in Greece. With the deepening of the economic crisis in the late 1970s this kind of public participation has become less important; it is especially notable in Portugal, where the State's contribution to the costs of owner occupancy has already been drastically reduced during the early 1980s and will probably be subject to even stronger cuts.

In spite of several attempts to solve the problems of the housing sector, contradictions and the gap between demand and disposable supply are increasing. Families are decreasing in size but there is a demand for higher standards, and the lack of houses for the poorest is very serious and, in Portugal at least, is worsening. In all four countries demand for second homes is also increasing and attracting investments which are thereby removed from the market for permanently occupied homes. This implies an increase in social inequalities which, sometimes, may also be increasing regional imbalances.

An important factor explaining part, but not all, of the housing dilemma in these countries is the short supply of urbanized land (that is, having the necessary infrastructure). The scarcity of supply furthers speculation and is one of the causes of the growth of the illegal markets in land and housing (Romanos 1970; Berlinger and Della Seta 1976; Ministère des Travaux Publiques 1980; Williams 1981). The solution to this problem is more political than technical or managerial; the State, central or local, must control the use of land and, at the same time, develop the technical and financial capacity to promote and maintain basic infrastructural provision. In some cases, particularly in Portugal, this will be possible only through a reduction in the standards demanded by legislation and by more flexible land-use planning.

Need for basic infrastructure

The most acute deficits are in Greece, Athens showing alarming shortcomings with respect to sewage systems and the provision of open space. In Spain and Italy, the recent inversion of the urbanization process may result in equipment becoming obsolete in the large cities while there are increased needs in other areas. In Portugal, in spite of major efforts by local authorities since 1975, the infrastructural network is still far from satisfactory. The main constraints are in water supply and sewage networks, the scarcity of water in some regions (especially the Metropolitan Area of Lisbon) being near catastrophic.

Besides the basic infrastructure shortage, each day raises more serious questions concerning environmental deterioration and a decline in the quality of life. Pollution and other forms of environmental decay, including destruction of the cultural and natural heritage was initially most serious in large cities and in tourist resorts. However, they have now begun to threaten— through new forms and patterns of urbanization— the smaller and medium sized centres, including some of the most dynamic rural areas. The pattern of diffuse industrial development which arose with the economic crisis may also seriously reduce the quality of the local environment, exhausting the capacity of existing infrastructure and destroying local productive capacity (for example, in agriculture) through pollution.

Problems of urban transport

Foreseeable changes in the pattern of urbanization in the four Southern European countries may increase their already quite severe problems of public transport provision, especially in the major cities. In large urbanized areas public transport is frequently operated by public enterprises, registering high financial losses and needing massive central and local State subsidies.

In most cases, State contributions to urban public transport benefit the urban areas which have the most developed transport networks. In this way the State is supporting the classes who live in the large urban agglomerations. The recent tendency for diffuse industrialization in rural and less urbanized regions accentuates the disadvantages of industrial workers who live in these areas and are poorly served by local public transport. For example, reduced fares (social passes and weekly, monthly or seasonal tickets) are almost entirely restricted to the large urban agglomerations where there is to be found an increasing proportion of tertiary sector jobs and a falling proportion of working class employment.

In addition to the generally accepted policy of using public transport to attain social goals, other factors have accentuated its lack of profitability.

One is the fact that, in some urban areas, there are a number of operators functioning without coordinated schedules. Another, and more serious factor, arises from the patterns of urban growth in the last 30 years. Some illegal developments, particularly those on the outskirts of large cities, are located so far from the urban centres and are so poorly serviced by roads that they give rise to the least profitable public transport routes. Also, in contradiction to the overt aims of public policy, private car transport has been favoured by road building programmes. At present, with the energy crisis, there is a strong policy desire to substitute public transport for cars. This would greatly help the public transport sector as well as reducing the congestion and pollution problems associated with reliance on individual motor cars.

In Greece, urban public transport is usually privately owned; only in Athens is it in the public sector, being run by three public enterprises which, together, accumulate enormous annual deficits. In Italy about one half of the total annual public transport deficit is accounted for just by the agglomerations of Milan, Rome and Naples. In Portugal, the public transport deficit is also accounted for by the larger cities, particularly Lisbon. The underground *metro* (operating only over a limited range within Lisbon) alone accounted for 10 percent of the total public transport budget in 1980. There has been a tendency in some of the large cities of southern Europe to increase underground transport networks; for example, new underground railways are planned for Athens, Barcelona, Madrid, Seville and Valencia and expansion of the networks of Lisbon, Rome and Milan is already in progress. This tendency has been criticized by some specialists who argue that it would be less costly and more profitable (economically and socially) to improve public transport conditions on the surface (trains, buses, trams) and to give these priority over individual motor cars (Gaspar 1981a).

Urban legislation and territorial boundaries: adjustment to social and economic realities

The excessive rigidity and narrowness of much existing urban legislation causes controls to be ineffective and encourages illegal development which, tacitly may be accepted by both central and local authorities. Such an atmosphere is propitious for corruption so that inefficient control may have extremely high indirect costs. The most visible consequence of the lack of respect for urban legislation is illegal developments which have come to represent an important part of the growth of some urban agglomerations.

Laws may be disregarded in many ways, and not only by the promoters-speculators. Frequently, the administration itself is the culprit: for example, local administrative procedures can cause excessive delays in drawing up and approving plans which may therefore not be completed before their legal deadlines.

Among the main deficiencies contained in legislation are:

1. Lack of coordination between the law and social and economic realities.
2. Slowness and rigidity of review and decision-making processes precisely as a result of the existence of unwieldly legislation.
3. Unjust allocations of resources arising from, and firmly entrenched in, general and partial urban plans.
4. The absence of well-defined implementation policies.
5. Lack of the means to permit interdepartmental coordination in the public sector.

Jurisdictional fragmentation at the metropolitan level also gives rise to various problems, the most serious being the difficulty or nonexistence of overall planning for land use, services, and development of the local economy. In addition, fragmentation of authority among a number of government entities creates inequalities in the receipts and expenditures of municipalities, thus giving rise to social and economic disparities. This further complicates attempts to coordinate activities at the metropolitan level. The fragmentation and weakness of local authorities permits one major municipality, usually the central city, to control overall metropolitan development and 'export' its problems to peripheral areas. Moreover, the southern European States have centralized administrations and these have usually favoured the central city, especially when it is the capital of the country. This increases conflicts of various types between the central State and the local authorities themselves.

The southern European countries are at different stages of institutional evolution in terms of their ability and skill to manage metropolitan areas. In Greece and Portugal there are functional metropolitan areas without any institutionalization; in Italy and in Spain these areas are institutionalized, even though planning may not be very effective.

6. Conclusion

Different degrees of economic development and urbanization may be observed among the four southern European countries, Italy and Portugal representing the extreme cases. The different level of economic development reached by each country is reflected in distinctive types and forms of urbanization. The lower the level of economic development, the greater the tendency towards imbalance in the urban network and the less the capacity to control this through the planning process. Illegal urban forms are also more evident in these situations, as are marginal forms of housing; in significant terms, slums only exist in Portugal whilst control over illegal development is most efficient in Spain and Italy.

Urbanization has displayed different forms in response to the onset of the present economic crisis. In the two more developed countries, Italy and Spain, a process similar to that in the more industrialized countries is occurring. The large cities cease to grow, cases of urban decline can even be observed, whilst in some areas (Valencia, Murcia and Alicante among others) diffuse urbanization can be found, with the urbanization of villages and growth of small towns; this is correlated with the expansion of small and medium-sized industrial production units, one of the important components here being the segmentation of the production process (Bagnasco 1977; Garofoli 1978, 1983; Balbo et al 1980; Vasquez Barquero 1983). In Greece and in Portugal, which in urban terms are strongly primate countries, the major metropolitan areas (Athens and Lisbon) have not stopped growing, but diffuse urbanization is evident, especially in Portugal.

The growth of urbanization which may be observed outside the larger urban areas, although perhaps representing an adaptation to the crisis (with corresponding savings of energy, infrastructure, housing, and even some equipment), may also indicate a movement towards restructuring of the settlement system to fit new social and economic realities. This may be summarized in the debate between the 'technological revolution' and the 'ecological revolution', but it may also be the least expensive way for the capitalist system to adjust to the crisis.

Although the patterns of urbanization observed recently in the four case studies show a tendency towards greater uniformity than is to be found amongst the more industrialized countries, their specificities, either in terms of development or of a differentiated urban culture, will give rise to distinctive forms of evolution in the short and medium term. It must also be stressed that future urbanization trends will be closely linked to foreseeable trends in the world economy. Energy will be especially important as the four countries are largely dependent on imports. In many respects trends already observed since the early 1970s (and noted above) are a consequence of the energy crisis and the overall economic depression.

With regard to the foreseeable common prospects of urbanization in the four countries, it can be argued that no large scale urban development is likely to occur; the idea of major new towns and growth poles seems to have been abandoned, the Sines project in southern Portugal being the newest venture and already apparently a failure. The larger cities will probably not exhibit growth: on the contrary, in some cases stagnation or even decline can be expected, especially in the major Italian and Spanish metropolitan centres. In contrast, some environmentally attractive areas, will continue to attract small and medium-sized industrial units, supporting, on one hand, development of small and medium-sized cities and, on the other, promoting counterurbanization or diffuse urbanization.

Recent trends in urbanization also suggest there will be urban development on the rural fringes of some metropolitan areas, especially where there exists a peasantry already articulated with the urban industrial-economy, either through the labour market or through the agricultural market. This may represent the rise of a new pattern of metropolitanization, more fluid, more hierarchical and probably (at least in the short run) with lower management costs and fewer negative externalities.

Significant growth will occur in the main metropolitan areas of the less urbanized of the four countries, Portugal, as well as in Thessaloniki and probably in southern Italy. In spite of vigorous measures undertaken recently, the important regional role of Athens in the eastern Mediterranean may jeopardize attempts to control its growth. In the Portuguese case, the deepening economic and financial crisis may contribute to the return (already noticeable) of shanty development, especially in the Lisbon city and metropolitan areas, accompanied by an increase in the 'black' economy.

Another negative prospect for the near future in some of the major cities is further obsolescence of the inner areas. In some cases this degradation may be accompanied by the growth of foreign ghettos, which may also develop in marginal localities on the periphery. There are already some examples in Italy (with North African, Somalian and Eritrean concentrations amongst others), in Portugal (Cape Verdians) and in Spain (Portuguese, partly of Gipsy origin).

[1] The author is grateful to C. Jensen-Butler for comments on this text.

References

Bagnasco, A. (1977) *Tre Italie. La Problematica Territoriale Dello Sviluppo Italiano*, Bologna, Il Mulino.

Bagnasco, A. (1981) Labour market, class structure and regional formations in Italy, *International Journal of Urban and Regional Research*, Vol. 5, pp40–44.

Bagnasco, C., Baldi, P. and Grasso, F. (1979) *Partecipazione e Territorio*, Florence, La Nuova Italia.

Balbo, M., Ceccarelli, P. and Ponti, M. (1980) *Tentencias Actuales de los Processos de Urbanization en Italia*, Comision de Planeamiento y Coordination del Area Metropolitana de Madrid.

Berlinguer, G. and Della Seta, P. (1976) *Borgate di Roma*, Rome, Editori Riuniti.

Bier, A.G. (1979) 'Vox Populi': El desarrollo de las Asociaciones de Vecinos en España, Naples, Papers, Vol. 11, pp169–183.

Bini, P.C. (1976) *Economia Periferica e Classi Sociali*, Liquori Editore.

Borja, J. (1974) Movimientos urbanos de las clases populares. Movimiento reivindicativo, movimiento democrático, dualidad de poder, *Papers*, Vol. 3, pp39–61.

Borja, J. (1977) Urban movements in Spain, in M. Harloe (ed) *Captive Cities*, Chichester, Wiley.

Boura, I., Jacinto, R., Lewis, J., Williams, A.M. (1984) Economic impact of returned emigrants: evidence from Leiria, Manguade and Sabugal, in M. Porto (ed) *Emigration and Return in the Central Region*, Coimbra, CCRC.

Burgel, G. (1981) *Croissance Urbaine et Développement Capitaliste de 'Miracle' Athénien*, Paris, Editions du Centre National de la Recherche Scientifique.

Castells, M. (1975) *Luttes Urbaines et Pouvoir Politique*, Paris, François Maspero.

Castells, M. (1978) Urban Social movements and the struggle for democracy: the Citizens' Movement in Madrid, *International Journal of Urban and Regional Research*, Vol. 2, pp133–146.

Ceccarelli, P. (1981) Urban Growth in Mediterranean Countries in the 1980s — Italy, *OECD Unpublished Report*.

Ceccarelli, P. (1982) Politics, parties and urban movements: Western Europe, *Urban Affairs Annual Review*, Vol. 22, pp261–276.

da Costa, R. (1975) *O Desenvolvimento do Capitalismo em Portugal*, Lisbon, Editorial Estampa.

Della Seta, P. (1978) Notes on urban struggles in Italy, *International Journal of Urban and Regional Research*, Vol. 2, pp303–329.

Dows, C. (1980) Comissões de moradores and urban struggles in revolutionary Portugal, *International Journal of Urban and Regional Research*, Vol. 4, pp267–294.

Dows, C., da Silva, F.N., Gonçalves, H. and Seabra, I. (1978) *Os Moradores à Conquista da Cidade*, Lisbon, Armazem das Letras.

Evanglinides, M. (1979) Core-periphery relations in the Greek case, in D. Seers, B. Schaffer, M.L. Kiljunen, (eds) *Underdeveloped Europe: Studies in Core-Periphery Relations*, Sussex, Harvester Press.

Ferreira, V.M. (1975) *Movimentos Sociais Urbanos e Intervenção Plítica*, Oporto, Afrontamento.

Fuá (1980) *Problemi Della Svillippo Tarvido in Europa*, Bologna, Il Mulino.

Garofoli, G. (ed) (1978) *Ristruturazione Industriale e Territorio*, Milan, Franco Angeli.

Garofoli, G. (ed) (1983) *Industrialization Difusa in Lombardia — Sviluppo Territoriale e Sistemi Produttivi Locali*, Milan, Franco Angeli.

Gaspar, J. (1980a) Urban Growth in Mediterranean Countries in the 1980s — Portugal, *OECD unpublished report*.

Gaspar, J. (1980b) Urban Growth Trends in Portugal, *EPRU 17*, Centro de Estudos Geográficos, Lisbon.

Gaspar, J. (1981a) Urban Growth in OECD Mediterranean Countries in the 1980s, (OECD unpublished report based on Ceccarelli (1981), Gaspar (1980a), Papayannis (1981), Ponsetti-Bosch (1981).)

Gaspar, J. (1981b) Os resultados preliminares do recenseamento geral da população, 16 de Março 1981, *Finisterra*, Vol. 32, pp328–341.

Gaspar, J. (1982) Regionalização: uma perspectiva sócio-geográfica, Problemas de Regionalização, *Sociedade de Geografia de Lisboa*, pp96–112.

Laganà, G., Pianta, M. and Segre, A. (1982) Urban social movements and urban restructuring in Turin, 1969–1976, *International Journal of Urban and Regional Research*, Vol. 6, pp223–245.

Lagopoulos, A. Ph. (1971) Rank-size and primate distributions in Greece, *Ekistics*, Vol. 32, pp380–384.

Leitão, L., Dias, A., Manuel, J. and Dianoux, L. (1978) Mouvements urbains et comissions de moradores au Portugal (1974–1976), *Les Temps Modernes*, Vol. 34, pp652–685.

Lewis, J. and Williams, A. (1981) Regional uneven development on the European periphery: the case of Portugal, *Tijdschrift voor Economische en Sociale Geografie*, Vol. 72, pp81–98.

Lewis, J. and Williams, A. (1984) Portugal, in M. Wynn (ed) *Housing in Europe*, London, Croom Helm.

Marcelloni, M. (1979) Urban movements and political struggles in Italy, *International Journal of Urban and Regional Research*, Vol. 3, pp251–268.

Ministère des Travaux Publiques (1980) *Rehabilitation des zones des constructions substandards clandestines, le cas de Rome*, Rome, Ministère des Travaux Publiques.

Naylon, J. (1981) Barcelona, in M. Pacione (ed) *Urban Problems and Planning in the Developed World*, London, Croom Helm.

Ocãna, M.C.O. (1979) Dinámica demográfica de las provincias españolas: Ensayo de classificación, *Revista de Geografia*, Vol. XII–XIII, pp63–89.

Papayannis, T. (1981) *Greece, Urban Growth in the 80s*, OECD unpublished report.

Ponsetti-Bosch, S. (1981) *Spain, Urban Growth in the 80s*, OECD unpublished report.

Puig, J.O. (1974) La conflictualidad urbana: algumas reflexiones sobre el reciente movimiento de barrios en Barcelona, *Papers*, Vol. 3, pp275–323.

Romanos, A. (1970) Illegal settlements and the housing problem, *Architecture in Greece*, Vol. 4.

Santillana, A. (1980) Política de vivienda, in Garner (Coord) *Política Economica de España II*, Madrid, Alianza Editoral.

Santos, B.S. (1982) O Estado, o direito e a questão urbana, *Revista Crítica de Ciências Sociais*, Vol. 9, pp9–86.

Vasquez Barquero, A. (1983) *Industrialization in Rural Areas — The Spanish Case*, report presented to the OECD Co-operative Action Programme Rural Entrepreneurial Capacities, Senigallia meeting 7–10 June.

Williams, A.M. (1981) Bairros clandestinos: Illegal housing in Portugal, *Geografisch Tijdschrift*, Nieuwe reeks XV, pp24–34.

The World Bank (1982) World Development Report 1982, Oxford University Press, on behalf of the World Bank.

CHAPTER 9

AGRICULTURE: ORGANIZATION, REFORM AND THE EEC

A.R. Jones

1. Introduction

Agriculture continues to perform a major role in the economies of Spain, Italy, Greece and Portugal contributing between 8–14 percent of the Gross Domestic Product (GDP) and between 12.8–28.5[1] percent of the working population, (Table 9.1). In the postwar period the contribution of agriculture to GDP and as a source of employment has fallen for all four countries, but the importance of agriculture remains significantly greater than that for the EEC as a whole, to which all four countries are linked politically and, or economically.

During the 1960s per capita incomes rose sharply, a change which was linked to rapid economic growth arising from the expansion and diversification of the industrial sector and of export trade, together with a sharp rise in tourism which opened new opportunities for work in the services sector and in construction. In Spain for example, over the period 1950–1965, astounding industrial and commercial growth rates were experienced, with some industrial sectors such as steel increasing production fivefold. The same period also saw a remarkable rise in the levels of tourism, with more than 24 million tourists visiting the country each year. Agriculture in southern Europe also witnessed a fundamental transformation from being essentially an inward looking sector to one increasingly oriented to and ultimately incorporated within the capitalist market economy of western Europe. An important aspect of this process has been the emergence of the EEC as a major trading partner for agricultural products.

[1] Note that there are small differences between these estimates and those given in Chapters 1 and 7.

Table 9.1 The importance of agriculture in southern Europe

	Contribution of agriculture to G.D.P. %		Agricultural workforce as a % of total workforce	
	1960	1980	1960	1980
Italy	19	8.0	32.8	12.8
Spain	20.0	9.0	42.3	17.4
Greece	24.9	14.3	57.0	28.5
Portugal	26.0	14.0	42.8	25.0

Sources: Yearbook of Labour Statistics, 1981.
          OECD, 1969.

The growth of the commercial and industrial sectors in southern Europe has had an important impact upon rural areas, with most peasant communities responding to the pull of urban regions such as Madrid, Athens–Piraeus, Milan and Lisbon with their seemingly abundant employment opportunities. More recently the spread of industrial enterprises into rural areas as in north-eastern Italy has created additional strains on traditional rural societies, as a result of agricultural exodus or the growth of part-time farming (see Chapter 7).

2. Agricultural populations

In southern Europe, 7.306 million people continue to depend on farming for their livelihood, but there has been a substantial decline in the proportion of agricultural employment over the last 20 years. The steady loss of workers from agriculture has developed from an imbalance between rural population pressures and agricultural productivity. Such features are not confined to southern Europe alone, since every western European country between 1960–1980 experienced a decline in the number of people employed in agriculture. However, the scale of this decline has been much greater in southern Europe (King 1983).

With industrial development both within and, more importantly, outside southern Europe, this movement away from agriculture turned into a massive rural exodus, characterized by national and international migration flows. In Italy, however, it was the north which experienced the greatest movement out of agriculture, while in southern Italy, at least up to the mid-1960s, the agricultural labour force was increasing. Much of rural southern Europe suffered chronic overpopulation, low standards of living and massive labour surpluses; the latter was the result of a number of factors including the organization of agriculture and, latterly, the introduction of machinery into farming practices. All of these factors contributed to reducing the peasantry to the margin of bare subsistence; emigration thus became a matter of life or death (see Chapter 6).

There is, though, an important distinction to be drawn between rural exodus and agricultural exodus, with the latter not necessarily implying movement out of the area, but into other forms of activity such as the tertiary and industrial sectors. The geographical aspects of the process of deruralization reflect the major regional differences in physical environment and organization of production which condition the response of agriculture to internal and external economic change.

The overall reduction in the agricultural population has been accompanied by far reaching qualitative changes in its composition which reflects the selective nature of most rural migration. The main characteristics of the working population engaged in agriculture in southern Europe, and certainly one having major social and economic implications, is the high proportion of elderly farmers. In Greece over 48 percent of all farm operators are over 55 years of age, while in Portugal the figure is just over 50 percent. This senescence of the agricultural population affects the degree of enthusiasm for change and therefore acts as a major obstacle to the technical and capital improvement of agriculture throughout the region. This has obvious implications for any agricultural reform programme. Another direct result of the exodus from the land has been the increasing feminization of the rural population, who continue to carry out farm work following traditional dimensions and methods, though given the inadequacy of their resources, their limited specialized knowledge and their innate reluctance to adapt to technical innovations, they achieve less than modest results. In Italy for example the proportion of women among all those employed in agriculture rose from 24 percent in 1951 to 33 percent in 1976 (Barberis 1979).

A further consequence of rural depopulation is the effect upon agricultural production and the concomitant impact upon the balance of trade. Outmigration has two major effects upon agricultural production. Firstly, rural migrants who move abroad often retain their plots of land, thus increasing the problem of land fragmentation and adding to the difficulties of agricultural mechanization and farming improvements. Secondly, outmigration can hamper agricultural expansion as a result of labour shortages. Moreover as Lane (1980) contends for Italy, even if labour is to be found, because the labourer has no direct stake in the results of his work, it is unlikely that it will be done conscientiously.

This scenario of the effects of outmigration upon rural communities in southern Europe has been refuted by one writer as a result of an indepth study of a Castilian village, just over 200 kms from Madrid (Aceves and Douglass 1976). While unfortunately no reference is made to the representativeness of the village, compared to those elsewhere in southern Europe, the study does throw up some interesting conclusions. A massive rural exodus (usually to Madrid) as a result of the parcelization of the land surrounding the nucleated village and the precarious nature of a farming system, based upon the cultivations of pears, potatoes and apples, has caused a revitalization and modernization of the village. This has come about through the freeing of large amounts of land by the emigrants to those left behind. While some emigrants retained their holdings, many of them leased these to resident villagers under varying systems of tenure. Additionally the rural exodus, through the creation of labour shortages, has affected the large landholders, who have consequently been forced to sell, rent or sharecrop the land which they previously worked under hire, thus increasing the fluidity of farm property.

In terms of international movement, trends in the labour market within western Europe since 1975 mean that a more recent phenomenon is that of return migration to southern Europe. Boura et al (1984) in a study of emigrants and retornados (the latter returning from overseas provinces particularly Angola and Mozambique) in three areas of Portugal suggest that 12 percent of their sample of *retornados* and over 14 percent of emigrants work in agriculture on returning. The input of new values, ideas, goals and initiatives into farming and overall rural life are likely to be considerable, especially if comparison is made to the experience of the *pieds-noir* in southern France. However, elsewhere there is little evidence that returned migrants do make a significant contribution to agricultural development (see Chapter 6).

Rural depopulation has also had a profound impact upon the peasantry in terms of its survival both as a social class and as a way of life. As Franklin (1969) states '. . . the whole kinship of peasantry has been subjected to change as the economic order of peasant life has experienced new pressures'. In recent decades these pressures have come in the form of a diffusion of small industrial concerns into rural areas, as for example in parts of the Po Basin in Italy, and in the development of tourism in southern Europe, which has, as in the case of Greece, facilitated the agricultural exodus (OECD, 1979).

Overall, the migration from rural areas that has occurred in the last few decades has come to symbolize the acceptance of the urban model of family existence and its associated aspirations as the preferred standard or objective of the peasant class.

Part-time farming

Another major characteristic of southern European agriculture has been the expansion of part-time farming over the last few decades. Although the term 'working-peasant' is a relatively recent feature of the agricultural scene, the custom of having an additional collateral activity to agriculture can be traced back to the preindustrial period in southern Europe (Pecora and Gregoli 1976). Part-time farming was regarded until quite recently as a transitory phenomenon; that is, an intermediate stage that agrarian societies passed through in an emerging industrial-based economy. Consequently it has received little or no attention from government policy makers (Bergmann and Laurent 1977).

Although part-time farming is regarded as a complex phenomenon (Brun 1977) it is broadly defined as '. . . a situation in which one or more members of a farm-based household are gainfully employed in work other than, or in addition to farming the family's holding' (Fuller and Mage 1976). The contribution of family labour becomes important when the operator works outside the farm. Indeed it is female work on the farm which frees the male labour force for nonfarm occupations, as Cavazzani (1976) notes for Marche in central Italy.

Problems arise though when classifications are made, since part-time farming can take a variety of forms depending on the socio-structural nature of the rural area, or region in which it occurs. As a result generalizations for southern Europe are difficult. Avoiding over-simplification, two main types of part-time farming have been outlined by Gasson (1977). Both exist throughout southern Europe. The first category relates to farmers who undertake nonagricultural work in an enterprise, usually located on the farm, and the second category relates to off-farm activities. In both cases the principal reason for the occurrence of part-time farming is that income from the farm is low and expanding the farm business is either not possible or not an acceptable means of improving it. Earnings from other sources are therefore needed to alleviate poverty (Bergmann and Laurent 1977).

While the existence of part-time farming has been recognized by many writers as a permanent structural characteristic of agriculture throughout southern Europe, considerable attention has been focussed on the Italian experience (Agostini 1977; Pecora and Gregoli 1976; Cavazzani 1977). In Italy two-thirds of all farmers work exclusively on their farms (compared to 52 percent in Spain) and the other third supplement their farm income by other (mainly) off farm work. The nature of part-time farming differs widely from one region to another, though in all cases the phenomenon reflects the country's long standing agrarian problems, that is, overpopulation, small farm size and fixity of resources. Three important types of part-time farming in Italy can however be distinguished, which are characterized by specific regional locations: part-time work in other agricultural activities, in nonagricultural activities, that is, industrial and service sectors, and part-time farming in the urban fringe.

Less than one-tenth of all Italian farmers derive supplementary income from working in other agricultural concerns, and this is mostly concentrated in southern areas where opportunities for off farm work in the industrial sector are limited. The extra work away from their own land usually occurs as a result of the demands for labour by large capitalistic concerns especially during the harvesting periods. Work in nonagricultural sectors characterizes 23 percent of Italy's farmers, and again has a particular regional dimension, occurring essentially in an area stretching from the Piedmont to the Venetian zones where industrialization has been most pronounced. Part-time farming may also be endemic on the rural–urban fringe where the reservoir of surplus labour on farms may be subject to strong employment influences from the nearby town.

In all cases the existence of part-time farming is likely to have a considerable impact upon production, land use and the effective utilization of land (especially the changeover from livestock to crop production). While in theory part-time farming could strengthen the structure of farm units, in practice it works only in keeping the peasant's family on the land. The impact of part-time farming has received often conflicting accounts. While King (1983) cites an example from central Italy which points to the fact that part-time farmers may be more dynamic than full-time farmers, Agostini (1977) maintains that investment by part-time farmers in essentials such as irrigation equipment and processing plants is already slowing down. The latter argument contrasts with Cavazzani's (1976) view that part-time farms are competitive, especially in terms of capital inputs (derived from savings from the other jobs). What is clear however is that part-time farming, especially on the rural–urban fringe, exacerbates problems of land fragmentation and circumscribes the limits to which full-time farmers can enlarge their farms in response to changing economic conditions.

3. Land tenure and modes of production

Land tenure is a vital element in the study of the structural problems of southern European agriculture. It comprises three principal components which act as major constraints to agricultural change and development: types of tenure, the distribution of land ownership, and land fragmentation. Natural change in farming is a painfully slow process, for such reasons as the peasant's affinity and close bond to his land, and the lack of alternatives to farming in many parts of rural southern Europe. While most of northern Europe has witnessed an overall trend towards increased size of farm holding through the process of farm amalgamation, this has not character-ized southern Europe to the same extent. For example, in Greece, average farm size only increased between 1961–1971 from 4.02 ha to 4.2 ha (OECD 1979).

There exists a considerable variety of land-tenure types in southern Europe, and there are an equal number of classifications. One distinction often made is that between family farms and large capitalistic concerns, the difference being that the latter relies essentially on hired labour. This use of hired labour is still important in parts of Italy and throughout most of Iberia. Another distinction is made between peasant and commercialized farming, with the latter being entirely market oriented. Differences in tenure can also be viewed from the angle of the relationship the farmer has with the land. This perspective throws up a multitude of tenure types which exist throughout most of southern Europe.

Distribution of land ownership

Table 9.2 shows the distribution of farms by size in southern Europe for the late 1970s. As is clearly evident there is a preponderance of small farms (that is under 5 ha.) in all four countries, ranging from 57 percent of all farms in Spain to 77 percent in Portugal. While average size of farm ranges from 4.39 ha in Greece to 11.5 ha in Spain, there are marked regional variations within each country. In Portugal, average farm size reveals a gradation from the northwest to the southeast, being least in the former (for example, 1.9 ha in Oporto) and largest in the latter (for example, 50.1 ha in Evora in the Alentejo). Similarly in Greece, average farm size varies with relief from 1.5 ha in the Ionian and Aegean Islands to 7.3 ha in Thessaly.

More significant is the degree of polarization of land holding, that is the percentage of land accounted for by large farms. Bearing in mind that the national census has in the past deliberately underestimated the true extent

Table 9.2   Distribution of farms by size

| Farm Size (ha.) | Percentage of farms | | | |
	Spain	Portugal	Greece	Italy
0–5	57.0	77.3	70.9	68.5
5–20	30.5	18.8	26.9	25.6
20–50	8.2	2.2	1.7	4.2
50+	4.3	1.3	0.2	1.7

| Farm size (ha.) | Percentage of utilized agricultural area | | | |
	Spain	Portugal	Greece	Italy
0–5	10.8	14.9	38.9	21.6
5–20	23.3	23.8	48.3	31.1
20–50	19.8	10.1	9.7	16.8
50+	46.1	51.2	3.1	30.5

Sources: Agricultural situation in the European Community 1982.
          Christodoulou (1976).

of land polarization for a variety of political and social reasons (Christo-doulou 1976), it can be seen that Portugal, Italy and Spain have most land concentrated in a few hands. Greece, on the other hand, has no such extensive polarization, as over 88 percent of its utilized agricultural area (UAA) is made up by farms of less than 20 ha in size.

Of the three countries with highly polarized landholding structures, two have had significant land reforms since 1945 — Italy in the early 1950s and Portugal in 1974. In Spain a service for agrarian and social reform was set up in the late 1930s leading to a modest degree of land expropriation within the perimeters of irrigation schemes for the purpose of establishing settlements, but most structural change has occurred through a policy of land consolidation.

The Portuguese land reform probably marks the last major land redis-tribution in Europe. Its occurrence in 1974/1975 was part of a process triggered off by events taking place in Portugal's overseas colonies (see Chapter 4). The land reform itself was confined to the Alentejo, a depressed and backward region in the south, mainly dependent on nonirrigated extensive agriculture, and characterized by a latifundist capitalist farming system (De Barros 1980). Holdings of over 50 ha, accounted for over two-thirds of all land throughout most of the south. The rural proletariat of the Alentejo identified the existence of the *latifundia* as the major factor behind the defects of the South's agrarian structure, and indeed the region had always been dominated by a conflict between the bourgeoisie and the rural proletariat over wages, working conditions and hours of work (Rutledge 1977). However the concern over wages and jobs soon gave way to the pursuit of agrarian reform, inspired by the Portuguese Communist Party.

The first seizures of land occurred in early 1975, on the initiatives of unemployed rural workers. It has been suggested (Cabral 1978) that these labourers did not want to become titleholders of their own plots, but merely achieve a guarantee of work. This view has, however, been refuted (Rutledge 1977). Within a matter of months over 1 million ha of land belonging to latifundist and very large capitalistic concerns was occupied. It was not until July 1975 that the agrarian reform acts were passed by the National Assembly which served only to legalize this fait accompli. The region where the reform developed became known as ZIRA (Agrarian Reform Zone). Reform, although radically transforming parts of southern Portuguese agriculture, did not eradicate completely the agrarian capitalist sector which continues to be important neither did it significantly affect the small and medium size southern farming sector, which still covers over 1 million ha.

A major feature of Portuguese land reform is the belief that larger size production units are the key to agricultural efficiency and development. It is indeed ironic that the collective production units (UCP) created by the reform are, in many cases, often double the size of the farms seized. Although Portuguese land reform is regarded as being politically significant, it has had only a limited economic and social impact, even within its geographically well-circumscribed area (De Barros 1980). The belief held by Christodoulou (1976) that land reform in the South has provided the dynamic for agrarian change throughout the whole of Portugal is questionable if we consider the following figures — the 1 million ha comprising the new production units represent only 33 percent of the cultivated area in the South (that is, South of the river Tejo), and that only 35 percent of the regional work force participate in the units.

While it could be said that land reform is the most solid achievement of Portugal's revolution (King 1978), events in recent years have raised fundamental doubts. A recent trend inspired by the Socialist party is to give back occupied land to its former owners, a policy which is based on the belief that a small to medium sized farming system provides the best solution to Portugal's agricultural quasi stagnation. Since 1979 the Democratic

Alliance (AD) which ousted the Socialist party has sought to promote land redistribution from the UCP's for its own political ends— namely weakening the base of support for the Communist party in the Alentejo. While land reform has given rise to certain structural and production changes (for example, from wheat/cereals to livestock) its future, and in particular that of the UCP's appears rather precarious.

The Italian experience of land reform differs greatly from that outlined for Portugal. Having occurred over 30 years ago its true impact upon Italian agriculture can more easily be assessed. Unlike that in Portugal, Italian land reform operated in an opposing structural direction by splitting up large latifundist estates, again in the south of the country, into small plots of between 2–10 ha. These small plots (*podere*) were intended to support the landless peasant (*braccianti*) and his family. In practise they had only limited success.

On economic grounds not only were they too small to support a family, but they also conflicted with overall Italian agricultural policy which foresaw the need for larger farming units especially with the increasing commercialization and export orientation of agriculture. In social terms, the reform policy created numerous problems; peasants used to the daily social contact patterns of large villages, often felt isolated in the new dispersed settlements. Consequently many abandoned their plots and returned to their former domiciles, either giving up their holdings completely or working these on a part-time basis.

As well as the politically emotive question of land reform, southern Europe has also witnessed other attempts at altering farm structures in the form of land consolidation schemes which, although not as comprehensive as, say, the French structural programme, have had nevertheless a profound impact upon farming structures in certain localities.

Land fragmentation and consolidation

Land fragmentation refers to a condition in which a holding is split into many separate, noncontiguous parcels (King and Burton 1981). Fragmentation has its origins in the Napoleonic code of equal inheritance whereby with each passing generation all direct heirs (usually sons) receive equal shares of the father's farmland. Large families characteristic of much of southern Europe have further added to the regional problem of fragmentation. Furthermore fragmentation is aggravated when the heirs do not agree as to how the land should be divided amongst them and, consequently, there have been further subdivisions. Fragmentation levels have an important regional dimension, and are particularly high in Crete (average of 10.5 parcels per farm) and Thrace (average of 7.6 parcels per farm) in Greece, Bragança and Viana do Castelo in Portugal (where between 45–63 percent of all farms have more than six parcels), and parts of Galicia in Spain where holdings on average have more than 30 parcels.

The problems raised by fragmentation are largely economic, though there are also notable socio-psychological, ecological and administrative disadvantages. Zaheer (1975) gives a representative view when he writes that '. . . fragmentation has a retarding effect on the agricultural economy . . . it is a system of perpetual handicap'. Farmers lose considerable time travelling back and forth between plots, thus the amount of time actually applied to the land falls off markedly with distance. Moreover, the often irregular shape and small size of fragments prohibit the effective use of machinery. Similarly, improvements to the land, such as fencing, are usually ruled out due to excessive cost. Another consequence is land abandonment and the problem of soil conservation which often leads to a reduction in agricultural production. Other disadvantages occur when decisions over land use need to be implemented, since consensus becomes less easy to achieve. Difficulties also present themselves for cadastral authorities attempting to monitor patterns of tenure.

The fragmentation of land can have a logical basis especially in response to soil and crop variation or to spread the risk of climatic or other hazards. For example, Galt (1979) has shown in his study of intensive viticulture on Pantelleria (an Italian island between Sicily and Tunisia), that fragmentation is an extremely rational adaptation to environmental conditions. However, there is generally no doubt that fragmentation constitutes one of the most serious obstacles to the technical and economic development of southern European agriculture.

The progress of land consolidation in southern Europe over the last thirty years has been variable (OECD 1969). In Portugal, Greece and Italy virtually nothing has been accomplished. A study by Thompson (1963) of Greek agriculture revealed an acute, pervasive and chronic fragmentation of Greek farm holdings. In one extreme case a holding of 15 ha was divided into 80 separate parcels. Since 1959 a scheme of compulsory consolidation has been incorporated within land-improvement programmes, though in its first 10 years of existence only 200,000 ha were consolidated, which covered less than 15 percent of all the land that was in need of consolidation. An important development, and one having particular implications for the success of all consolidation schemes, is that the land which has been consolidated is now threatened with a new round of fragmentation as a result of the continued existence of the inheritance laws.

In Portugal, fragmentation continues to be a major handicap to agricultural development, yet little consolidation has occurred. Indeed, in some northern districts such as Aveiro and Oporto, fragmentation is increasing, which Lewis and Williams (1981) explain in terms of the growth of diffuse industrialization and part-time farming.

Similarly, until quite recently land consolidation has received relatively little attention in agrarian policy in Italy. Most consolidation programmes have taken place under the umbrella of integrated joint management schemes which have had only a limited acceptance among rural populations (Cesarini 1979). Substantial structural changes were among the first results of the establishment of joint managements. For example, in the 12 cooperative units which were first set up in Abruzzio, Molise, Campania, Sicily and Sardinia (areas characterized by heavy emigration and rapid ageing and feminization of the population), the number of plots was reduced from 1929 in 1970 to only 208 in 1972. Furthermore, the average size of the plots on the land rose from 0.49 to 4.53 ha. Cesarini's (1979) analysis of 61 cooperatives in the Italian South revealed radical structural transformations as a result of land consolidation. In Molise the number of plots of those farms involved in the scheme fell from 2652 in 1970 to 86 in 1975, while considerable increases were also recorded in the average size of plots (see Table 9.3).

Table 9.3   Structural change on 61 joint management schemes in southern Italy, 1970–1975

Region	Number of plots		Average size of plots (ha.)	
	1970	1975	1970	1975
Abruzzo	3,467	968	0.3	1.1
Apulia	20	1	2.4	48.4
Basilicata	591	159	2.1	7.2
Calabria	38	23	2.2	3.6
Campania	154	65	2.8	11.5
Molise	2,652	86	0.6	21.0
Sardinia	1,336	41	1.4	38.6
Sicily	155	39	4.2	17.1
Total:	8,413	1,382	0.9	5.2

Source: Cesarini (1979).

The country where land consolidation has made most progress in recent decades is Spain. The first Spanish agricultural census of 1963 revealed that fragmentation of farmland had reached alarming proportions with an average 13.7 plots per farm (Guedes 1981). Fragmentation was particularly acute in Galicia where there were on average 32 parcels per farm. Indeed, O'Flanagan (1980) maintained that the severe fragmentation of Galician farmland was one of the main factors preventing the local rural society from reaping rich rewards from a generally favourable physical environment. In areas where the rural landscape consists of tiny plots, up to 20 percent of the cultivated area may be lost to boundaries (King and Burton 1981). While the problem of fragmentation was not universally acute throughout Spain (areas like Cadiz, for example, had only 1.8 plots on average per farm) it was recognized in 1957 that approximately 8 million ha were in need of consolidation (Naylon 1959).

The consolidation of farmland started in 1952 when a Service for Parcelary Concentration was established, which had three main aims. Its major intention was to make small farms more viable through parcelary concentration; thus a farmer would be assigned a single plot equal in area and quality to the several plots he previously possessed. Secondly, the new holding would be sited with easy access to the farmstead and, to this end, new roads would be constructed (Guedes 1981). Thirdly, the new holding would become legally confirmed by its inclusion in the property register. The need for land consolidation is greatest in the northern half of the country (except in the Basque Provinces and Catalonia, where a tradition of passing land to the oldest son exists) whilst in the south large capitalist estates are predominant; consequently, most consolidation schemes have been directed towards the northern area. While consolidation was slow throughout the 1950s, with only 578,000 ha consolidated between 1955–1963, the rate of progress increased in the 1960s with 350,000–400,000 ha being consolidated annually (OECD 1969). In the 1970s consolidation rates have fallen due to rising administrative and technical costs. By 1977 therefore only 4,728,351 ha had been consolidated, that is just over half of the land regarded as being in need of consolidation. Other problems associated with consolidation also exist. Although there is some legislation to prevent the subdivision of plots under a minimum size, the overall lack of legislation to prevent re-fragmentation, as noted for Greece, continues to be a problem. Furthermore the consolidation programme fails to take into account differences in local agrarian structures, as noted for Galicia by O'Flanagan (1982). Overall the policy has been relatively successful, though it is likely that greater costs will have to be incurred in the future so that the pace of consolidation can be increased.

4. Southern European agriculture and the EEC

Structure of agricultural production

All four countries show marked similarities in terms of the composition of their agricultural production, with a definite emphasis on the production of Mediterranean crops (Musto 1982). The EEC has defined Mediterranean agriculture as one in which citrus fruits, fruit and vegetables, olives, wine, flowers, tobacco, rice, durum wheat and sheepmeat comprise at least 40 percent of total agricultural production. Although there are sizeable percentages of non-Mediterranean items grown in each country, especially in Italy, Spain, and, to a lesser extent, in Portugal, all four countries can on the basis of this definition be regarded as having largely Mediterranean agricultural production structures. For example, in Spain fruit and vegetables alone account for 25 percent of the final agricultural product (EEC 1982, 6) while in Greece Mediterranean products account for just under half of total agricultural production (EEC 1983, 7).

More important perhaps than the portrayal of a static picture of agriculture in these countries, is an analysis of trends in production over the last decade. Table 9.4 shows the indices of production for principal agricultural products in Greece, Italy, Portugal and Spain for the period 1969–1981, using 1969 as the base year. It becomes apparent that there has been a trend towards an increasing specialization in Mediterranean products. For example, Greece's biggest increases in agricultural production have been registered with respect to most fruit and vegetables, especially apricots, peaches and tomatoes. These increases have been due in part to government encouragement in the form of production subsidies (EEC 1981, 3). Large increases in the production of barley, potatoes, poultry and eggs have led to the country becoming almost self-sufficient in these products, though considerable shortages of beef meat, milk products and fodder grains still exist (OECD 1979).

While substantial increases have occurred in the production of most products in Greece, the experience of Portugal over the last decade has been quite different (Tsoukalis 1981). Due to the profound upheavals in the political and economic situation of the country (some of the agricultural implications of which were outlined earlier), production and productivity have stagnated. Almost all agricultural items have experienced a consider-

Table 9.4   Indices of agricultural production 1969–1981 (1969 = 100)

	Greece	Italy	Portugal	Spain
Cereals	154	116	63	98
Wheat	147	91	50	71
Rice	88	108	63	114
Barley	121	305	58	120
Potatoes	136	79	77	120
Olives	149	102	47	52
Tomatoes	171	125	88	123
Onions	111	112	106	52
Peaches	243	143	97	189
Lemons and Limes	137	92	111	384
Oranges	146	114	92	80
Tang/Clem/Mand	116	120	118	218
Apricots	281	115	85	128
Wine	124	112	67	134
Tobacco	139	156	120	158
Sheep ('000 head)	104	115	117	80
Beef and veal (slaughtered)	81	102	105	111
Mutton and Lamb (slaughtered)	110	120	133	101

Sources: FAO. Production Yearbook 1981.
        Own calculations.

able fall in their levels of production, and most notable amongst these have been cereals (especially wheat and barley) and fruit and vegetables (especially olives, apricots and tomatoes). Although the production of most meat products has increased (especially sheepmeat), consumption has continued to outstrip production levels which has led to massive food import bills.

Although agriculture in Spain has declined in importance in terms of its percentage of GDP from 20 percent in 1960 to 9 percent in 1979 (EEC 1982, 6), total agricultural production has risen rapidly often as a result of increases in the area of irrigated land. Indeed, over 10 percent of the utilized agricultural area is irrigated compared with only 5 percent in France. The most remarkable increases in production over the last decade have been with respect to dairy products and fruit and vegetables. Significant increases have been recorded for citrus (especially lemons and limes), peaches, tobacco, wine, tomatoes, rice and potatoes, which taken together now make up 60 percent of all crops grown (Spanish Embassy 1982). However, supply of these products far exceeds domestic requirements. Massive surpluses exist for citrus, for which Spain is 243 percent self-sufficient (mandarins 377 percent, oranges 206 percent, lemons 177 percent), olive oil 147 percent (despite a fall in the level of production over the period), wine 125 percent, and rice for which Spain is 121 percent self-sufficient. Like Greece and Portugal, Spanish self-sufficiency in cereals and meat products is low. Spain is only 32 percent self-sufficient in maize, and less than 89 percent self-sufficient for beef and veal, despite increases in production over the period as a result of a switch away from mutton and lamb. Spain also continues to have a slight deficit for dairy products, especially cheese (94 percent self-sufficient) and milk (99 percent).

For Italy 38.9 percent of final agricultural production is made up of Mediterranean products (Table 9.5) but for the South this proportion is 56 percent. Southern agriculture is a large portion of the total Italian agricultural sector, accounting for 40 percent of agricultural output and 54 percent of agricultural employment (Podbielski 1981). Trends in production must therefore be seen against the backcloth of the dualistic nature of Italian agriculture, between the Mezzogiorno on the one hand and the rest of Italy on the other; that is between labour- and capital-intensive forms of production. Furthermore, production trends must also be seen in the light of the operation of the Common Agricultural Policy (CAP) which provides

Table 9.5   Composition of agricultural production in Italy 1973–1977

	Italy	South
	(Percentage averages 1973–77)	
Mediterranean Products (of which)		
Vegetables	13.0	16.2
Fruit and citrus fruit	3.2	10.9
Wine	9.7	11.0
Olive oil	5.3	12.1
Total:	38.9	56.2
Continental Products		
Cereals	12.1	10.7
Other crops	9.8	11.8
Meat	25.0	13.8
Milk	10.3	5.3
Other livestock products	3.9	2.7
Total:	61.1	43.8

Sources: Podbielski (1981).
　　　　Pasca (1979).

varying degrees of support for groups of products.

Italian agriculture in general has experienced many changes over the last two decades, especially in terms of a move away from mixed farming towards increasing regional specialization in the production of particular products by intensive methods (Pinna and Ruocco 1980).

Although the production of wheat has fallen over the period, Italy continues to be the second largest producer in Western Europe, after France. While wheat production levels have fallen, often as a result of the conversion of much of the wheatland area into orchards and market gardens, barley production has risen substantially. As in both Greece and Spain, the fruit and vegetable sector has experienced sizeable production increases, often as a consequence of increases in cultivated land. For example, the area covered by vegetables increased from 280,000 to 400,000 ha between 1960 and 1975, which has had a profound impact upon regional landscapes. Moreover, it has rendered Italy over 117 percent self-sufficient in vegetables (Pearce 1981). Similarly for fruit, especially citrus, the total land use area has doubled and production has tripled over the period, resulting in self-sufficiency levels of 133 percent for fresh fruit, and giving rise to a situation in which Italy accounts for 99 percent of the EEC's citrus production. For other Mediterranean crops such as wine, tomatoes, olives and tobacco, increases in production levels have been recorded often as a result of new plantings or the increasingly intensification of production, as with tomatoes and tobacco (Vedel and Pisani 1979).

Like Greece, Spain and Portugal, Italy suffers from shortages both in the meat sector and in dairy products. Despite production increases in most meat products over the decade (see Table 9.6) Italy is still only 62 percent self-sufficient in beef and veal and only 74 percent self-sufficient in pig-meat, while for dairy products self-sufficiency levels are often lower; butter 69 percent, skimmed milk products 13 percent (EEC 1982, 4).

The trends in agricultural production identified for the four countries, indicate an expansion in the production of Mediterranean products, and this has given rise to high levels of domestic self-sufficiency. Trade, especially that with the EEC, has been an important element in facilitating this expansion.

Cooperatives

The social and economic role played by agricultural cooperatives in southern Europe should not be underestimated, though the range and scope of their activities in Italy and Greece, and in the non-EEC member countries

Table 9.6   Self-supply rate in principal agricultural products (%)

	Portugal	Greece	Spain	Italy
Wheat	59	111	104	82
Barley	92	97	116	37
Maize	27	33	32	65
Rice	57	108	121	271
Sugar	4	120	94	93
Olive oil	104	107	147	—
Wine	122	120	125	137
Citrus fruit	100	156	243	114
Tomatoes	100	100	110	—
Potatoes	94	107	102	100
Sheep and Goat meat	100	66	99	64
Beef and Veal	70	63	89	62
Pigmeat	92	99	94	74
Eggs	100	101	103	95
Cows milk (fresh)	99	100	99	99
Butter	52	79	89	69

Sources: Agricultural Aspects of Enlargement, *Green Europe*, Vol. 190.
  Agricultural Situation in the Community, 1982 Report.

of Spain and Portugal is much more narrow than for the EEC as a whole.
Even within the EEC, differences in the degree of involvement by cooperatives can be identified between southern France and southern Italy. One
sector in which the cooperatives do not play a major role in Greece,
Portugal, Spain and Italy is that of agricultural marketing. The underdevelopment of the marketing structure has indubitably presented serious
obstacles to agricultural development in southern Europe and has given rise
to increased activity by middlemen leading to a wider divergence between
producer and retail prices. An improved and expanded system of cooperatives could play an important role in overcoming some of the structural and
marketing problems currently facing southern European agriculture, and
to this end the EEC has given increased emphasis to a series of marketing
measures included in its Mediterranean package.

Agricultural trade

There are certain complications involved in the analysis of the agricultural
trade links between the four countries and the EEC, since each country has
a different political/institutional, and thus ultimately a different economic
relationship with the Community (Jones 1981). Italy is a long standing

member of the European Community and therefore a participating member of the CAP, which provides that agricultural trade may take place freely between member countries, and that trade with nonmembers is subject to common rules. It is in this latter light that the EEC's agricultural trade with Spain, Greece and Portugal must be viewed. The Community has not however offered similar treatment to the three nonmember countries especially in terms of trade privileges in the agricultural sector. Greece's relationship with the EEC, for example, dates back to an association agreement of 1962 with the eventual aim of Greek accession, which was realized in January 1981. This agreement was indeed the first to be signed by the Community with any Mediterranean state, and some commentators have attributed this fact to the rather generous nature of the accords in terms of agricultural products (Karabetsis 1976). The association agreement also provided that Greek agriculture should be harmonized with the EEC's CAP over a 12-year period (Kalamotousakis 1976).

For Spain and Portugal, preferential trade agreements were signed with the EEC in 1970 and 1972 respectively. In terms of the treatment given to Spanish agricultural products, the agreement fell significantly short of those privileges offered not only to Greece, but also to many other Mediterranean states, such as Tunisia and Morocco, where the possibility of EEC accession did not exist (Jones 1981; Tovias 1979).

Despite these legal differences Greece, Spain and Portugal have come to depend greatly on the EEC as their major food trading partner. For example, even before Greek accession, the Community was providing just under 30 percent of Greece's food imports and taking 51 percent of her food exports (EEC 1981, 3). Similarly for Spain and Portugal, the Community has come to represent an essential trading partner for agricultural items, taking 59 percent and 49 percent respectively of their total agricultural exports, and providing 10 percent and 11 percent of their agricultural imports (EEC 1981, 3).

In somewhat simplified terms this agricultural trade is composed of an exchange between fruit, vegetables and wine for the three on the one hand and animal products (meat and milk) for the EEC on the other (Tsoukalis 1981). The importance of the EEC however as an export market cannot be disputed and this is certainly so if we analyse the composition of each country's world exports of agricultural products, and the percentage of these major exports taken by the Community. As regards Spain, 54 percent of its total agricultural exports comprise Mediterranean items, for which the EEC is often the sole market outlet — 88 percent of citrus exports and 87 percent of vegetable exports are directed towards the Community's markets (EEC 1981, 3).

Similarly for Portugal, wine, vegetables and food crops account for 58 percent of total agricultural exports, with the EEC taking over 62 percent of each category. Greece's trade reveals a similar situation, with 75 percent of total Greek agricultural exports consisting of fresh and preserved fruit and vegetables and unmanufactured tobacco, with the larger part being exports to the EEC (OECD 1979).

Before analysing Italy's trade in the Community it would be relevant to discover how important Greece, Spain and Portugal are for the Community, especially for the provision of Mediterranean products. The three countries taken together provide only 6 percent of the EEC's total agricultural imports and take only 5.2 percent of EEC agricultural exports (EEC 1982, 4). However, on a sectoral level the importance of the three countries to the EEC is more pronounced, especially for Mediterranean products. Table 9.7 serves to demonstrate the close links that exist between production structures in the three and their dependence upon the Community as an export market for these products. Spain continues to occupy a very important position in the EEC market with regards to the supply of Mediterranean agricultural produce, despite receiving less favourable treatment in that market. For example, the Community applies a 20 percent *ad valorem* duty on imports of Spanish oranges, while the corresponding figure for the Maghreb is 7.2 percent and Greek oranges enter duty-free (Taylor 1980).

Table 9.7   Production and EEC dependence

Trade in five 'typical' Mediterranean products
(a) = percentage of EEC imports from Greece, Portugal and Spain
(b) = percentage of exports from Greece, Portugal and Spain destined for the EEC

	%	Oranges	Tomatoes	Potatoes	Olive Oil	Wine
Spain	(a)	46.2	57.4	18.6	28.0	38.2
	(b)	92.2	96.0	93.3	38.0	34.1
Greece	(a)	1.6	0.1	7.9	13.0	9.0
	(b)	17.4	13.0	87.4	84.0	47.5
Portugal	(a)	—	—	0.1	0.2	11.6
	(b)	—	—	26.1	4.4	36.8

Source: *Green Europe* 1982.

Italian agricultural trade with the EEC differs in that it operates within the framework of the CAP which provides support for groups of products, and also implies free movement of agricultural products between member states. Italian agricultural exports to EEC members are concentrated mainly in the Mediterranean sectors, and production benefits from varying degrees of support (Pasca 1979). Indeed Italian agriculture provides a useful case study to illustrate both the effectiveness of the CAP in terms of its price support for Mediterranean products, and its effectiveness in restricting the import of similar products from nonmember states.

Although the CAP to date is regarded as the single most important achievement of the EEC in terms of its progress along the road to economic unity, the policy has been fraught with problems of both an economic and political nature and has rightly been accused of being regressive (Rodriguez Alcaide 1978). Moreover the CAP has paid only lip service to the problems of Mediterranean agriculture stemming from a marked sectoral and geographic allocation of budgetary resources in favour of those regions already in a privileged position.

The European Commission has recognized the problems of Mediterranean agriculture (EEC 1977, 1), but this concern has not been reflected to any great extent in Community expenditure, either from Agricultural guarantee and guidance funds (EAGGF), or in terms of regional and social policy. Although some writers have suggested that the bias towards northern temperate products compared with Mediterranean products is a misconception, this view must be refuted on the basis of the levels of price support and total support expenditure for Mediterranean products. In addition, the operation of the CAP, even within Italy, has been shown to aggravate existing regional differences in levels of farm income between temperate and Mediterranean product-producing regions (Podbielski 1981). Consequently, for the EEC as a whole the incomes of those working on farms in the more prosperous northern parts of the Community are around seven times higher than those in areas like southern Italy.

Although expenditure on Mediterranean products as a percentage of total guarantee expenditure has increased from 12.6 percent in 1977 to 23.1 percent (proposed) in 1983, temperate product expenditure still accounts for roughly two-thirds of Community price support. Crucially, expenditure on Mediterranean products has been substantially and consistently below the contribution of Mediterranean products to EEC agricultural output (Table 9.8). Fennell (1979) has shown that for Mediterranean products there is effective support for durum wheat, rice, olive oil and tobacco; weak support for wine, citrus fruits, grapes, pears, peaches and tomatoes, and no support for other fruit and vegetables. One of the principal reasons given for

Table 9.8   European Agricultural Guidance and Guarantee Fund (EAGGF) guarantee expenditure by sector 1980–1982

	1980		1981		1982	
	million ECU	%	million ECU	%	million ECU	%
Cereals	1669.0	14.8	1921.4	17.2	2031.3	15.2
Rice	58.7	0.5	21.7	0.2	67.5	0.5
Milk products	4752.0	42.0	3342.7	30.0	4018.5	30.2
Olive oil	317.9	2.8	439.8	3.9	679.0	5.1
Sugar	575.2	5.1	767.5	6.9	1225.5	9.2
Beef and veal	1363.3	12.0	1436.9	12.9	1407.6	10.6
Pigmeat	115.6	1.0	154.6	1.4	166.1	1.2
Sheepmeat	53.5	0.5	191.5	1.7	224.0	1.7
Fruit and vegetables	687.3	6.1	641.1	5.8	852.6	6.4
Wine	299.5	2.6	459.4	4.1	416.0	3.1
Tobacco	309.3	2.7	361.8	3.2	597.7	4.5
Others	115.8	1.0	184.5	1.7	265.0	2.0
Total common organization of markets =	11,016.4		10,902.8		13,042.1	

Source: EEC Commission Brussels.

the low thresholds of price support is the perishable nature of Mediterranean products (Pearce 1981).

Italy is the major producer of Mediterranean products in the EEC, producing 72 percent of the Community's total output of tomatoes, 91 percent of its peaches and 99 percent of its citrus fruit. It is important however to estimate the effectiveness of the support offered to Italian Mediterranean products under the CAP against the effectiveness of the trade privileges (and hence their ultimate share of the EEC market) granted to Spain, Greece and Portugal for their Mediterranean agricultural exports. An analysis of this type has been undertaken by Pasca (1979) who concluded that the trade concessions led to the three countries prevailing in the Community's fruit and wine markets, while CAP protection for olive oil and certain vegetables led to Italy retaining its position for these products.

The fact that the three countries have been able to make sizeable inroads into Community markets for Mediterranean products, despite certain trade restrictions, illustrates clearly the worries that Italian (and French) Mediterranean producers have concerning EEC enlargement, whereby not only will the trade restrictions be removed, but also certain of the three countries' Mediterranean products will be included in the CAP support system.

Italian agriculture is also included within the structural policies of the CAP's guidance fund which facilitates the reorientation of agricultural production. Although guidance policies only accounted for 6 percent of total CAP expenditure in 1982, they have been given a prominent role in the EEC's agricultural policies towards its Mediterranean regions. Furthermore, structural policy may well take on a greater significance in dealing with the problems that are likely to develop as a result of Community enlargement.

Structural measures for Mediterranean regions

Because the price and marketing regimes for most Mediterranean products offers so little assistance the recent Community approach to 'the Mediterranean problem' — characterized by a high proportion of the population working in agriculture combined with a low level of agricultural productivity — has been very largely concentrated on structural improvements in the form of irrigation, processing, marketing and forestry. In 1978 soon after the application for Community membership by Spain and Portugal, a 'package' for the Mediterranean regions came out of Brussels which, in brief, perceived the problems of the Mediterranean regions of the EEC as being not entirely confined to agriculture but bound up with low levels of economic development and infrastructure. With enlargement in mind, the Commission also proposed a series of crop diversification and quality improvement schemes for sectors such as citrus and wine, that is those areas in which it foresaw problems of structural surplus in an enlarged Community context (EEC 1982, 5). The success of these schemes, at least in Italy, have received little or no research attention, Bartoli's study of vineyard conversion in the Languedoc-Roussillon between 1976–1979 does provide however a welcomed exception. His findings are particularly pertinent for other Mediterranean areas of southern Europe, where certain types of production are traditional. His analysis suggests that the programme has had only a modest impact with only 13,000 ha affected, that is less than 3 percent of the region's vineyards. Moreover, the policy has had little impact in those areas such as the monocultural *plaine viticole* of the department of Herault, for which the policy was largely intended (Bartoli 1981). The reasons suggested for the overall lack of success of the policy are technical, economic and social rigidities of production, which include the difficulties and costs of conversion, the small and weak structure of many viticultural holdings, and the uncertainties about other types of product combined with a senescence of the farm population and the importance of viticulture as a part-time activity. These structural constraints, as we have seen, exist throughout southern Europe.

Consequently, for all its wide scope the Mediterranean package has no real depth since it fails to tackle the fundamental structural, social and economic problems of Mediterranean agriculture and merely reflects the conflict between price support and structural policy in the CAP. This point is well illustrated if we consider one of the Commission's latest (February 1983) programmes to help the Community's Mediterranean areas, this consists of a £4,000 million integrated scheme to help agriculture, fishing, tourism, reafforestation and craft industries (EEC 1983, 7). While in round figures the plan calls for spending of Community money on every one of the six million Greek citizens, £53 on each of the 33 million Italians covered by the scheme, and £56 on each of the 17 millions living in the French areas involved, just under half of all the money is to be spent on price support. More important is that this support is destined for products such as tomatoes, peaches, wine and olive oil, that is, items which are already in surplus in the EEC 10 and are likely to be further so if Portugal and Spain join. Such spending corresponds to the divergent interests of the French and Italian governments over Mediterranean agriculture, with the French pressing for higher guaranteed minimum prices for Mediterranean products and the Italians seeking greater support for major structural reform (Leigh 1978). Indeed, in the Italian view structural policies were expected to act as a corrective to the less favourable treatment accorded to Mediterranean agriculture by the price and market policies. In fact, however, the results appear to have been very modest in spite of the strengthening of measures specifically designed to meet the needs of the Mezzogiorno in recent years, such as Community regulation No. 1362/1978 for irrigation works and No. 355/1977 for marketing structures (Podbielski 1981).

One of the major reasons for this apparent lack of success is, as we have seen, the small amount of finance made available by the guidance section of the CAP. Although Italy receives on average 30–35 percent of these allocations, the absolute amounts are too small to make any significant differences in agricultural structures.

As well as the measures outlined above, the EEC has also been anxious to see greater use being made of existing policies such as the modernization and retirement grants. Although these have had some degree of success in France, where Community legislation is supplemented by effective regional organizations such as the Société d'Aménagement Foncier et d'Établisment Rural (SAFER) (Naylor 1982), the familiar administrative and financial incapacity of Italian governments, combined with a general EEC ignorance of the special conditions prevailing in backward agricultural areas, has limited the success of these structural policies. This is reflected in the EEC's policy towards the modernization of holdings which is based upon the criterion of full-time farming and the preparation of a development programme by each farmer. Such criteria do not lend themselves well to a backward area where, as we have already seen, part-time farming is a significant aspect of agricultural activity.

It is apparent, therefore, that the problems of the Italian Mezzogiorno are perhaps beyond the capabilities of the CAP and that greater financial measures are required in the form of regional, social and agricultural action schemes. Whether these funds will be forthcoming depends very much on the enlargement process, since major changes in Mediterranean agriculture are likely to occur as a result of the future membership of Spain and Portugal of the EEC, both for the current southern European members and for the applicants, and furthermore both the potential new members will add their voices to the demands for greater EEC attention to the Mediterranean regions (see also Chapter 10).

5. Conclusion: future prospects for southern European agriculture

The problems which Greek, Portuguese and Spanish agriculture pose for the Community are in many respects very similar, though they differ greatly in their importance. Because of the relatively small size of Greek agricultural production, combined with the fact that Greece was already regarded as a de facto member of the Community in terms of its agricultural sector through the agricultural harmonization clause of its association agreement, Greek agriculture can be absorbed into the EEC without too much dislocation to either party (Gallus 1979). This view was further reflected in the rather smooth nature of the accession process which resulted in Greece's full membership in January 1981.

For Portugal and Spain the negotiations have been more protracted and as a consequence the prospect of EEC membership has become more remote, especially with the threat of a French and/or Italian veto looming over any enlargement decision (Leigh 1978). Portuguese agriculture, like that of Greece, is unlikely to cause any major headaches in terms of its absorption and integration with the CAP, especially compared with the size of the Spanish agricultural sector (Trigo de Abreu 1978). Unfortunately, and indeed much to the annoyance of the Portuguese government, it has been the linking of the Portuguese application with that of Spain's which has been the main factor delaying full entry.

Spanish accession is regarded as being likely to present far greater problems for Community agricultural markets and policy as the agricultural area of the EEC will increase by 30 percent and the farm workers by 25 percent. By comparison, the accession of Portugal will enlarge the agricultural utilized area by only 4 percent and increase the labour force by 12.8 percent (EEC 1978, 2).

There are three aspects to the problem of Mediterranean agriculture in an enlarged Communtiy — static effects, dynamic effects and the resulting budgetary effects (Hudson and Lewis 1982). For all these aspects the integration of Spanish agriculture presents the greatest difficulties. Most fears centre on the productive capacity of Spanish agriculture, and in particular the problems that are likely to be incurred for specific sectors of Mediterranean agriculture. For example, if we analyse Spanish production as a percentage of the production of the EEC 9 for certain Mediterranean products, we discover values of 96 percent for citrus fruit (122 percent oranges, 400 percent grapefruit), 86 percent for apricots and 82 percent for olive oil. In addition to the purely quantitative factors likely to lead to severe market imbalances in terms of excess supply over demand for Mediterranean products, the extension of the *acquis communautaire* to Spain is likely to create further problems of structural surplus.

Conflict between state policies in the agricultural sector and the price support offered by the CAP could prove to be a major problem area. Levels of state intervention in the agricultural market taken overall, especially in Spain, are greater than the support offered by the CAP. For example, the common organization of markets which covers on average 95 percent of the agricultural production of the EEC 9, covers less than three-quarters of Greek agricultural production. However, for certain products, price levels in the EEC are often higher than those operating in Spain, Portugal and Greece, and this could lead to shifts in the pattern of production towards more favourably priced products. For example, prices for olive oil and tobacco are substantially higher in the EEC than in Greece.

Although analyses of price differentials between the applicants and the EEC for particular products are frequently employed as an indicator of expected changes in production type and production levels (for example, Lewis and Williams 1982), they must however be used with some degree of caution since they fail to take into account such important considerations as fluctuating currencies, transport costs, marketing deficiencies, distance and geographical location (Ródríguez Alcaide 1978). However, with this in mind it is possible to make some tentative predictions about those sectors where the greatest difficulties in terms of surplus might be incurred as a result of higher prices operating in the Community. Although all three governments support their agricultural production to varying degrees, for example 50 percent of Portuguese agricultural production receives financial support, levels of support for certain Mediterranean products are often higher in the EEC. On this basis, wine, olive oil and certain fruit and vegetables have been singled out as those products likely to present the most problems in an enlarged Community as a result of surplus and the dynamic effects of membership. This has crucial implications for those existing Mediterranean regions of the EEC such as the Languedoc-Roussillon region of southern France, and parts of the Italian south, as well as for the EEC nonmember countries of the Mediterranean basin (Jones 1981). If we consider the olive oil sector, with the accession of Greece the Community's deficit in olive oil diminished sharply as the level of self-sufficiency rose from an average of 86 percent (EEC 9) to 95 percent (EEC 10). Olive oil production in the EEC is shared by three countries with Italy producing 70 percent, Greece producing 26.9 percent and France producing 0.4 percent (EEC 1982, 6).

The annual production of olive oil in Spain is 82 percent of the production of the EEC 9 and almost 60 percent of the production of the EEC 10. The accession of Spain alone will have the effect, if consumption remains the same, of increasing the level of self-sufficiency in the EEC of Eleven to about 109 percent. Moreover, the inclusion of Spanish olive oil production in the CAP, combined with a trend of decreasing olive oil consumption in the EEC, as well as increased competition from other vegetable oil, could lead to massive Community surpluses (Vedel and Pisani 1979).

In the fruit and vegetables sector Spanish accession will compete not only with similar produce grown in the existing Mediterranean regions of the Community, but also with out-of-season glasshouse producers in northern Europe. Although the situation will be different for each product, the overall conclusion is that this sector is likely to cause the most problems in terms of structural surplus (especially through Spanish production potential) and the depression of prices. It is the Italian Mediterranean producers who seem likely to take the full brunt of Spanish accession in this sector (Pasca 1979).

The difficulties likely to be posed in the agricultural sector after enlargement will require major changes in the Community's financial and policy mechanisms, if only to protect the unity of the EEC from a revival of national self-interest. Several suggestions at both local, national and Community levels have been put forward to deal with these expected problems:

1. Assuming that enlargement does take place, long transitional periods could be implemented, say 10 to 12 years, in order to bring the Spanish and Portuguese prices into line with those of the Community. This is important because the adoption of the CAP will also have a significant impact upon the new members in the form of higher prices for cereals, dairy products, etc., which would have inflationary implications as well as aggravating existing trade deficit problems, especially for Portugal.

2. Suggestions have been put forward for increasing the price support given to Mediterranean products, in order to redress the imbalance within the CAP (House of Lords 1978). But high prices may give rise to surpluses, particularly for fruit and vegetables and exacerbate those for olive oil and wine, especially with the accession of Spain.

3. One of the most popular suggestions has related to a major structural reform programme for the Mediterranean regions of an enlarged Community (for example, Keller-Noellet 1979), involving both guidance and regional and social funds. While the limited success of similar schemes in the past has already been discussed for the EEC 9, its application to the EEC 12 would involve a massive transfer of funds from 'northern' members to the Community's southern periphery. With several of the northern members, such as the United Kingdom and W. Germany already complaining, sometimes bitterly, over their existing contributions to the EEC budget, the prospect of a financial transfer of the magnitude necessary to facilitate major structural reform in the Community's Mediterranean regions appears remote.

At the time of writing, the enlargement negotiations have come to a somewhat protracted deadlock with agriculture presenting the biggest stumbling block. Opposition to enlargement, especially in the Mediterranean regions of the EEC, is increasing and frequently manifests itself in demonstrations and violent outbreaks in the French *midi* against imports of

Spanish wine, fruit and vegetables. Moreover the enlargement issue has led to the Mediterranean regions of the Community turning against each other, causing a situation comparable to the northern battle over budgetary contributions. For Portugal and more especially Spain, prospects of membership appear far off, with any eventual agreement likely to include numerous safeguard clauses and diluted promises.

EEC enlargement is, however, not simply a question of accession; it is intricately bound up with the contradictions and constraints that European union faces. The Community has to find some answers to these before it can even contemplate enlargement, though this can only place enlargement even further off so that full membership in its correct usage may not come to Spain and Portugal until the late 1990s or early 2000s, that is almost 40 years since the first Spanish approaches to the Community.

With so much of Spanish and Portuguese agricultural (and industrial) trade gravitated towards western Europe and the ultimate desire of both countries to become full members of the EEC, the Community must find solutions to the problems that enlargement will bring. Short-term financial palliatives, introduced to placate existing member states, are, it seems, no solution to the fundamental difficulties that the accession and more importantly the integration process will present both for the Community and for the applicants.

References

Aceves, J.B. and Douglass, W.A. (1976) (eds) *The Changing Faces of Rural Spain*, Schenkman, Cambridge, Mass.

Agostini, D. (1977) Part-time farming in the rural–urban fringe in Italy, in R. Gasson (ed) *Place of Part-time Farming in Rural and Regional Development*, Kent, Wye College.

Barberis, C. (1979) *Famiglie senza giovani e agricoltura a mezzo tempo in Italia*, Milan.

Bartoli, P. (1981) *La politique de reconversion viticole. Resultats de la prime d'arrachage en Languedoc-Roussillon 1976–1979*, Montpellier, INRA.

Bergmann, D.C. and Laurent, C. (1977) Research needs and priorities, in R. Gasson (ed) *Place of Part-time Farming in Rural and Regional Development*, Kent, Wye College.

Boura, I.M., Jacinto, R.M., Lewis, J.R. and Williams, A.M. (1984) The economic impact of returned emigrants: Evidence from Leiria, Mangualde and Sabugal, in M. Porto (ed) *Emigration and Return in the Central Region*, Coimbra, CCRC.

Brun, A. (1977) Part-time farming, in R. Gasson (ed) *Place of Part-time Farming in Rural and Regional Development*, Kent, Wye College.

Cabral, M.V. (1978) Agrarian structures and recent rural movements in Portugal, *Journal of Peasant Studies*, Vol. 5, pp411–45.

Cavazzani, A. (1976) Social determinants of part-time farming in a marginal region of Italy, in A.M. Fuller and J.A. Mage (eds) *Part-Time Farming, Problem or Resource in Rural Development*, Norwich, Geo Abstracts.

Cavazzani, A. (1977) Part-time farming and the Common Agricultural Policy, in R. Gasson (ed) *Place of Part-time Farming in Rural and Regional Development*, Kent, Wye College.

Cesarini, G. (1979) *Rural Production Cooperatives in Southern Italy*, Arkleton Trust.

Christodoulou, D. (1976) Portugal's agrarian reform: a process of change with unique features, *Land Reform, Land Settlement and Cooperatives*, Vol. 2, FAO.

De Barros, A. (1980) Portuguese agrarian reform and economic and social development, *Sociologia Ruralis*, Vol. 20, pp82–96.

Fennell, R. (1979) *The Common Agricultural Policy of the European Community*, London, Granada.

Franklin, S.H. (1969) *The Rural Peasantry: the Final Phase*, London, Methuen.

Fuller, A.M. and Mage, J.A. (1976) (eds) *Part-Time Farming, Problem or Resource in Rural Development*, Norwich, Geo Abstracts.

Gallus, G. (1979) Agricultural problems of the accession of Greece, Portugal and Spain to the EC, *Intereconomics*, Vol. 1, pp6–10.

Galt, A.H. (1979) Exploring the cultural ecology of field fragmentation and scattering in the island of Pantelleria, *Journal of Anthropological Research*, Vol. 35, pp95–108.

Gasson, R. (1977) (ed) *Place of Part-Time Farming in Rural and Regional Development*, Kent, Wye College.

Guedes, M. (1981) Recent agricultural land policy in Spain, *Oxford Agrarian Studies*, Vol. 10, pp26–43.

House of Lords (1978) *Select Committee of the House of Lords, Thirty-Third Report: Mediterranean Agriculture*, London.

Hudson, R. and Lewis, J. (1982) The regional problem in an enlarged European Community, Paper presented to the Institute of British Geographers, Southampton, January 8, 1982.

Jones, A.R. (1981) The EEC's Mediterranean Policy, *Unpublished MA Thesis*, University of Durham.

Kalamotousakis, G.J. (1976) Greece's association with the European Community: an evaluation of the first ten years, in A. Shlaim and G.N. Yannopoulos (eds) *The EEC and the Mediterranean Countries*, Cambridge, Cambridge University Press.

Karabetsis, C. (1976) The legal foundations of the Greek association with the EEC, *Occasional Paper No 2*, Amsterdam, Europe Institute.

Keller-Noellet, M.J. (1979) Politique commune des structures: Un tournant, in M. Tracy and I. Hodac (eds) *Prospects for Agriculture in the EEC*, Bruges.

King, R.L. (1978) Shifting progress in Portugal's land reform, *Geography*, Vol. 63, pp118–9.

King, R.L. (1983 forthcoming) Agriculture and rural change, in H.D. Clout et al (eds) *Western Europe: Geographical Perspectives*, London, Longman.

King, R.L. and Burton, S. (1981) An Introduction to the Geography of Land Fragmentation and Consolidation, Leicester, *Occasional Paper No 8*, Department of Geography, University of Leicester.

Lane, D. (1980) Mini-farming in the Italian south, *The Geographical Magazine*, Vol. 53, p3.

Leigh, M. (1978) Nine EEC attitudes to enlargement, *Mediterranean Challenge*, Vol. I, Brighton, University of Sussex European Research Centre.

Lewis, J.R. and Williams, A.M. (1982) Desenvolvimento regional desequilibrado em Portugal: situação actual e impacto provavel da adesão a CEE, *Desenvolvimento Regional*, Vol. 14/15, pp79–139.

Musto, S. (1982) Enlargement and the structures of Western Europe, in D. Seers and C. Vaitsos (eds) *The Second Enlargement of the EEC: The Integration of Unequal Partners*, London, Macmillan.

Naylon, J. (1959) Land consolidation in Spain, *Annals of the Association of American Geographers*, Vol. 49, pp361–73.

Naylor, E.L. (1982) Retirement policy in French agriculture, *Journal of Agricultural Economics*, Vol. 33, pp25–36.

O'Flanagan, T.P. (1980) Agrarian structures in north-western Iberia: responses and their implications for development, *Geoforum*, Vol. 11, pp158–169.

O'Flanagan, T. (1982) Land reform and rural modernisation in Spain: a Galician perspective, *Erdkunde*, Vol. 36, pp48–53.

OECD (1969) *Agricultural Development in Southern Europe*, Paris, OECD.

OECD (1979) *The Agricultural Policy of Greece*, Paris, OECD.

Pasca, R. (1979) Conflicts arising from the enlargement of the Community: an Italian perspective, in M. Tracy and I. Hodac (eds) *Prospects for Agriculture in the EEC*, Bruges.

Pearce, J. (1981) *The Common Agricultural Policy*, 13, London, Royal Institute of International Affairs.

Pecora, A. and Gregoli, F. (1976) On some aspects of structural deficiencies of Italian agriculture: small farmers and non farming labour, in A. Pecora and R. Pracchi (eds) *Italian Contributions to the 23rd International Geographical Congress 1976*.

Pinna, M. and Ruocco, D. (1980) (eds) *Italy: A Geographical Survey*, Tokyo, 24th International Geographical Congress.

Podbielski, G. (1981) The Common Agricultural Policy and the Mezzogiorno, *Journal of Common Market Studies*, Vol. 19, pp333–50.

Ritson, C. (1982) Enlargement and its impact upon agriculture, in D. Seers and C. Vaitsos (eds) *The Second Enlargement of the EEC: The Integration of Unequal Partners*, London, Macmillan.

Rodríguez Alcaide, J.J. (1978) Spanish agriculture and the Common Market, Paper presented to UACES. Conference on Spain, Portugal and the EEC.

Rutledge, I. (1977) Land reform and the Portuguese revolution, *Journal of Peasant Studies*, Vol. 5, pp79–98.

Spanish Embassy (1982) *Spanish Agriculture*, London.

Taylor, R. (1980) *Implications for the Southern Mediterranean Countries of the Second Enlargement of the European Community*, Brussels, European Information.

Thompson, K. (1963) *Farm Amalgamation in Greece*, Athens, Centre for Economic Research.

Tovias, A. (1979) EEC enlargement: the southern neighbours, *Mediterranean Challenge*, Vol. 3, Brighton, University of Sussex European Research Centre.

Trigo de Abreu, A. (1978) Portuguese agriculture and the EEC, Paper presented to UACES Conference on Spain, Portugal and the EEC.

Tsoukalis, L. (1981) *The European Community and its Mediterranean Enlargement*, London, Macmillan.

Vedel, G. and Pisani, E. (1979) (eds) Europe et Mediterranée, *Cahiers de l'Institut de Recherche Sociale*, Perpignan, Université de Perpignan.

Zaheer, M. (1975) Measures of land reform: consolidation of holdings in India, *Behavioural Science and Community Development*, Vol. 9, pp87–121.

European Communities (EEC):
1. Mediterranean Agricultural Problems, *Newsletter of the Common Agricultural Policy* (May), Brussels 1977.
2. *Opinion on Spain's application for membership*, Brussels 1978.
3. *Agricultural Situation in the European Community*, Brussels 1981.
4. *Agricultural Situation in the European Community*, Brussels 1982.
5. *Agricultural Aspects of Enlargement*, Green Europe, Brussels 1982.
6. Agricultural Aspects of Spain's entry into the EEC, *Economic and Social Committee*, Brussels 1982.
7. *Telex Mediterranean*, February 1983.

CHAPTER TEN

THE EUROPEAN COMMUNITY AND THE MEDITERRANEAN REGION: TWO STEPS FORWARD, ONE STEP BACK

M. Blacksell

1. Introduction

The relationship between the European Community and the Mediterranean countries along its southern flank has always been an uneasy one. The economic vitality of the region and the need for its political support are clearly of considerable importance to the Community, but the interests of the Mediterranean lands have never, and probably will never be able to coincide neatly with those of the predominantly industrial north European nations that have dominated the Community since 1958. Repeated efforts have been made to strengthen economic and political ties, but they have tended to be fragmentary and directed towards individual countries or specific problems, so that the grandoise claims about an overall Mediterranean policy have always had something of a hollow ring to them.

The accession of Greece to the Community in 1981 and the formal negotiations about membership that have been going on with Portugal and Spain since 1978 and 1979 respectively have, however, given a new sense of urgency to the need for a more positive approach and for policies geared to the actual needs of the Mediterranean region. If the negotiations with all three countries turn out to be successful, their combined populations (54 millions) will comprise some 14 percent of the Community (313 millions) and thus become a force with which to be reckoned, especially in view of the fact that significant proportions of two of the original member countries, France and Italy, are essentially Mediterranean in their orientation and outlook already. The latter point is doubly significant, because the first enlargement of the European Community in 1973 shifted the emphasis decisively northwards, with Denmark, Eire and the UK forming some 25 percent of the then total population, thereby relegating the special needs of the Mediterranean economies to a relatively lowly position.

The key to the current changes is going to be the outcome of the negotiations with Spain. Just as the UK dominated the first enlargement of the Community in 1973, so Spain, the second largest country in Europe (504,750 sq km) with a population of 36 millions, is dominating the second. Neither Greece nor Portugal is sufficiently large to affect significantly the overall structure and orientation of the Community. Spain on the other hand poses problems other than its sheer size: of all the countries in Western Europe it has been the most isolated from the various moves towards political and economic integration in the post-World War II era, and it also has a well-developed foreign policy of its own that is strongly influenced by its links with a former colonial empire (Minet, Siotis and Tsakaloyannis 1981). It only became a full member of the OEEC in 1959 and joined NATO as recently as 1981. It has never seriously attempted previously to become a member of the European Community (Rudnick 1976), and has also never belonged to EFTA. With such a background and the somewhat fragile state of the democratic institutions that have been gingerly put together since the end of the Franco dictatorship in 1975 (see Chapter 5) it is hardly surprising that achieving membership of such an aggressively democratic grouping as the European Community has proved a difficult proposition.

2. Mediterranean policy within the European Community

The policies of the European Community have always been first and foremost economic, seeking to remove barriers to free trade internally and to develop common policies, notably with respect to agriculture. Nevertheless, the ironing out of regional economic disparities has been a constant underlying concern and, throughout the 1960s, a very important aspect of the task was to improve conditions in the southern fringe of the Mediterranean, particularly in the *Mezzogiorno* of southern Italy. It is also worth recalling that in the late 1950s Mediterranean problems loomed much larger in the domestic policies of France, for until 1962 Algeria was effectively a member of the Community as one of the overseas *départements*, prior to it becoming an independent state. In the early years, between 1958 and 1972, over 90 percent of the £1,400 millions loaned by the European Investment Bank went to projects in Italy and the Mediterranean regions of France (Commission of the European Communities 1982a). Even after the first

enlargement in 1973, these two countries continued to get generous allocations of the available funds for regional development, with Italy claiming 40
percent of the £540 millions shared out by the European Regional Development Fund in its first three years between 1975 and 1978. Taking the whole
of the period over which they have operated, from 1958 and 1973 respectively, the European Investment Bank and the European Regional
Development Fund have together devoted some 45 percent of their total
resources to Mediterranean projects. If the European Social Fund and the
European Guidance and Guarantee Fund are also taken into account, then
between 1975 and 1981 the *Mezzogiorno*, the south of France and Greece
have received altogether £2,622 millions in grants and £3,381 millions in
loans.

The true scope of these monies, however, is put into perspective when
compared with the total budget of the Community and with the various
national budgets. All the agencies described above spend rather less than 15
percent of Community funds, while agricultural support still accounts for
well over 60 percent, having at one time in the late 1960s consumed over 90
percent. Since the bulk of this support goes to subsidizing the production of
temperate European crops and animal products, Mediterranean agriculture
with its heavy investment in fruit, wine, vegetables and olives fares
relatively badly. In any case the Community budget is only equivalent to
about 2.5 percent of the national budgets of the member countries, so that it
is really not in a position to compensate to any really significant extent for
differences in overall economic performance. Under these circumstances it
is entirely predictable that the economic imbalance between the north and
the south of the Community has continued to widen. In all the Mediterranean regions agriculture still employs between 20 percent and 60 percent
of the working population, figures that have not been approached in the
industrial parts of western Europe for more than a generation, and in the
Mezzogiorno and Greece GDP per head remains less than half the Community average.

3. The second enlargement

The second enlargement of the Community is proving a long-drawn-out
affair, compared with the first. Rather than applying as a group and
succeeding or failing together, Greece, Portugal and Spain lodged their
applications at different dates and the negotiations are all now at different
stages. Greece's application has been successful and it has been a full

member since January 1981, although it will be between the five and seven years, depending on which sectors of the economy are involved, before it is fully integrated into the Community. As far as Portugal and Spain are concerned, there appears to be no immediate prospect of an early breakthrough in the negotiations and the earliest date that either could join would seem to be 1985. Assuming that the transition periods will also be rather longer than in the case of Greece, probably extending for up to 10 years, it seems unlikely that the second enlargement will actually be complete before 1995 at the earliest.

Greece has had an association agreement with the Community since 1962 and, although negotiations and new developments were frozen, it remained in force as far as trade was concerned throughout the period of the military junta from 1967 to 1974 (Tovias 1977, p45). The whole purpose of this agreement was that it would lead to eventual customs union, so that full membership was the logical, ultimate outcome. The initial impact of the accession of Greece on the Community as a whole has been slight, as was widely predicted (Georgakopoulos 1980; Pepelasis, Yannopoulos, Mitos, Kalamotousakis 1980). However, the initial impact on Greece itself has been variable. As reported in Chapter 2, net budgetary gains have been offset partly by the adverse effects on the balance of trade between Greece and the remainder of the Community. Food prices have risen as a result of high-cost EEC imports replacing those from other countries. The worst hit sector has been manufacturing and Greece has had to take a step backwards in this area, reimposing some protective tariffs.

As a member of EFTA, Portugal has had a formal trading agreement with the Community since 1972, concluded as part of the first enlargement, giving preferential access for most of its industrial products. There is some concern within the Community about structural weaknesses in the Portuguese economy and a feeling that these need to be attended to before exposure to the full rigours of the customs union, which full membership would entail. Nevertheless, studies of the impact of membership on specific sectors of the economy have concluded that for most agricultural products, rye and maize being exceptions, the prospects will improve, as they will for many industries, notably textiles, paper, wood and cork, nonmetallic minerals and metal products (Lewis and Williams 1982). Only two areas of industry seem likely to be seriously disadvantaged, chemicals and base metals. It would seem that Portugal has much to gain from membership (at least in some sectors) and the Community little to lose.

As has been pointed out earlier, the real problems of the second enlargement are posed by Sapin, whose only formal connection with the Community has so far been a preferential trade agreement, signed in 1970, which was restricted to specific products, such as citrus fruit, and did not allow for future negotiations and development. Reservations about Spanish membership stem from a number of different questions, many of which apply also to Greece and Portugal, but which because of their sheer size loom larger and appear more intractable in the case of Spain.

Agriculture

Of most immediate concern is Spanish agriculture, not so much because of its importance in the national economy, which is steadily declining, but more because of the overwhelming share that the CAP devours of the Community's own budget and the preoccupation amongst the present members with reform. If Spain does become a member, the area of farmed land within the Community will increase by some 30 percent, the agricultural labour force by 25 percent and the number of farm holdings by 32 percent, but, significantly, the number of consumers will only grow by some 14 percent (Taylor 1980). The simplistic implication of these figures is clearly that were output from Spanish agriculture to approach the levels in the Community as a whole, then membership would mean that the market would be flooded with cheap food and prices would be forced down. In practice the potential impact would seem likely to be both more complex and less traumatic than the crude figures might lead one to suppose.

While agriculture in Spain shares many features in common with the industry elsewhere in the Community, the mix of crops and livestock is markedly different from that in the countries of northern Europe, with the emphasis firmly on products that the Community has defined as 'Mediterranean'— citrus fruit, fruit and vegetables, olives, wine, flowers, tobacco, durum wheat and sheep meat. Many of these are products in which the Community is not self-sufficient, so that the main difficulty is to find ways of protecting small-scale producers already within the Community from sharper competition.

This will prove most difficult with citrus fruit, where Spain accounts for 20 percent of world exports, of which in 1981 some £200 millions worth (90 percent) found their way into Community markets. As far as the Community is concerned the main question is how to hold prices. Under the existing preferential trade agreement Spain has restricted imports when prices threatened to fall too low, so producers in Italy, France and latterly Greece have been protected. Once it became a full members, however, such restraint would be abandoned and prices would almost inevitably fall. Ironically, this would not only put pressure on producers in France, Italy and Greece, and in the other Mediterranean countries that also export citrus fruit to the Community, it would also probably reduce world prices generally and, therefore, be detrimental to Spanish producers as well. Indeed there would appear to be little that citrus growers in Spain have to gain from Community membership in the short-term, for they have already penetrated this market very successfully and, even when tariff concessions were forfeited completely for short periods, it did not appear to affect unduly the general export performance (Leigh 1977). The situation with fresh vegetables is similar, in that enlargement to 12 members is likely to make the Community more or less self-sufficient, so that the producers most likely to suffer are those elsewhere in the Mediterranean region, whose existing preferential agreements will be undermined by the removal of all restrictions on producers in Spain, Greece and Portugal.

In the long-term the most intractable agricultural problems for the Community will probably turn out to be how to absorb Spanish olive oil and wine. Spain produces over 40 percent of the world's olive oil and output is currently valued at £70 million. At present some 38 percent of this is bought by the Community, most of it finding its way to Italy, but demand is weak and has been falling since the mid-1970s. The reason is not difficult to identify, for olive oil is between three and four times as expensive as other cooking oils and increasingly large numbers of consumers are turning to these substitutes. If Spain becomes a member of the Community, the price of olive oil will undoubtedly fall, unless there is intervention on a massive scale through the CAP. It seems unlikely, however, that any price reductions will be sufficiently large to stem the overall decline in demand, so that ways must be found to persuade producers to turn to other crops. If such a strategy is not successful, overproduction and an unsaleable glut would seem to be inevitable.

Wine producers face the same sort of problems: Spain has a massive and relatively poorly utilized capacity, which full membership of the Community could stimulate and thus provide very unwelcome competition in a market that is arleady saturated. In fact Spain sells some 34 percent of its £115 million (1981) of wine exports to the Community at the moment, so that once freed of tariff restrictions exports there should be no difficulty in improving substantially on its share of the market. Anticipating these changes, Spanish wine producers have recently been concentrating on improving the quality of their product and expanding the range of wine for export, with much greater emphasis on red, rather than the traditional Spanish white wines.

The reluctance of existing Community members to involve themselves in yet further complications over agricultural policy — given their abject failure to reform the CAP— is understandable, yet the impact of Spanish agriculture need not necessarily be entirely negative. Spain is a net importer of grain and, as its still relatively modest meat and dairy production sectors expand, demand for animal feed is bound to grow too. At present grain imports are purchased on world markets, mainly from the USA and Latin America, where prices generally are substantially lower than in the Community. Once Spain became a full member, it would have to contend with much higher prices because of the Community import levy and farmers in its new partner countries would be in a much better position to sell grain there. Although this inducement is attractive to the existing members of the Community, it is not without pitfalls. There is considerable scope for Spanish farmers to increase their domestic production of grain and other fodder crops, particularly if they are forced to abandon the more traditional olive groves and vineyards on a large scale. Equally the US and Latin American grain producers will exert all available pressure to ensure that their traditional markets in Spain are not wrested from them by blatant protectionism (Tovias, 1979). At the very least, it seems certain that Latin American countries will demand the same concessions as those currently enjoyed by the ACP nations under the Lomé Convention and Spain, because of its historic colonial connections with the region, will doubtless support them.

On balance, therefore, it seems unlikely that Spanish membership will do anything other than exacerbate the already unsatisfactory and costly system of agricultural mangement developed within the CAP. At the very least, the existing members are going to demand a long transition period, so as to give them time to put their own houses in order. In all probability they will procrastinate for as long as possible, before even taking a decision in principle about Spanish (and Portuguese) membership.

Fisheries

An understandable reluctance to upset agreements painstakingly thrashed out over a period of years within the present Community explains much of the hesitation amongst the members about committing themselves to a further enlargement. Spain has one of the biggest fishing fleets in Europe and to incorporate it under the umbrella of the Common Fisheries Policy

(CFP), only agreed after 10 years of negotiation in January 1983, will mean that important aspects of the policy have to be renegotiated. Inevitably old grievances will be reopened and the temptation for states to break ranks, and unilaterally protect what they see as their own national interests, will be almost unstoppable.

There are two quite distinct aspects to the CFP: on the one hand the principle of equal access for all Community fishermen to the territorial waters of member states and, on the other, a complex system of catch quotas, devised so as to give fair shares to all and prevent overfishing (Churchill 1980). Of the two, the question of access will probably prove the easiest to solve. There is no prospect of varying the exclusive fishing zones agreed for the UK around the British coast and there will probably be little pressure from the Spanish to do so. It seems likely that the main difficulty will arise with the French objecting to the Spanish fleet having completely unrestricted access in the Bay of Biscay, and they may well try to negotiate exclusive fishing rights for themselves there. It is the discussions about catches, however, that are likely to prove the most delicate. These have largely been agreed for reasons of conservation, so as to ensure the long-term preservation of the fishstocks, and the increase of a quarter in the size of the fishing fleet, which Spanish membership would entail, will obviously throw the calculations completely awry. Spain (and Portugal) will of course contribute its own exclusive fishing grounds around the Iberian peninsula to the Community pond, so that the trade-off will not be entirely oneway, but the balance will have been upset. There is little reason for supposing that renegotiating will prove any easier than when the CFP was first agreed.

Despite these undoubted difficulties and the sensitivity of the issues involved, fisheries are unlikely to prove critical in the negotiations over enlargement. Spanish accession will confer considerable benefits as well as costs on the Community fishing industry. Overall Spain has a deficiency in fish and already imports considerable quantities from elsewhere in Europe. The prospect of easier access to this market will go some way to quelling the fears amongst existing Community members. In the final analysis, however, fisheries will not be decisive under any circumstances, because the industry carries too little weight, both in the Community and in the individual member states. Unlike agriculture, it commands only a very small part of the Community budget and nowhere, with the possible exception of Denmark, does the fishing industry exert anything other than local pressure. None of the larger member states is likely to have to bow to pressure from fishery interests and oppose enlargement, although it may well be used as a ploy to delay progress.

Industry

In the seemingly endless debate about the problems that Spanish agriculture will cause in an enlarged Community, it is easy to forget that Spain is an industrial country, not unlike either Italy or France, and that manufacturing industry comprises well over 40 percent of the GDP, growing vigorously in recent years until the recession (see Chapter 1). The major sectors are: textiles and clothing, which are in gradual decline; food processing, which is virtually static; and metal manufactures, which are growing strongly. As far as the Community is concerned, most Spanish industrial products already enjoy almost unrestricted access to its markets under a series of agreements concluded in the early 1970s, so that enlargement is not going to open its industries to any new and damaging competition. On the other hand, Spanish markets are still protected by a complex web of import controls and other restrictions and removal of these would expose domestic industries to much fiercer competition.

Opinion is divided as to how industry in Spain would respond to being fully integrated into the Community customs union. On the negative side it is argued by Tovias (1979) that many of the weaker firms, particularly in the more traditional sectors of textiles and clothing and food processing, rely on the protected domestic market for their survival. Equally much of the new foreign investment has been attracted to Spain by concessions and incentives that would disappear once it became a member of the Community. A more positive interpretation is that, despite its recent success, Spanish industry is suffering from a lack of competition, that is delaying much needed restructuring and reform. There are too many small firms, relying on paying wages that are too low and not backed up by adequate social security provisions. Membership would see these anomalies gradually removed and, to keep themselves competitive, firms would have to improve their productivity and adopt more aggressive marketing techniques. As a result Spanish industry would, in theory, emerge much stronger and with better overall long-term prospects.

These kinds of argument may be attractive in a period of economic expansion, when demand is high and new markets are crying out to be served. During a recession, such as has afflicted western Europe and the whole of the world trade system during the late 1970s and the 1980s, they are much less alluring. Indeed the growth of diffuse industrialization can be viewed as one response to this crisis (see Chapter 7). Furthermore, restructuring is synonymous with contraction and unemployment in the

Community of 10 stood at 12 millions in 1982. To increase the total productive capacity still further would simply impose intolerable burdens, in the eyes of some member countries, on an economy that is already overstretched. It would mean that the small amounts of money for regional aid available from Community funds like the European Social Fund and the European Regional Development Fund would have to be spread even more thinly. Despite the relative success in developing basic manufacturing industries such as car assembly, Spain's two largest industrial regions, the Basque country and Catalonia, have experienced sharp increases in unemployment in the 1980s. Many of the more traditional industries, such as ship-building, would have to compete in a Community market where there is currently chronic over-capacity. A further difficulty is the regional disparities within Spain. Manufacturing industry is heavily concentrated in a narrow band in the east and north of the country, the areas closest to the Community and, therefore, best placed to compete in the enlarged, open market. Aside from the capital, Madrid, most of the remaining two-thirds of Spain to the south and west is still predominantly agricultural, and the fear is that income disparities would increase. They are already wide by European standards, with the poorest region Extremadura having an index of 69.8, as compared with a national average of 100 and a figure of 123.3 for the richest region, Madrid. In recent years these per capita disparities have in fact fallen somewhat, due to population migration from the poorer agricultural areas, but there is a suspicion that Community membership could once more reverse the trend (Hebbert 1982).

Despite the many imponderables about the impact of enlargement on industrial development in both the Community and Spain, the reality, as with agriculture, may well prove less traumatic than the prospect. More than half Spain's exports already go to the Community and a third of imports come from it. Indeed, the latter proportion is much higher if imports of oil and natural gas are excluded. This suggests that Community industries have a firm hold in many Spanish markets despite protective measures and that, while the terms of trade may improve somewhat with enlargement, the basic pattern will probably alter relatively little. For its part, Spanish industry already has more or less unrestricted access to the Community and, even though as a nonmember it could theoretically be unilaterally excluded through the imposition of import controls and other similar measures, such action seems highly unlikely on any significant scale. The fears that foreign industrial investment might be driven away by the prospect of Spain coming into line with the rest of the Community on such things as wage rates and social security payments seems equally fanciful. More probably foreign investment will actually be attracted by the prospect of guaranteed access to the whole of the Community market.

Movement of labour

One particular facet of the economic impact of the second enlargement that is politically extremely delicate is the free movement of labour. In the early years the right of workers to seek employment anywhere in the Community, regardless of nationality was much cherished, even though in practice it did little more than confirm what was already the status quo. Until the mid-1970s, there were very large movements into the industrial heartland of the Community from the agricultural regions of both member and nonmember countries in the Mediterranean region. Although the total numbers have declined a little from a peak in the mid-1970s, there were still in 1982 over 5 million foreign workers in Community countries, with more than half a million each originating from both Portugal and Spain. In the current recession the Community is seeking every possible avenue to restrict immigration and also to reduce further the numbers already working there. Since as early as 1974 most member states have banned the recruitment of labour from outside the Community, including Portugal and Spain, and there have even been moves to try and curb internal movements, notably from the UK. The prospect of unrestricted access for workers from the two Iberian states is, therefore, an alarming one, especially for France and West Germany, where immigrant workers still comprise nearly 7 percent of the total population. Both countries will adamantly oppose free movement in the short-term and, even if they agree to its eventual introduction, are certain to demand a very much longer transition period than the seven years that was agreed in the case of Greece. For their part, Portugal and Spain are likely to try and insist on this part of the original Treaty of Rome being implemented in full. Portugal has had the greatest difficulty in absorbing the estimated 800,000 *retornados* displaced from its former colonies and both it and Spain set great store by the remittances sent back by immigrant workers, even if the economic importance of these monies has often been exaggerated (see Chapter 6).

The Community budget

Much of what has been said above underlines the fundamental difficulties involved in trying to integrate states with widely different levels of economic activity into a single economic unit. Spain has a per capita GDP only marginally greater than that of Eire and Greece, the poorest members of the present Community, while Portugal's GDP is significantly smaller (Deubner 1980). The policies of the Community are still, more than a decade after the first enlargement, biased heavily towards the interests of the six original members. The overwhelming emphasis is on the customs union and internal free trade in industrial goods, coupled with massive support for temperate agriculture through the CAP. This balance has been a source of constant friction over the past ten years, because it has meant that the UK, the biggest of the countries to enter in the first enlargement, has been a net contributor to the budget, despite being one of the poorer countries in the Community. This has led to repeated wrangles, which have been quieted but still not removed, largely by increased West German financial contributions.

As most Mediterranean farm products are not covered by the CAP, it is quite possible that both Portugal and Spain would be net contributors to the Community budget as well, even though they would be two of the least well-off countries. West Germany has already indicated its unwillingness to continue to resolve the recurrent crisis over UK contributions, let alone those created by the admission of any new members. For their part, Portugal and Spain are playing down the very real problems that their membership will cause in the absence of radical reform of the Community budget. The difficulties for the UK were also widely predicted prior to the first enlargement, but were discounted because of the wider benefits which, it was assumed, would accrue from membership. The Community is unlikely to allow itself to fall into the same trap twice, but to avoid doing so it must either reform the budget prior to any further enlargement, or impose conditions on entry which preclude Portugal and Spain from claiming, let alone getting, the kind of rebates, that the UK has been claiming and sometimes getting since 1979. Any such exclusion would, however, have serious repercussions, for it would be the first step towards recognizing two classes of Community membership, something that has frequently been mooted, but so far always been firmly rejected as being against the spirit of the ideal of an integrated Europe (Wallace 1976).

4. The overall Mediterranean approach

The relationship between the countries bordering the Mediterranean and the Community has traditionally been a close one (Figure 10.1), but has not been marked by the kind of global agreement concluded with the ACP

Figure 10.1 Relationship of Mediterranean countries to the European Community.

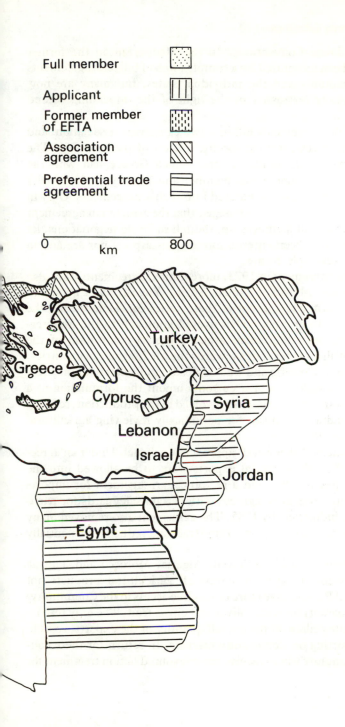

Full member

Applicant

Former member
of EFTA

Association
agreement

Preferential trade
agreement

0   km   800

Turkey

Greece

Cyprus

Syria

Lebanon

Israel

Jordan

Egypt

states under the Lomé Conventions. In the Mediterranean the former colonial ties have been recognized by a complex web of bilateral agreements between the Community and the individual states, but many are now having to be radically reassessed in the light of the impending second enlargement.

In broad terms the agreements fall into two categories: association, and more limited preferences covering specific aspects of the economy. The association agreements are similar to that which Greece had with the Community before it became a full member and Turkey (1963), Malta (1971) and Cyprus (1973) have all entered into such arrangements. Only in the case of Turkey, however, is it envisaged that the association agreement will eventually lead to full membership, though so far no negotiations, let alone a time-scale, have been entered into on this aspect, nor are any in prospect in the foreseeable future.

Before the first enlargement in 1973, more limited agreements were also signed with Tunisia, Morocco, Israel, Spain, Yugoslavia, Egypt and Lebanon, but the form and content of these varies considerably and the Community decided to embark on an overall approach to the Mediterranean area. There were four main aspects: the harmonization of the external policies of all member states towards the Mediterranean countries; agreement on reciprocal tariffs and quotas, leading ultimately to the creation of either a free-trade area or a customs union; the formulation of a common policy towards third countries involved in the production, refining or export of oil; and a mechanism for periodically reviewing agricultural concessions (Tovias 1977).

The first beneficiary of the overall approach was Israel. Under an agreement signed in 1975, all industrial exports were to be allowed into the Community duty free by 1977 and a reciprocal arrangement for imports from the Community was to be agreed, with certain safeguards for particularly vulnerable industries, by 1985. The agreement also removed many of the quotas on agricultural exports from Israel and reduced substantially the tariff levels.

Further agreements quickly followed. Algeria, Morocco and Tunisia accepted arrangements in 1976, whereby all agricultural products not governed by the CAP could have more or less free access to the Community, thus opening up markets for wine, olives and citrus fruit. The only restriction was an absolute ceiling on the overall quantity of the exports, so as to prevent gluts occurring on Community markets. In return for these concessions, the Community was to receive most favoured nation treatment for its exports.

In 1977 agreements were signed with Egypt, Jordan and Syria, removing almost entirely tariffs and quotas on nonagricultural products, and introducing reduced tariff levels for agricultural products as well. Finally, a more limited agreement was concluded with Lebanon, because of the unstable political situation there, and moves were made to implement a nonpreferential trade agreement with Yugoslavia, that had first been signed in 1973.

With all these agreements it is vital to remember that the emphasis was on cooperation. Nearly every one included aid provisions, whereby the Community would try to strengthen the industrial base of the country concerned and actively encourage trade links at all levels. For all the Mediterranean countries the Community is an important market and in the cases of Egypt, Algeria, Morocco, Syria and Israel accounts for over 30 percent of their imports and exports (Taylor 1980). The second enlargement is particularly worrying for Morocco, Algeria, Tunisia and Malta, because all three applicant countries produce both industrial and agricultural products that compete directly with their own. The degree of concern actually varies considerably: Morocco and Tunisia facing a very uncertain future for their exports if the enlargement goes ahead, while Algeria with its huge oil reserves is much more secure.

It would be wrong, however, to lay too much stress on the second enlargement, when trying to explain the relatively small success of the Community's overall Mediterranean approach in improving the standard of living and the general economic performance of the countries in the region. Almost as soon as the agreements were signed, the world recession and the worsening economic situation within the Community resulted in voluntary agreements to restrict exports of products that might affect adversely production from domestic industries. Of these, the most significant related to textiles, as it affected all the Mediterranean countries, even though some, such as Egypt, Tunisia and Morocco, will feel the affects more seriously than others, because of the size of their textile industries. The main problem with the second enlargement is that it threatens to turn many of these supposedly temporary measures into a permanent disadvantage. Both the industry and agriculture of Greece, Portugal and Spain are very similar to that of many of the other Mediterranean countries and at present all three are, or recently were, subject to the same restrictions. Full membership of the Community will see these restrictions progressively dismantled as the transition periods elapse and the nonmember countries will then have the greatest difficulty in reestablishing themselves in the Community market.

The Community is all too well aware of the dilemma in which it finds itself. On the one hand, its overall approach has failed to achieve most of its stated objectives (Commission of the European Communities 1982b). In addition, the general economic recession has severely reduced the demand for labour, so that new immigrant workers from the Mediterranean countries are now all but barred from working in the Community. This latter development has effectively removed one of the closest links between the Community and its southern neighbours, as well as a valuable source of foreign exchange for any of the poorer countries. On the other side, the Community wants to cement its relationships with Greece, Portugal and Spain and realizes that anything short of full membership will almost certainly prove unsatisfactory, especially now that formal negotiations are well advanced with all three countries. The choices are difficult and the only prospect of the Community building a really close and fruitful relationship with the whole of the Mediterranean area is a return to general economic expansion and, thus, a desire for the removal of economic protection on all sides (Commission of the European Communities 1982c).

5. European security and the Mediterranean region

The European Community has always been primarily an economic community, its policies geared towards greater integration within the European economy as a whole. Yet despite its atempts to stand above party and even national politics in economic matters, it has repeatedly dabbled in issues of wider international concern. Even before the Treaty of Rome was signed in 1956, there was an abortive effort to create a European Defence Community and again in more recent years there have been numerous attempts by individual member states to try and get the whole of the Community to speak on their behalf and thus add the weight of all 10 voices to their argument. All but Eire are members of NATO, even if the degree of commitment varies, and all firmly support democratic government, so that there is a genuine, fundamental identity of outlook, even if disagreements inevitably arise over the details of policy.

In the states of northern and western Europe that are not members of the Community, the governments are politically very stable and they share, at least in principle, the latter's overall objectives, even if for a variety of reasons, they feel unable to join. Such stability and unity of purpose does not characterize the Mediterranean states. Many have unstable or totalitarian governments, or both; only Turkey is a member of NATO; and some, such as Syria and Libya, have close military ties with the Soviet Union. The Community is therefore concerned to increase its influence in this region, so as to ensure that the Mediterranean does not become the front line in East–West power politics. What cannot be guaranteed is that the accession of Spain and Portugal, following on from that of Greece, will strengthen the political unity of the Community. Greece has already taken an independent line on a number of issues for which the Community has formulated general political views and PASOK's aims previously have included complete withdrawal from NATO and strengthening relations with the Balkan states. At present, none of the Communist parties in southern Europe have immediate prospects of acceding to government but their strengths do represent possible sources of weakness in any overall western European security strategies.

In 1982 the European Commissioner with special responsibilities for Mediterranean affairs, Vice-President Lorenzo Natali, in a speech about the need for a coherent and positive approach to the region, argued that, 'Geopolitical reasons in themselves made an impressive case for the necessity of a coherent European community policy on the Mediterranean. A glance at the map proves it. Look first at the Balkans and the mouth of the Atlantic. Take in the Dardanelles and the petrol producing region of the Near East: remember too that the Mediterranean is the inescapable north–south axis for links between Europe and Africa. We must question whether the Community could survive a serious disturbance in the Mediterranean region. . . .' (Natali 1982, p1). Clearly what he was advocating was an approach on the part of the Community that would guarantee the support of the Mediterranean countries, because it would be in its best strategic interests. Whether the means to that end are economic, political or military is almost besides the point. There is nothing new about this theme and over the years its importance has been stressed repeatedly. In 1971 Lambert wrote that '. . . the Mediterranean is the pond in the Community's backyard, and to those who traditionally consider it as a European sea . . . there cannot fail to be something at once disturbing and provoking in the sight of the American and Soviet fleets playing hide and seek in it' (Lambert 1971, p38–9). Yet despite such exhortations, the members of the Community have been reluctant to assume a sufficiently high political and economic profile to dominate the course of events in the Mediterranean region. Those Mediterranean countries that are not already members have little evidence on the basis of past policy for believing that the Community is truly committed to their future, notwithstanding the overall approach and the promise of new initiatives in the wake of the second enlargement.

6. Conclusion

Naylon (1982, p122) has recently described the Mediterranean enlargement of the Community as 'a troublesome enlargement' and that it is certainly proving to be, though no more so in its way than the first in 1973. There is, however, a major difference in the current negotiations, in that the members are under considerable political pressure to ensure that they succeed, yet are filled with doubts about the economic wisdom of what they are doing. The situation is made even more confused, because most of the public argument is over the economics of the proposed enlargement, though what is being done in the name of economics is actually part of a political process that is using economic integration as a means rather than an end. All the members of the Community welcomed and encouraged the return to democracy in Greece, Portugal and Spain and their joining is seen as an insurance against a return to dictatorship. The economic freedoms embodied in the Community are really only an aspect of a much wider freedom that membership confers. However, the ambivalence that always surrounded the political relationship between the Community and the national governments of its member states, has made it very difficult to argue the case for joining in anything other than economic terms.

Indeed, it is ironic that the immediate political strains are likely to be increased if the enlargement goes ahead, as all the Mediterranean members will have Socialist governments, while the Conservatives hold sway in most of the north. Furthermore, the Community may find itself involved in increasing numbers of political disputes between its members. It is, for example, already being drawn into the controversy between the UK and Eire over Northern Ireland and it is hardly conceivable that it could avoid involvement in the dispute between the UK and Spain over the sovereignty of Gibraltar. It should also be recalled that, had Spain been a member in 1982, it would have been far more difficult to put together unified EEC support for Britain's actions in the Falklands. Spain's accession will also be likely to involve the Community in the dispute with Morocco over the former's colonies in North Africa. Portugal's accession brings the least global political difficulties (although control of Timor is still in dispute with Indonesia) but, looking further ahead, future Turkish membership could bring that country's dispute with Greece over the Aegean right into the heart of Brussels. Enlargement will create as many new strategic political problems as advantages.

To the end of the century the Community is in fact faced by hard and difficult choices. The second enlargement has concentrated attention on incorporating the fledgling democracies on its southern border, even though the EC hitherto had little success in narrowing the economic disparities between rich and poor countries and regions. There is no guarantee that the bulk of the populations of Greece, Portugal and Spain will be economically better off inside rather than outside the Community. What is absolutely certain is that the Community itself will be faced with immeasurably more difficult problems of regional disparity and, so far, its record of coping with them is far from impressive. All the concentration on the Mediterranean has also diverted attention away from links elsewhere. The residual group of Alpine and Scandinavian countries in EFTA have been largely ignored by the Community as such in recent years and there are grounds for believing that this may be encouraging a dangerous fragmentation (Hager 1982). Many members are reluctant to see their former allegiances in other parts of Europe wither, especially at the expense of a Mediterranean adventure that is fraught with difficulty and where the fruits of success are likely to be few. Some national governments might simply turn their energies away from the Community and it could die of neglect, rather than as a result of any conscious political decision to alter it. Although such a demise is unlikely, the stability of the Community certainly cannot be taken for granted and the political limbo caused by the slow pace of the negotiations on the second enlargement is a genuine cause for concern.

References

Churchill, R. (1980) Revision of the EEC's Common Fisheries Policy, *European Law Review*, Vol. 5, pp3–37 and pp95–111.

Commission of the European Communities (1982a) The Community and the countries and regions of the Mediterranean, *European File* 19/82.

Commission of the European Communities (1982b) On a Mediterranean policy for an enlarged Community *COM(82)* 353 final.

Commission of the European Communities (1983c) Problems of enlargement, *COM(82)* 757 final.

Deubner, C. (1980) The southern enlargement of the European Community: opportunities and dilemmas from a West German point of view, *Journal of Common Market Studies*, Vol. XVIII, pp229–45.

Georgakopoulos, T.A. (1980) Greece and the EEC, *Three Banks Review*, Vol. 128, pp38–50.

Hager, W. (1982) Little Europe, wider Europe and Western economic cooperation, *Journal of Common Market Studies*, Vol. XXI, pp171–97.

Hebbert, M. (1982) Regional policy in Spain, *Geoforum*, Vol. 13, pp107–20.

Lambert, J. (1971) The Cheshire cat and the pond: EEC and the Mediterranean area, *Journal of Common Market Studies*, Vol. X, pp37–46.

Leigh, M. (1977) Mediterranean agriculture and the enlargement of the EEC, *World Today*, Vol. 33, pp207–14.

Lewis, J.R. and Williams, A.M. (1982) Desenvolvimento regional desequilibrado em Portugal: situação actual e impacto provaval da adesão a CEE, *Desenvolvimento Regional*, Vol. 14/15, pp79–139.

Minet, G., Siotis, J. and Tsakaloyannis, P. (1981) Spain, Greece and Community Politics, *Mediterranean Challenge*, Vol. VI, Brighton, University of Sussex European Research Centre.

Natali, L. (1982) L'élargissement de la Communauté Européenne vers le sud, A speech delivered at the Konrad Adenauer foundation, Brussels, 2–3 December.

Naylon, J. (1981) 'Spain, Portugal and the EEC: A troublesome enlargement', *Bank of London and South American Review*, Vol. 15, pp122–30.

Pepelasis, A., Yannopoulos, G., Mitos, A., Kalamotousakis, G. and Perdikis, N. (1980) The tenth member— economic aspects, *Mediterranean Challenge*, Vol. IV, Brighton, University of Sussex European Research Centre.

Rudnick, D. (1976) Spain's long road to Europe, *The World Today*, Vol. 32, pp134–41.

Taylor, R. (1980) Implications for the southern Mediterranean countries of the second enlargement of the European Community, *Europe Information* X/225/80–EN.

Tovias, A. (1977) *Tariff preferences in Mediterranean diplomacy*, London, Macmillan.

Tovias, A. (1979) EEC Enlargement: the southern neighbours, *Mediterranean Challenge*, Vol. III, Brighton, University of Sussex, European Research Centre.

Wallace, W. (1976) Wider but weaker: the continued enlargement of the EEC, *World Today*, Vol. 33, pp104–11.

INDEX

Abruzzi, 170, 247
Abyssinia, 17
ACNP, 116, 119
Aegean, 35, 43, 242, 285
Africa, 5, 6, 17, 91, 146, 150, 156, 157, 188, 284, 285
agriculture, 8, 14, 33, 38, 41, 69, 85–86, 137, 138–139, 154–155, 166–168, 201, 225, 236–264, 270, 271, 272–274
  irrigation, 138, 250, 258, 259
  labour force characteristics, 237–238
  part-time, 201, 240–241
  size structure, 42, 101, 155, 242–249
Albania, 4
Alentejo, 99, 101, 242, 243–245
Algeria, 157, 158, 160, 269, 281, 282
Alicante, 213, 231
Almeria, 139
Alto Adige, 170
Amoral, 95
Andalusia, 138, 139, 40, 151, 161, 165, 191, 213, 214
Andreotti, 78
Angola, 91, 92, 101, 239
Apulia, 170
Arias, 121, 123
Armed Forces Movement (MFA), 22, 97–98, 99, 218
army, *see* military
Asia, 5, 6, 188, 200
Asia Minor disaster, 17, 35
Asturia, 121
Athens, 41, 43, 46, 47, 157, 168, 169, 190, 201, 211, 214, 227, 229, 231, 232, 237

Attica-Beotia, 190
Austria, 118
autarky, 7, 9–10, 13, 18, 19, 137
Aveiro, 247
Azevedo, 101
Azores, 109, 214

Badajoz, 138, 166
balance of payments, 6, 10, 11, 12, 13, 38, 41, 93, 107, 109, 137, 138, 194
Balearic Islands, 191, 213
Balsemião, 95, 105
banks, 24, 38, 68, 85, 99, 107, 109, 190
Barbosa, 85
Barcelona, 121, 138, 165, 213, 217, 222, 229
Bari, 157
Basic Labor Law 1939, 9
Basilicata, 167, 170
Basque Country (and Basque Separatism), 7, 26, 121, 127, 139, 140, 147, 166, 169, 183, 190, 191, 213, 248, 277
Belgium, 149, 159
Berlinguer, 77
Bilbao, 139
Biscay, Bay of, 275
bloco central, 106, 110
Bologna, 80
bourgeoisie political movements, 16, 17, 65, 84, 118
Braga, 86, 214
Bragança, 246
Brazil, 7, 90, 149, 150
Bretton Woods, 5
Brindisi, 166

Burgos, 121

Cabo Verde, 86, 157, 232
Cáceres, 166
Cadiz, 213, 248
Caetano, 20, 21, 94–97
Calabria, 165, 167, 170, 173
Campania, 247
Campos, 96
Canada, 150
Canary Islands, 213
capital accumulation, 17, 19, 92, 117, 184–191
Captains' Movement (Movimento dos Capitāes), 98
Carlists, 116
Carlos, 99
Carneiro, 105
Carrero, 121
Carvalho, 101
Cassa per il Mezzogiorno, 68, 70, 190–191
Castellon, 213
Castile, 164, 168, 191, 213, 214, 239
Catalonia, 7, 123, 139, 140, 166, 170, 190, 191, 213, 222, 248, 277
CDE, 95
Centre Union Party (UCD), 36, 124, 140
CEUD, 95
chemicals industry, 42, 88, 138, 156, 187, 188, 199, 271
China, 91
Christian Democratic Party, 21, 62, 63, 65, 66, 67, 68, 69, 72, 76–78, 79, 80, 220
Church (and Catholicism), 17, 18, 21, 33, 64, 66, 76, 100, 118, 119, 128, 131
clientelism, 8, 14, 22, 23, 24, 33, 38, 44, 46, 53, 62, 68, 72, 79, 82
clothing industry, see textiles
Coimbra, 86
Cold War, 66, 67, 69
Colonels, Greece, 18, 19, 21, 36–37, 271
colonial wars, 10, 91–92, 97–98, 215, 222
colonies (see also decolonization, 5, 6, 17, 25, 86–87, 88, 92, 102, 108, 214, 281
comitati di quartieri, 218
Commercial Bank, 14
Committee of Democratic Coordination, 123
Confererazione Generale dei Sindicati dei Lavoratori, 69
Confederazione Generale Italiano del Lavoro, 69

consenso pactado, 124
constitution, 22, 26, 45, 79, 99, 100, 101, 109, 126, 140
continuismo, 121
cooperatives, 50, 163, 247, 252, 253
COPCON, 101
Córdoba, 166
core-periphery, 6–7, 12–13, 25, 49
corporatism, 18, 21, 75, 80–81, 114, 117–120, 125–126, 128–129, 130–133, 133–136
da Costa, Amaro, 105
da Costa, Nobre, 103
Council of the Revolution, 22, 99, 105, 109
counterurbanization, 174
Cova da Beira, 189
Craxi, 23, 63, 75, 78
Crespo, 105
Crete, 35, 43, 247
Cunha, 97
Cunhal, 100
Cyprus, 21, 35, 37, 45, 46, 216, 281

Damīao, 91
decolonization, 2, 101–102
Democratic Alliance (AD – Alianca Democratica), 20, 104–106, 107, 244–245
Denmark, 54, 269, 275
dependency, 12–15, 17, 24, 35, 38
devaluation, 10, 57, 73, 138
development, 1, 4–7, 8–20, 70–71, 85–97, 116, 120
Dias, 85
diaspora, 34
dictatorship, 1, 16–21, 36–37, 65, 85, 94–95, 109, 113–125, 215–217
Diu, 91
Douro, 92
Drama, 43

Eanes, 101, 103, 105, 110
EC, 5, 7, 10, 14, 33, 39–40, 42, 50, 55–58, 67, 69, 80, 87, 96, 108, 149, 158, 175, 180, 188, 197, 249–260, 268–287
accession, 20, 24, 25, 46, 53–55, 81, 88, 104, 109, 175, 180–181, 189, 254, 268, 284
agriculture, 25, 34, 56, 57, 81
Common Agricultural Policy (CAP), 55, 251–252, 254–260, 263, 272, 274, 279, 281

Common Fisheries Policy (CFP),
274–275
EAGGF, 256
enlargement, 81, 203, 259, 260–264,
268–269, 270–279, 281–283, 286
European Investment Bank, 189, 269,
270
European Regional Development Fund,
25, 56, 82, 270, 277
European Social Fund, 25, 56, 82, 270,
277
ECSC, 67
EDIK, 47, 49
education, 36, 58, 86, 94, 209
EFTA, 10, 87, 88, 180, 269, 271, 286
Egypt, 157, 281, 282
elections, 36, 46–53, 58, 63–64, 66, 76–78,
95, 96–97, 99–100, 103–106, 140
electrical and electronics industries, 88,
188, 199, 203
emigration, 5, 7, 11, 15, 20, 24, 25, 39, 68,
70, 90–91, 93, 138, 139, 145–164, 208,
212, 238–239, 278, 283
  culture, 162, 168
  employment, 152–153, 163
  remittances, 11, 12, 41, 70, 90, 138, 160,
  161, 184–186, 190, 209, 212, 278
  retornados, 101, 102, 104, 214, 239, 278
  return, 150, 153, 157–164, 174, 209, 239
Emilia Romagna, 173, 201
employment, 11, 42, 69, 93, 107, 139, 188,
237–238
ENI, 199
Epirus, 35, 43, 47
Estado Novo, 9, 18, 87
ETA, 127, 140
Ethiopia, 157
Euratom, 67
Eurocommunism, 23, 47, 130
European Defence Community, 283
European Monetary Agreement, 86
European Payments Union, 86
Évora, 242
exports, 1, 7, 10, 39, 57, 67, 73, 80, 87, 88,
102, 108, 160, 181, 188, 193, 194–197,
273, 277, 281, 282
export platform production, 197, 201
export processing production, 194, 201
Extremadura, 138, 139, 213, 214, 277

Falange, 117
family law, 22, 24, 58

Fanfani, 76, 80
fascism, 1, 18–19, 65, 68, 76, 114, 116,
117–118, 120, 124, 131
fishing, 189, 259, 274–5
Florence, 170, 218
Florina, 43, 47
Fokida, 47
food processing industries, 7, 39, 88, 138,
192, 194
Fraga, 124, 140
France, 4, 17, 24, 90, 147, 148, 149, 150,
152, 153, 158, 160, 164, 175, 194, 197,
215, 245, 250, 252, 253, 257, 258, 259,
260, 262, 263, 269, 270, 272, 273, 275,
276, 278
Franco, see also Francoism, 2, 11, 18, 19,
20, 21, 114–122, 123–124, 128, 216, 220,
222
Fthiotida, 47
Funchal, 214

Galaxia plot, 129
Galicia, 138, 164, 167, 191, 213, 246, 248
de Gasperi, 67
GATT, 80
GDP, see also GNP, 8, 12, 15, 33, 38,
39–40, 41, 43, 44, 68, 85, 93, 102, 107,
138, 179, 181, 182, 236, 250, 276,
279–280
Genoa, 61, 157, 170, 174
geopolitics, 283–4
Germany, 5, 17, 39, 113, 149, 150, 158,
160, 161, 162, 164, 175, 179, 181, 187,
188, 189, 197, 263, 278, 279
Gibraltar, 285
Goa, 91
golpismo, 123, 124, 127, 129
Gomes, 97, 99
Gonçalves, 99, 101
González, 23, 133, 140
Gramsci, 65
Granada, 166
GRAPO, 127
Greek Civil War, 7, 10, 23, 35, 58
Greek Communist Party see also KKE, 36
grémios, 9
growth, economic, 1, 2, 5, 8, 12, 34, 38, 39,
68, 69, 82, 85, 87, 93, 96, 108, 137–139,
182, 191–192
growth poles, 70, 82, 139, 166, 191, 213,
232
Guerra, 95

Guinea, 91

Harmonization of the Autonomies, 127–8
Heraklion, 214
historic compromise, 77–78
Hong Kong, 197, 203
Hot Autumn, Italy, 12, 14, 22, 64, 72,
    73–74, 76, 78, 79, 82
housing, 12, 38, 40, 41, 71, 169, 215,
    217–219, 222, 225–227
    state, 218, 220, 226–227
Huelva, 213

IBDR, 92
ideology, 19, 20, 21, 35, 38, 45, 49, 55–56,
    117, 118, 119, 128
Il Manifesto, 218
IMF, 10, 13, 86, 107, 137
immigration, 156–157
imports, 41, 57, 80, 88, 93, 108, 181, 193,
    272, 274, 275, 277
import substitution, see also import
    reproducing, 10, 38, 194, 201
incomes, 43, 71, 102, 139
India, 91
industrialization, 9, 19, 38, 41, 71–72, 82,
    179, 192, 208, 213, 225
    diffuse, 8, 14, 75, 174, 190, 200–201,
    203, 212, 224, 228, 231, 276
inflation, 11, 12, 17, 40, 63, 74, 75, 80, 93,
    102–107, 263
informal economy, see also 'black'
    economy, 14, 42, 173, 224, 232
INI, 14, 37
international division of labour, 15, 24,
    180, 199
investment, 38, 39, 85, 102, 107, 137, 138,
    184–191
    foreign, 10, 11, 14, 24, 38–39, 42, 86,
    91–92, 180, 184–189, 197–199, 276,
    277
    state, 14, 20, 38, 39, 70, 85, 91–92, 96,
    190–191, 197, 199, 202
Ioannides, 20, 37
Ionian Islands, 35, 43, 242
Ireland, 42, 54, 269, 279, 283, 285
IRI, 14, 82, 199
Israel, 91, 281, 282
Italian Communist Party (PCI), 62, 65, 66,
    67, 70, 75, 76–78, 79, 80, 81, 218, 220
Italian Socialist Party, 62, 65, 66, 67, 70,
    76–78, 79

Itea, 187

Jaén, 166
Japan, 8, 113, 181, 188, 192
Jordan, 282

Karamanlis, 21, 37, 45, 46, 53, 54, 55
Kastoria, 47
Kiklis, 43
KKE, 45, 47, 52, 55
KKE Interior, 47. 55
KODISCO, 55

labour, 8, 15, 93, 102, 145–147, 200–201,
    215
    costs, 9, 10, 11, 73, 74–75, 80, 153, 155,
    188, 200, 224
Land Laws, 224
land and land reform, 14, 24, 70, 99, 109,
    135, 155, 166, 167, 218, 238, 241,
    242–249
Larissa, 214
Lateran Pacts, 65
latifundia, 14, 67, 138, 166, 243–244–245
Lebanon, 281
Lei das Atribuições e Competências, 106
Lei das Finanças Locais, 106
Lei do Fomento Industrial, 95
Lei da Nacionalização dos Capitais, 86
Leixões, 189
Leon, 213, 214
Levante, 213
Liberal Party, 65, 66, 78
Libya, 284
Lisbon, 86, 92, 94, 96, 101, 169, 211, 214,
    218, 219, 220, 224, 226, 228, 229, 231,
    232, 237
literacy, see education
local government, 26, 106, 215, 220–221,
    222–223, 230
Lombardy, 7, 183
Lomé Convention, 274, 281
Lotta Continua, 218

Macau, 109
Macedonia, 35, 43, 47
Madeira, 109, 214
Madrid, 139, 165, 168, 170, 190, 213, 214,
    216, 229, 237, 239, 277
Malta, 281, 282
Mancini, 72
Mani, 167

manufacturing industry, 14, 38, 41, 42, 57, 63, 69, 92, 137, 200, 276–278
small firms, 42, 50, 75, 189, 199–201, 276
Marche, 170
Marshal Aid, 5
Martins, 95
Megali Idea, 35, 56
Mellado, 129
Melo e Castro, 95
metals (base) and metallurgical industries, 39, 70, 88, 138, 156, 194, 199, 271, 276
Metaxas, 17, 18, 19, 35
Mezzogiorno, *see also* South of Italy, 9, 15, 21–22, 61–62, 65–66, 67–68, 70–71, 82, 164, 166, 170–173, 190, 199, 202, 213, 226, 232, 245, 247, 251, 259–260, 262, 269, 270
Middle East, 15, 175, 203
migration, 15, 70, 71, 139, 164–173, 212, 213–214, 222, 225, 277
Milan, 61, 68, 71, 73, 157, 165, 171, 173, 174, 218, 229, 237
military, 1, 18, 19, 22, 35, 36, 45–46, 91, 97, 98, 101, 116, 117, 123, 126–130
military coup, Portugal, 2, 21, 97–98
minifundia, 14, 138
mining, 187, 194
Molise, 170, 247
Monarchists, 76
Moncloa Pacts, 127, 134
Moro, 72, 80
Morocco, 156, 157, 158, 254, 281, 282, 285
Mota, 95
Mozambique, 91, 92, 239
MSI-DN, 76, 77
multinational companies, 7, 13, 39, 61, 133, 182, 184, 187–188, 197
Murcia, 231
Mussolini, 1, 18, 19, 21

Naples, 157, 218, 229
Natali, 284
National Bank, Greece, 14
national unification, 17, 34–35, 67
NATO, 4, 8, 44, 45, 46–47, 50, 55, 56, 58, 67, 129, 269, 283, 284
Navarre, 213
Navarro, 139
neighbourhood associations, 64, 79, 216, 218, 220
Nenni, 72
Netherlands, 4, 160, 189

New Democracy Party (ND), 20, 22, 45–46, 47–49, 52, 55
Newly Industrialized Countries, 15, 181, 197, 203, 208, 225
Nigeria, 157
North Vietnam, 91

OEEC, 269
oligarchic rule, 16, 49
oil crisis, 6, 11, 73, 97, 139, 149, 158, 218, 232
Oporto, 86, 96, 169, 211, 214, 218, 219, 222, 247
Opus Dei, 116, 119, 137

Pacheco, 85
Pantelleria, 246
Papdopoulos, 20, 33, 36, 37
Papagos, 37
Papandreou, 23, 36, 44, 45, 49, 53
paper industry, 26, 88, 187, 271
parasyntagma (parallel constitution), 35, 45
parliamentary government, 16, 20–24, 44–46, 50–51, 98–102, 103–106, 113–114
PASOK, 23, 37, 41, 45, 47–53, 55–56, 58–59, 284
Patras, 214
patronage, *see* clientelism
Peace Movement, 79
peasants, 36, 169, 239, 240, 242, 245
Peloponnese, 43, 47
petrochemicals, 26, 70, 179, 199, 202, 203
Philippines, 157
PIDE, 86, 95
Piedmont, 7, 241
pieds-noir, 239
Pintado, 95
Pinto, 103
Piraeus, 157, 169
Po Valley, 165, 170, 239
Poland, 56
political parties, support, 23, 47–49, 66
pollution, 8, 11, 26, 41, 187, 224, 228
Popular Alliance (AP), 22, 124, 140
Popular Front, 118
Popular Monarchists (PPM), 95, 104–106
Popular Party, 66
population, *see also* rural, depopulation, 43, 90, 211, 268
Portugese Communist Party (PCP), 23, 25, 99, 100–101, 102, 106, 217–219, 244
Potere Operario, 218

pronunciamentos, 118
Pylos, 26, 191
Pyrenees, 167

Radical Party, 63, 64, 78, 79
Rallis, 46
referendum, 64, 79, 122
regional disparities, 15, 43, 68, 70, 82, 94, 139, 209, 211–212, 213–214, 223, 225, 269, 277
regional government, 26, 64, 79, 132, 163, 221
regional planning, 96, 202
regionalism, 22, 24, 26, 120, 127, 131, 132–133, 140, 215
Republican Party, 63, 65, 66, 78
research and development, 15
retornados, see emigration
Rodopi, 47
Rome, 157, 170, 171, 174, 218, 229
rousfeti, 44
rural areas, 47, 68, 86, 152, 153–156, 161, 209, 237–238
    depopulation, 43, 70, 90–91, 139, 165, 166–169, 209, 213, 214, 238–239

Sá Carneiro, 95, 103, 104–106
SAAL, 218, 219
Salazar, 2, 18, 19, 84–85, 86, 87, 91, 92, 94, 108, 222
Salgueiro, 95
Santander, 139
Sardinia, 166, 170, 247
SEDES, 95
semiperiphery, 6, 7, 12, 24, 125
service class, 19, 116–117, 123–124
service employment, 8, 19, 40–41, 62, 70, 166, 186, 213, 225
Setúbal, 86, 169, 214, 218
Seville, 213, 214, 229
shanty towns, 216, 218, 219, 220, 232
Sicily, 79, 145, 156, 157, 161, 173, 247
Simão, 95
Sines, 96, 191, 232
Singapore, 203
Siracusa, 70, 166
Soares, 23, 94, 96, 106
Social Democratic Centre (CDS), 100, 103–106
Social Democratic Party, Italy, 66, 72, 78
Social Democratic party (PSD) Portugal, 22, 100, 104–106

social provision, 43, 44, 86, 94, 106, 209, 215, 218–219
Socialist National Confederation of Workers, 132
Socialist Party (PS), 22, 100, 103–104, 106, 218–219, 244–245
Socialist Workers' Party (PSW), 133, 140
South America *see also* Latin America, 5, 6, 17, 25, 147, 149, 156, 157, 274
South Korea, 192
South Vietnam, 91
Spadolini, 63, 80
Spanish Civil War, 2, 7, 10, 18, 23, 117, 118, 137
Spanish Communist Party (PCE), 124, 127
Spínola, 97, 99
Stabilization Plan, Spain, 138, 180
State economic policies, 38, 40, 44, 68, 80–81, 95, 137
Suárez, 123, 124, 126, 129, 140
Sudan, 157
svolta sindacale, 75
Switzerland, 145, 147, 149, 150, 160, 162, 164
Syndical Union, 132
Syria, 282, 284

Tagus, 179
Taiwan, 7
Taranto, 70, 166, 179
Tarragona, 26
technology, 11, 15, 38, 39, 40, 137, 200, 203, 231
Tejero, 22
terrorism, 63, 64, 77, 79, 127
textiles, 7, 39, 57, 88, 156, 184, 188, 192, 193, 199, 200, 271, 276, 282
Thessaloniki, 43, 47, 169, 179, 211, 214, 232
Thessaly, 35, 47, 246
Timor, 109, 285
Tomás, 96, 97
tourism, 7, 8, 11, 12, 20, 26, 92, 138, 139, 212, 225
trade, 7, 54, 56–57, 80, 88, 96, 253–258, 269, 281
    protection, 10, 16, 20, 24, 57, 87, 273, 274, 276, 277, 282
trade unions, 9, 16, 17, 21, 58, 63, 68–69, 71, 72–73, 74–75, 81, 117, 123, 125, 132, 188, 189
transfer payments, 70, 82, 174, 190, 212

transformation, 1, 8, 64, 69, 70, 115, 186, 236
transport, 11, 15, 96, 174, 188, 228–229
Treaty of Rome, 149, 175, 278, 283
Trentino, 170
Tunisia, 156, 157, 158, 254, 281, 282
Turin, 61, 68, 71, 73, 74, 157, 171, 173, 174, 218
Turkey, 4, 6, 17, 24, 35, 37, 45, 46, 58, 146, 158, 159, 209, 281, 283, 285
Tuscany, 171, 201
tzakia, 16

UCPs (collective farms, Portugal), 99, 101, 244–245
UK, 4, 5, 17, 54, 87, 91, 153, 179, 181, 197, 263, 269, 275, 279, 285
Umbria, 170
unemployment, 11, 40, 63, 68, 71, 276–277
uneven regional development, 15, 197, 201–202
União Nacional (National Union), 95
Unione Italiana del Lavoro, 69
United Nations, 10, 137
urban obsolescence, 213, 218, 225, 228, 231
urban planning and policies, 174, 216, 220, 222–224, 229–230
urban political/social movements, 22, 26, 214–221

urban primacy, 209, 211, 231
urbanization, 43, 86, 165, 173, 208–214, 231
USA, 4, 5, 6, 10, 17, 24, 45, 46, 49, 50, 55, 56, 58, 91, 147, 149, 150, 175, 181, 188, 274, 284
USSR (including Russia), 5, 91, 284

Valencia, 138, 213, 229, 231
vehicle production, 70, 138, 188, 192, 194, 277
Veneto, 170, 173, 201, 241
Venezuela, 148, 140
Venizelists, 16
Viana do Castelo, 94, 246
Vila Nova de Gaia, 86
Volos, 214

wood and cork industries, 88, 187, 200, 271
workers councils/commissions, 64, 73, 79, 123, 132
World Bank, 10, 137

Yugoslavia, 4, 157, 158, 209, 281, 282

Zaragossa, 139, 213
ZIRA, 244